Troubleshooting

Microsoft®

Access Databases

Covers Access 97 and Access 2000

Virginia Andersen

Microsoft®

PUBLISHED BY
Microsoft Press
A Division of Microsoft Corporation
One Microsoft Way
Redmond, Washington 98052-6399

Library of Congress Cataloging-in-Publication Data
Andersen, Virginia, 1929-
    Troubleshooting Microsoft Access Databases / Virginia Andersen.
        p. cm.
    Includes index.
    ISBN 0-7356-1160-2
    1. Microsoft Access.   2. Database Management.   I. Title.
QA76.9.D3 A635 2000
005.75'65--dc21   00-048704

Printed and bound in the United States of America.

1 2 3 4 5 6 7 8 9   QWT   6 5 4 3 2 1

Distributed in Canada by Penguin Books Canada Limited.

A CIP catalogue record for this book is available from the British Library.

Microsoft Press books are available through booksellers and distributors worldwide. For further information about international editions, contact your local Microsoft Corporation office or contact Microsoft Press International directly at fax (425) 936-7329. Visit our Web site at mspress.microsoft.com. Send comments to *mspinput@microsoft.com*.

Acquisitions Editors: Christey Bahn and Alex Blanton
Project Editor: John Pierce

Acknowledgements

It's a very exciting and challenging endeavor to pioneer a new book series. The *Troubleshooting* series is so innovative, it's all the more so. It was a great pleasure to work with the Microsoft Press team to help carve out this most-helpful PC-user resource. My sincere thanks to Christey Bahn, the acquisitions editor who introduced me to the project, and to Alex Blanton, who has so ably assumed that chair upon Christey's departure.

I would also like to express my appreciation of Laura Sackerman, Jenny Moss Benson, and Wendy Zucker for their focus and guidance that has led to the introduction of the series. My special thanks go to the ever-patient John Pierce, who took on the dual role as my developmental and technical editor for *Troubleshooting Microsoft Access Databases*. He's managed to keep me focused on the intent of the series and was always helpful with new ideas and approaches to tackling Access problems.

I also must thank my ever-alert agent, Matt Wagner, of Waterside Productions, for connecting me to Microsoft Press and opening this important and challenging opportunity.

Finally, my patient husband, Jack, and all the cats deserve thanks for putting up with me for all these months. At least sitting in front of a computer for hours each day provided a lap for the cats, and they were never reluctant to take purring advantage.

Quick contents

Contents

About this book

Troubleshooting Microsoft Access Databases presents a new way to diagnose and solve problems you might have encountered with your database or some of its tables, forms, reports, or other elements. Even if you know only the basics of how Access stores, analyzes, and presents your data, you'll find it easy to locate solutions and fix your problems with Access.

I've written this book with two goals in mind: ease and simplicity. If a creative form that you designed isn't displaying any data, for example, you'll be able to quickly figure out whether the form shows no data because there's a problem with the way you designed it or because there just isn't any data to show. This book shows you how to locate your problem, describes what might be causing the problem (without going into too many details), and then leads you through a solution that will help you get back to what you were doing.

How to use this book

You don't need to read this book in any particular order, or even from cover to cover. It's designed so that you can jump in, quickly diagnose your problem, and then get the information you need to fix that problem—whether you've just begun to learn about databases and database management programs or whether you're knowledgeable enough to get right to the source of the problem. The problems you're most likely to have are grouped into chapters that are listed alphabetically; the chapter titles are kept simple so you know at a glance what kinds of topics each chapter covers. Each chapter is broken into two specific elements: the flowchart and the solutions.

Flowcharts

The first thing you'll see when you go to a chapter is a dynamic, easy-to-use flowchart. The flowchart starts by asking you a broad question, and then it takes you through

Assumptions about Access versions

Troubleshooting Microsoft Access Databases covers both Access 97 and Access 2000. Differences between the versions in either the source of the problem or the solution are noted. The illustrations show dialog boxes and other screen elements from Access 2000. Readers who are using Access 97 might see some differences in appearance, but the steps and explanations are the same unless otherwise noted.

simple, yes-or-no questions to help you pinpoint your problem. If the solution to your problem is a simple one involving just a handful of steps, you'll be given a quick fix right on the flowchart. Your problem will be solved, and you'll be right back to work. If your problem requires a little more explanation and a few more steps, you'll reach a statement of the problem along with the page number on which you can find the solution. And if your problem isn't shown on the flowchart, you'll find a list of related chapters in which your problem might be addressed.

Solutions

The solutions are where the real troubleshooting takes place. I'll describe the source of the problem you're experiencing and then tell you how to fix it with clear, step-by-step instructions. The solutions contain plenty of illustrations that show you what you should be seeing as you move through the steps. I also provide some background information for a deeper understanding of why you might have encountered your problem. Tips and sidebars contain additional, related material you might find interesting; warnings tell you what you should or shouldn't do before you begin.

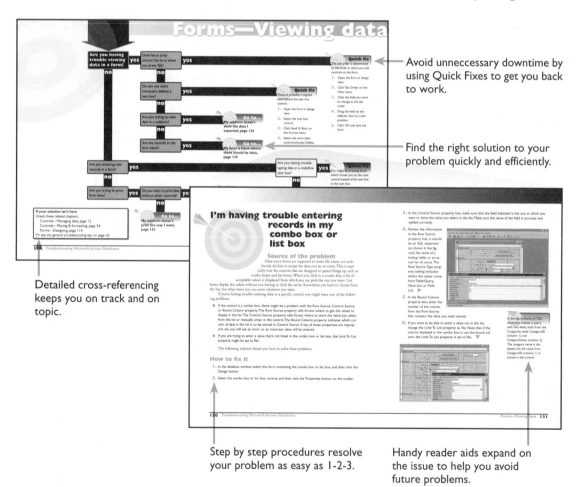

Avoid unneccessary downtime by using Quick Fixes to get you back to work.

Find the right solution to your problem quickly and efficiently.

Detailed cross-referencing keeps you on track and on topic.

Step by step procedures resolve your problem as easy as 1-2-3.

Handy reader aids expand on the issue to help you avoid future problems.

Troubleshooting tips

To troubleshoot, as defined by the *Microsoft Computer Dictionary*, is to "isolate the source of a problem in a program, computer system, or network and remedy it." But how do you go about isolating the source of the problem in the first place? The source often isn't readily apparent, it might be a symptom masquerading as the source, or it might reveal itself to be something other than what you initially thought.

message, or you just got the wrong results. If necessary, reconstruct the steps you took that caused the problem in the first place.

Turn to the chapter that deals with the task you're having trouble with, such as "Queries—Selection criteria." Then you can follow the path in the flowchart to the right solution—either a quick fix right on the flowchart or a reference to a more detailed solution later in the chapter.

How to troubleshoot

The easiest way to isolate a problem is to stand back and take a look at what you're trying to do at the moment. (I'm trying to extract data from a table with a query, for example, or I'm trying to design a report that will display subtotals.) Then narrow down the scope of the problem. (I can't enter the right criteria in the query design; I can't get the calculation to work.) Write down a list of what you tried to do, how you went about it, and what happened, specifically. For example, you heard a beep, you saw an error

Let Access help

Access doesn't exactly hold your hand as you trek through the jungle of creating and using a database, but it isn't far from your side. Most of the error messages you see (and I've seen a lot of them) include a Help button. You can click the Help button to see a brief description of the error and what you did to bring it on.

Access also makes its presence known as a generous helper by providing the What's This? button in a lot of the dialog boxes. If you're not sure whether you've set an option or property correctly, click the What's This? button (the question mark in the top right corner) and then click the item in question. You'll see a description of the item, often with advice about your choices.

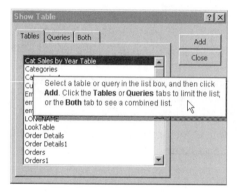

If quick information isn't enough to help you determine what's wrong, you can always resort to the complete online Help topic relating to the activity that's giving you trouble. You can use the Contents tab to browse through topics, or you can search for a topic using the Index tab or, in Access 2000, the Answer Wizard.

Make sure the database isn't read-only

It's hard to make important changes to the design of a form or report with your hands tied behind your back. If you open the database as read-only, you can't add or edit data and you can't make any changes in the design of forms, queries, reports, or tables. If you selected the Read-Only option in the Open dialog box, close the database and reopen it using the plain old Open button.

If you use an Access 97 database in Access 2000, it opens read-only. To make design changes in an Access 97 database, you must open the database in Access 97 or convert it to Access 2000. After making the changes in Access 2000, you can convert it back to an Access 97 version if you need to.

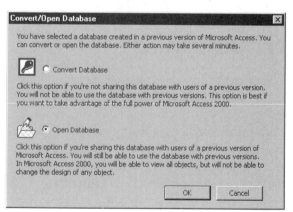

Take it slow

Many of us get frustrated when clicking buttons doesn't solve our problem, so we just click more of them. Doing so won't solve your problem, and it usually compounds the problem exponentially until you have a really snarled-up mess. Then all you can do is give a big sigh and start all over.

A far better strategy is to move slowly, one step at a time, to determine the cause of the problem. You can sort of sneak up on a solution. Keep track of what you do, and keep looking over your shoulder for an escape route. Try not to get boxed into a corner with no way out but Ctrl+Alt+Delete. Once you emerge from the tunnel into the light of a solution, jot down the path you took for future reference. This might help guarantee you'll never have that problem again—Murphy is alive and well!

If you're still stuck

I've endeavored to anticipate common problems you're likely to run into when using Access, but obviously the list can't be exhaustive. There's even a chance that my solutions won't solve your particular problem. If you run into a dead end, you can turn to Microsoft product support or to other resources, such as the following:

- *http://microsoft.com/office*, the Microsoft Office product Web site
- *http://search.support.microsoft.com/kb*, the Microsoft searchable Knowledge Base
- *http://www.microsoft.com/office/access/*, the Microsoft Access product Web site
- *http://www.zdnet.com/zdhelp/*, a popular technology Web site with helpful tips

Troubleshooting Web site

With the purchase of this book you have access to the Microsoft Troubleshooting Web site (*mspress.microsoft.com/troubleshooting*), which complements the book series by offering deeper, more extensive troubleshooting information that's updated monthly. (Remember, the updates on the Web site are free, but connect time charges may apply.) If you have a problem that isn't addressed in this book, you can check the Web site to see if it's there. Even if you don't have a specific problem you're looking to solve, you might find some useful information that you can apply anyway. To access the site, you need this code: **MSA1276**

The Troubleshooting Web site is just as easy to navigate as the book, and it keeps in mind the goals of helping you quickly locate your problem and its solution without going into too much detail.

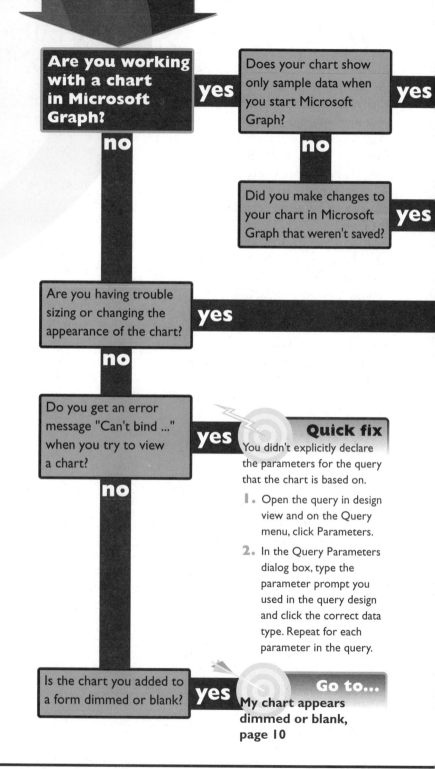

Are you working with a chart in Microsoft Graph?

yes →

Does your chart show only sample data when you start Microsoft Graph?

yes

no ↓

Did you make changes to your chart in Microsoft Graph that weren't saved?

yes

no ↓

Are you having trouble sizing or changing the appearance of the chart?

yes →

no ↓

Do you get an error message "Can't bind ..." when you try to view a chart?

yes →

Quick fix

You didn't explicitly declare the parameters for the query that the chart is based on.

1. Open the query in design view and on the Query menu, click Parameters.

2. In the Query Parameters dialog box, type the parameter prompt you used in the query design and click the correct data type. Repeat for each parameter in the query.

no ↓

Is the chart you added to a form dimmed or blank?

yes →

Go to...

My chart appears dimmed or blank, page 10

Quick fix

Access replaces the sample data with your real data the first time you view the chart in the form or report.

1. Open the form or report in form view or print preview.

Go to...

I made changes to a chart in Microsoft Graph, but they were not retained, page 4

Does the chart fail to resize with the form?

yes

Quick fix

If your chart size doesn't change when you resize the chart control, you need to change the chart's graph area.

1. Double-click the chart.

2. In Microsoft Graph, drag the sizing handles on the chart to match the width and height you have set in the chart control on the form.

3. Return to form view, and click Size To Fit Form on the Window menu.

no

Are you working on the column order?

yes

Go to...

The columns in my chart aren't in the order I want, page 8

no

Are you trying to change the labels in the chart's legend?

yes

Go to...

The legend labels on my chart don't say what I want, page 6

If your solution isn't here:
Check these related chapters:
Or see the general troubleshooting tips on page xiii.

I made changes to a chart in Microsoft Graph, but they were not retained

Source of the problem

You work hard making a chart look the way you want it. You finish it and save it, but when you view it again, the rascal has kept some of your settings and ignored others. Chances are that without realizing it, you set conflicting properties or values in the underlying record source, in the chart's properties, or in Microsoft Graph. The information shown in your chart comes from all three of those places, and information in one place may take priority over information in another.

Access recomputes and redraws a chart every time you preview or print it, so changes you made in one of these three places might be overwritten by properties or values you set in another. You can use Microsoft Graph to make changes to the appearance of the graph and to change the colors and formatting of labels, titles, and the legend. These sorts of changes will be retained. But if you tried to change the x-axis labels by editing the datasheet in Microsoft Graph, for example, or if you tried to update the names of the legend labels or any of the chart's data, the changes will be overwritten by the values in the underlying query or tables.

Here's how to be sure that changes you make to your chart will stick.

How to fix it

1. If you made changes to a chart in Microsoft Graph that were overwritten by the underlying data or values, you need to return to the query or table the chart is based on and make your changes there.

2. If the form or report containing the chart isn't open, switch to the database window, select the form or report that includes the chart, and then click the Design button.

3. Right-click the chart, and then click Properties on the shortcut menu.

4. In the Row Source property box, identify the query or table the chart's data is based on. ▶

5. Close the form or report.

6. In the database window, select the underlying table or query, and then click the Open button.

7. Make the changes to the data or the field names that need to be updated in your chart. ▶

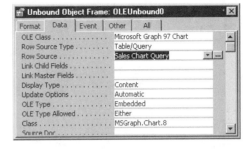

The nature of chart priorities

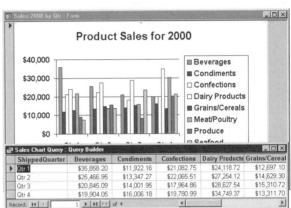

You have three places to make changes to your chart. Where you do so depends on what information you want to change. You can think of these places as levels, with the top level taking precedence over settings you make in the others.

Top Level: The underlying data, which can be a table, a query, or an SQL statement created by the Chart Wizard. The data overrides changes at other levels if a conflict arises.

Middle Level: The Row Source property for the chart itself. Here you can change the chart's title or labels, for example. Changes made at this level can be overwritten by changes in the data. An exception is when the Row Source property contains a calculated field that includes formatting characters. This format supersedes the format of the underlying data.

Low Level: Microsoft Graph. Only changes to the chart's appearance will be retained. Changes made here to the data in the chart run the risk of being overwritten.

The legend labels on my chart don't say what I want

Source of the problem

The Chart Wizard creates the labels in the legend from field values in the underlying data. The labels are not always as informative as you want them to be because the wizard copies the values in the fields used in a series of data. For example, if you are tallying up sales of various categories of products during the four calendar quarters, the categories are part of a series. The quarters appear on the chart's x-axis, and the sales totals become the values shown on the y-axis. The categories might be identified only by a number. Often, that's not very helpful.

Charts that are based on a query show the query column headings as legend labels. In a chart based on a query that totals the values in a field—for example sales of individual product categories by quarter or year—the legend label for the resulting aggregate field would read SumOf<*field name*>. That doesn't look very professional. In cases like this, the Row Source property of the chart is an SQL statement that constructs the data for the chart. You can modify the SQL statement to make the labels more useful.

The following solution shows you the way to make the legend list in your charts more to your liking.

How to fix it

1. In the database window, select the query the chart is based on and click Design.

2. Find the name of the field that has values you want to display differently in the chart.

3. Replace the field name with an expression that includes the text you want to display in the legend list beside the value from the field. ▶

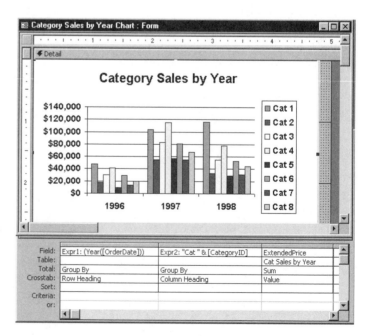

For example, for a legend that shows only the category ID number, you could replace the CategoryID field name with the expression **"Cat" & [CategoryID]**. Be sure to enclose any text you add in double quotation marks.

4. View the chart again in form view to confirm that the label is correct.

To change the legend text when you are working with a chart that displays SumOf <*fieldname*>, edit the SQL statement by following these steps.

1. In the database window, select the form or report containing the chart and open it in design view.

2. Right-click the chart and then click Properties on the shortcut menu.

3. At the right of the Row Source property box, click the Build (...) button.

4. In the query design window, click SQL View on the View menu.

5. Edit each of the AS clauses in the SQL statement to remove the SumOf prefix. You can also revise the text between the brackets of the AS clause to read as you want your legend list to appear. ▶

6. Save and close the SQL statement window.

7. Switch to form view to see the new text in the legend. ▶

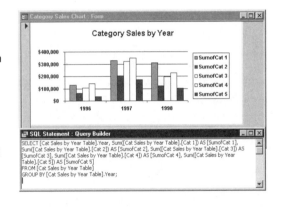

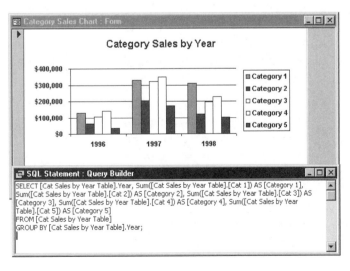

The columns in my chart aren't in the order I want

Source of the problem

The column order in a chart is determined by the order of the fields in the table or query that the chart is based on. To change the order of the columns in the chart, you need to modify the order in which the fields are sorted in the table or query. Suppose that when you create a bar chart to compare the number of orders by month, you want to point out which months had exceptional orders rather than list months chronologically. To do this, you need to tell Access how to sort the values for the sales.

You do this by rearranging the field columns and specifying the sort order in the query design grid. If you used the Chart Wizard to create the chart, the query will be in the form of an SQL statement when you access it. But you can still work in the query design grid by selecting the query view instead of SQL view in the Query Builder window.

The following solution shows how you can arrange the columns in a chart in the order you want.

How to fix it

1. In the database window, select the form containing the chart and click the Design button.

2. Right-click the chart, and then click Properties on the shortcut menu.

3. At the right of the Row Source property box, click Build (...) to open the query design grid.

4. Change the sort order for the field by which the chart columns are arranged. In the example illustrated in the figure, you might want to rearrange the columns in the bar chart so that the months are listed on the chart's x-axis in descending order of popularity. To do this, you set the Sort cell to Descending in the Count2: Count(*) field. ▶

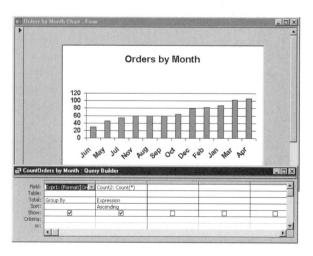

5. If you want to sort on more than one field, arrange the fields in the query design with the primary sort field at the left and the other fields to the right in order of precedence.

6. Close the Query Builder window, and display the chart in form view to review the column order.

Tip

If you set the order of the columns in Microsoft Graph, the underlying query will probably change the order to match the real data. That's because the data—not the appearance of the data—determines the column order.

Just a few chart definitions

The *Category (x)* axis is the horizontal line at the bottom of the chart that tells you what category of data the chart displays. The *Value (y) axis* is the vertical line that shows the values in the chart data. A *series* is a group of related data values from one field in the record source. For example, in the Quarterly Orders by Product chart shown below, each product's sales volume represents one of a series of values that are grouped by quarter. The *legend* is the color-coded list of members of the data series. The *labels* are derived from the data in the query or table the chart is based on.

Several features in a chart are provided by and can be customized in Microsoft Graph. Chart titles are optional. They can be placed at the top of the chart and next to each axis. Gridlines are horizontal or vertical lines that appear across the chart at the tick marks, which are the short lines that appear on the axes at evenly spaced intervals.

A chart's scale refers to the range of values in the chart and the increments that are marked as the Value axis with tick marks.

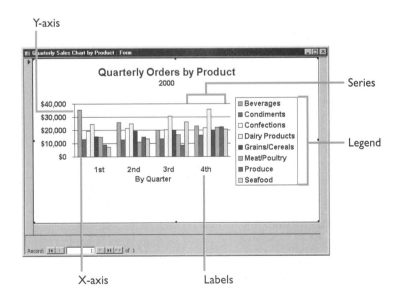

My chart appears dimmed or blank

Source of the problem

You went to all that work to create a chart showing how dramatically your company's sales have skyrocketed. Now you open the report containing the chart and see that your work of art is dimmed or completely blank.

The most likely cause of this unsettling problem is that the chart's Row Source property isn't valid. It's the Row Source property that tells Access which query or table it should use to get the data to display in the chart. You might have changed the name of the underlying query or table or deleted it altogether. When Access can't find the data you told it to use in the chart, it just shrugs and shows you nothing.

The problem of dimmed or blank charts might also occur if you are working with a record-bound chart. A *record-bound* chart is one that is linked to a specific field in a record. In this case, the field linking the chart and the form that includes the chart might not be correctly specified. For example, if your chart shows sales performance for several regions separately, the chart would be bound to the Region field. But if you chose Product as the field linking the chart and the form, there would be no match. The table or query the chart's based on must contain the field you are using to link the form and the chart. You designate this field in both the Link Child Fields and Link Master Fields properties. Both properties usually show the same field name, especially if you used the Chart Wizard to create the chart.

How to fix it

To make sure the chart's Row Source property is correct, follow these steps:

1. In the database window, select the form or report that includes the chart and open it in design view.

2. Right-click the chart control, and then click Properties. Check the name entered in the Row Source property, and make sure it shows a valid table or query name. If the name isn't valid, you'll need to correct it. ▶

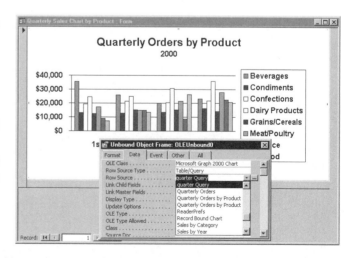

3. If you have renamed the query or table that's selected in the Row Source property, rename it here as well. If the query or table was deleted, you'll need to re-create the chart and base it on a query or table that's still part of your database.

4. Switch to form view or click Print Preview (if you are working with a chart in a report) and see whether the chart now displays the information you expected.

If you're working with a record-bound chart, open the form or report in design view and follow these steps:

1. Right-click the chart control, and then click Properties.

2. In the Link Master Fields property box, check to be sure the field name matches the Link Child Fields. Select the matching field if it does not. ▶

3. Switch to form view or click Print Preview (if you are working with a chart in a report) and see whether the chart now displays the information you expected.

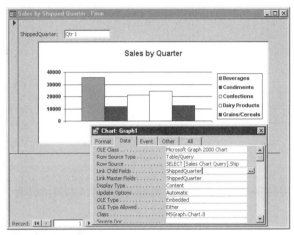

Tip
You can link more than one set of fields. Separate the field names in the property box with semicolons(;). The fields don't have to have the same names, but they must contain the same type of data. In the Link Child Fields property box, make sure the field name selected is included in the table or query that the chart is based on.

Charts and disk space

Charts take up a lot of disk space on your computer. If you are short of disk space, you can convert a chart to a static image. But you can do this only with charts that are not linked to individual records (record-bound charts). If you convert a chart to an image, you will not be able to edit the chart in place after the conversion. And you can't convert an image back to a chart. To convert a chart to an image, open the form or report in which the chart appears in design view. Click the chart control. On the Format menu, click Change To, and then click Image.

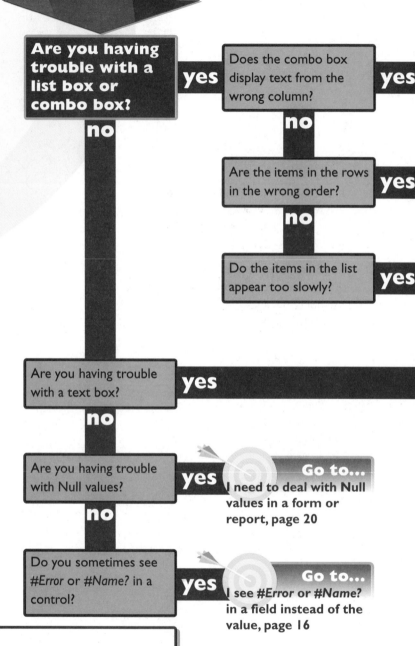

Are you having trouble with a list box or combo box?

yes → **Does the combo box display text from the wrong column?** yes

no

Are the items in the rows in the wrong order? yes

no

Do the items in the list appear too slowly? yes

no →

Are you having trouble with a text box? yes →

no

Are you having trouble with Null values? yes → **Go to...** I need to deal with **Null** values in a form or report, page 20

no

Do you sometimes see *#Error* or *#Name?* in a control? yes → **Go to...** I see *#Error* or *#Name?* in a field instead of the value, page 16

If your solution isn't here
Check these related chapters:
Data—Setting field properties, page 44
Expressions, page 90
Or see the general troubleshooting tips on page xiii.

Quick fix

The width of the column you want to see is set to 0.

1. Right-click the combo box, and then click Properties.

2. In the Column Widths property box on the Format tab, enter the width (in inches) of each column from left to right, separated by semicolons.

3. Set the width of any column you don't want to see to 0.

Go to...

The order of the rows in my list box or combo box isn't right, page 14

Go to...

The items in my list box or combo box take too long to appear, page 23

Does the text box fail to resize based on the amount of text it displays?

yes

Quick fix

You need to set the Can Shrink and Can Grow properties.

1. Open the report or form in design view.

2. Right-click the text box, and then click Properties.

3. Set the Can Shrink and Can Grow properties to Yes.

no

Are labels getting in the way?

yes

Go to...

The text box control labels are in the way, page 22

no

Are you having trouble with conditional formatting?

yes

Go to...

I don't get the right results with conditional formatting, page 18

The order of the rows in my list box or combo box isn't right

Source of the problem

Nature has a way of putting what you want in the last place you look for it. Similarly, it's lousy when the item you choose most often is the last one on a list. It would be helpful if a list box or combo box displayed alternatives in a different order so that you wouldn't have to scroll to find the value you want. To change the order of the rows in a list box or combo box you need to sort the records in the list. If you used one of the clever Access wizards to build the list or combo box, the rows are automatically sorted by the values in the first visible column. To reorder the rows, you can use the Query Builder. The following solution shows you how.

How to fix it

1. In the database window, select the form that contains the list box or combo box and then click the Design button.

2. Right-click the list box or combo box control whose values you want to rearrange, and then click Properties on the shortcut menu.

3. Click in the Row Source property box, and then click the Build button (...).

4. In the Query Builder, find the field the list is sorted by and change the setting from Ascending to Descending or from Descending to Ascending. ▶

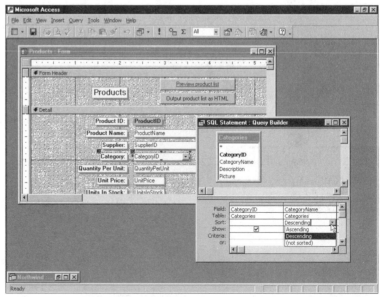

5. Close the Query Builder window, and click Yes in the message box asking whether you want to save the changes.

6. Click the Form View button. Open the list box or combo box, and check the new order of the rows.

If this set of steps doesn't put the rows in the order you want, you can save a query to use as the row source for the list box or combo box as follows:

1. Create a new query, basing it on the table that contains the fields you are working with in the list box or combo box.

2. Drag the field you want in the first column of the list box or combo box to the query grid.

3. Set the sort order you want for this field, Ascending or Descending.

4. Drag the second field you want in the list to the query grid.

5. Save and name the query.

6. Open the form with the list box or combo box in design view.

7. Right-click the list box or combo box, and then click Properties on the shortcut menu.

8. In the Row Source property box, select the name of the query you just created.

> **Tip**
>
> A combo box has two confusing properties: Row Source and Control Source. Row Source indicates where the list of options displayed in the drop-down list comes from. Control Source tells the combo box where to store the selected or entered data.

Referring to list items in a calculation

After selecting an item from the list in a list box or combo box, you might want to use that value in a calculation. When you use the Column identifier to refer to a column other than the bound column (the column tied to the underlying field), you may get unexpected results. One reason could be that you are not referring to the column correctly. You must refer to the column using the index number that identifies it. The index begins with 0, so the first column is Column(0), the second is Column(1), and so on. For example, the statement Forms![Products]![Category].Column(1) refers to the second column in the Category combo box on the Products form.

I see *#Error* or *#Name?* in a field instead of the value

Source of the problem

It's really frustrating to view data in a form you've worked hard on only to see a text box or a list box display *#Error* or *#Name?* where you expected to see a value. Several situations can cause this unwelcome event, and there are several corresponding cures. If the control is bound to a field, *#Name?* usually occurs when the control can't find the data you want it to display. If the data displayed in the control comes from an expression, one or more of the following situations could be the source of your trouble:

- The expression in the Control Source property box might not be preceded by an equal sign.

- The expression might include the names of fields or controls with spaces in them that are not enclosed in square brackets.

- The expression might include the name of the control itself. This creates a circular reference that Access can't resolve.

- The expression might refer to another control incorrectly so that Access can't evaluate the expression.

Tip

If you are using Access 97, renaming the field could also cause the problem. With Access 2000, you can activate the Name AutoCorrect feature. This feature helps prevent this problem by finding and changing a field name everywhere it occurs after you change the field name in the table or query. To activate this feature, click Options on the Tools menu. Click the General tab, and check the boxes for the Name AutoCorrect feature.

How to fix it

1. In the database window, select the table or query the form is based on and click the Design button. Review the fields in the table or query, and make sure that the field you're having trouble with is still included. If the field isn't in the table or query, it's best to delete the field from the form.

2. If the field is still there, close the table or query window, and then select the form in the database window.

3. Click the Design button to open the form in design view.

4. Right-click the troublesome control, and click Properties on the shortcut menu.

5. In the Control Source property box, check the spelling of the field and correct it if necessary.

If you are using an expression in the Control Source property, check that the expression is correct.

1. Be sure you've included an equal sign if you typed the expression yourself.

2. Check the field or control names used in the expression. If a field or control name in the expression contains a space, enclose the name in square brackets. For example, =[%State Tax]*[Total Amount of Sale].

3. Check to make sure that matching pairs of quotation marks (single or double) enclose text and other literal values in an expression.

4. Make sure you haven't used the name of the control in the expression. For example, the Control Source property of the BestBet field control is =[Field1]+[Field2]+[BestBet], which creates a circular reference. ▶

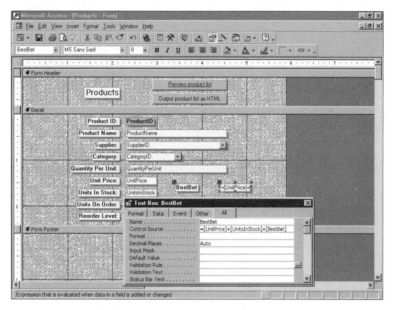

5. If you need to change the name of the control to fix the circular reference, make the change in the Name property box.

6. If you are referring to another control in the expression, make sure you are using the right format for the expression. For example, an expression such as =Forms![Orders]![OrderID] fully identifies the OrderID control on the Orders form. You could use this expression on a different form where you needed to refer to the OrderID control. On the other hand, you don't need the full identifier if you're referring to fields that are included on a form. For example, the expression =[SubTotal]+[Freight] might display the sum of the two values on a form that contains both the SubTotal and Freight fields.

Tip

If you have to change the name of a control, make sure you change it everywhere it occurs.

I don't get the right results with conditional formatting

Source of the problem

The conditional formatting feature is pretty helpful. It's new to Access 2000. It lets you emphasize values in a text box or combo box with a different appearance when the values meet the condition you've specified. If one of your sales reps exceeds her goal for the quarter, for example, you can automatically highlight the new threshold on future reports to make it stand out from the pack. But you have to get everything right. The condition can be as simple as matching a single value or something more complex, such as an expression comparing values. If you don't get the results you expect, one of these problems might be the culprit:

- You might have set an interval in your expression that includes (or does not include) the values at the limits of the interval.

- You might have set multiple conditions that conflict or override one another.

- You might have referred incorrectly to another control in a formula.

The following solution shows how to correct each of these problems.

How to fix it

1. In the database window, select the form or report that includes the control you've applied (or want to apply) conditional formatting to.

2. Click the Design button.

3. In the design view window, select the control, and then click Conditional Formatting on the Format menu.

4. In the Conditional Formatting dialog box, review the conditions set for that control.

5. If you want to include the values at the beginning and end of a range in the conditions you are trying to define, use the Between...And operator. ▶

6. If you want to set upper and lower limits without including the values at the beginning and end of the range, combine the Greater Than and Less Than operators in two conditions.

7. If more than one condition evaluates to true for the same field value, change the sequence of the conditions and put the one you want to prevail as the first condition. ▶

Using conditional formatting to manage controls

Did you know that you can use conditional formatting to make a control inactive under specific conditions? For example, if an order is to be shipped COD to a trusted customer, you can make the controls that contain credit card information inactive when COD is selected from the combo box. The credit information fields will no longer be in the tab order, which can save time during data entry. To use conditional formatting to make a text box or combo box inactive, open the Conditional Formatting dialog box (see step 3), enter the condition, and then click the Enabled button at the far right of the condition box.

I need to deal with Null values in a form or report

Source of the problem

When you don't know the value that goes in a field, you just leave it blank, right? That's okay on paper, but in Access, blank (or *Null*) values can generate unexpected results. You can get in real trouble, for example, if a field with blank values is used in a formula or another expression. Think about dividing a number by a field that is blank. You won't get the results you need. If the work you need to do with a field prohibits the use of blank values, set the field's Required property to Yes when you add the field to a table. If blank fields are a problem in a form or report but values of zero are okay, here's the way to solve your problem.

How to fix it

1. In the database window, select the form or report and then click the Design button.

2. In the toolbox, click the Text Box tool. Click on the form to add a new text box to the form or report.

3. Click the Properties button on the toolbar.

4. In the Control Source property for the text box, enter the expression **=Nz([FieldName])**. For FieldName, enter the name of the field that contains the Null values giving you problems. The Nz function changes blank values to 0 (for a number field) or to a zero-length string (for a text field). ▶

Warning

If you try to format the field value right in the bound text box control, you will cause an error. You must use a separate control for the formatting function.

Tip

If you want to display some informative text (such as *Need info*) in a blank field, use the expression =Nz([FieldName],"Need info").

Nz function : Form

ReaderName:	Rabbit
FieldName:	
Get Data	Need info

Text Box: Text3

Format | Data | Event | Other | All

Control Source	=Nz([FieldName],"Need info")
Input Mask	
Default Value	
Validation Rule	
Validation Text	
Enabled	Yes
Locked	No
Filter Lookup	Database Default

More expressions for dealing with Null values

There are other expressions you can use to work with a field with Null values in certain situations. If you are using the field in an expression that calculates the value of another field, you need to check for blank values before completing the calculation and convert them to a numeric 0, which can be used in the expression. To do this, you can combine the Nz function with the IIf function (IIf stands for Immediate If) in an expression such as =IIf(Nz([TotalCost])>100, "High", "Low"). Here, if the TotalCost field is blank, the Nz function changes it to 0, which can be compared to 100 like other calculated numeric values. If the calculated value of TotalCost is greater than 100, the control displays "High"; if the calculated value is less than or equal to 100, the control displays "Low."

Another way to get around blank values is to use the IIf function with the IsNull function in an expression such as =IIf(IsNull([MiddleInitial]), "NMI", [MiddleInitial]). If the middle initial field is blank, the control displays the text "NMI"; otherwise the middle initial itself is shown. ▶

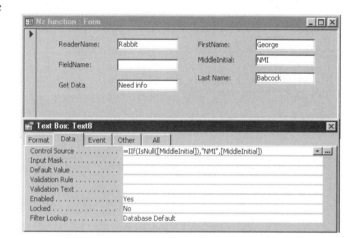

The text box control labels are in the way

Source of the problem

Every time you add a text box control to your form or report, Access thinks you want to use the label that goes with it. This is not always what you want, especially if you are pressed for room in the design or if the labels don't really match the values you see in the field.

The following steps show you how to add text boxes without automatically attaching a label.

How to fix it

1. In the database window, select the form or report you're working with and click the Design button.

2. If the toolbox is not already open, click the Toolbox button on the toolbar.

3. In the toolbox, click the Text Box tool.

4. Click the Properties button on the toolbar.

5. In the properties dialog box, click the Format tab and set the Auto Label and the Add Colon properties to No. ▶

Tip

Changing the settings for the Auto Label and Add Colon properties affects only the form or report you are working on. It doesn't change the default setting for all text boxes.

Tip

If you remove an attached label from a text box control, you can reattach it later. Select the label you want to use, and click Cut on the Edit menu. Then select the control, and click Paste on the Edit menu.

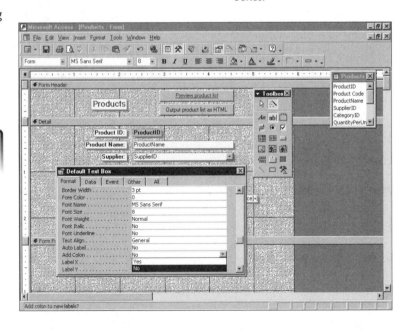

The items in my list box or combo box take too long to appear

Source of the problem

Sometimes it seems like a list box or combo box takes forever to display its values on the screen. The delay is caused by the time it takes to retrieve information from the database.

How to fix it

One way to speed up the display of information in the list is to base the list box or combo box on a saved query instead of on the SQL statement created by the List Box or Combo Box wizard. Follow these steps:

1. In the database window, select the form and click the Design button.

2. Right-click the combo box or list box, and then click Properties on the shortcut menu.

3. Click in the the Row Source property box, and then click the Build (...) button at the right.

4. In the Query Builder window, click the Save button.

5. In the Save As dialog box, enter a name for the query and then click OK. ▶

6. Close the Query Builder window, and click Yes when asked to save changes to the query design.

7. Save the changes to the form's design.

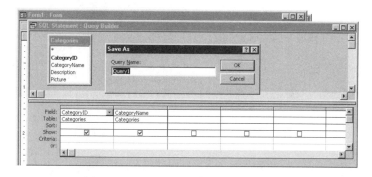

Are you trying to change a control property or type?

yes

no

Are you having trouble adding an option to an option group?

yes

Go to...
My option group doesn't work the way it should, page 26

no

Are you having trouble with a command button control?

yes

no

Are you having trouble with a tab control?

yes

Go to...
I'm having trouble creating, organizing, and sizing a tab control, page 28

no

Are you having trouble with a hyperlink?

yes

Are some or all of the properties blank?

yes

Quick fix

Only the properties that the selected controls have in common show up.

1. Hold down Shift and deselect the nonmatching control.

2. If you see no properties, you are in Edit mode. Press Esc to leave Edit mode and recover the property sheet.

no

Do you want to change a control to a different type?

yes

Quick fix

1. Select the control.

2. Point to Change To on the Format menu.

3. Click the control type from the displayed list. The dimmed types are not allowed.

Are you trying to include an & in the control title?

yes

Quick fix

On its own, an ampersand character in a control title creates a shortcut key for the command button action.

1. To include an ampersand in the title, type two of them: Jack && Jill.

no

Are you trying to put a custom image on a button?

yes

Go to...
I can't make an image fit on a command button, page 30

Go to...
I get an error message when I click a hyperlink, page 32

If your solution isn't here
Check these related chapters:
Forms—Designing, page 114
Reports—Creating, page 246
Or see the general troubleshooting tips on page xiii.

My option group doesn't work the way it should

Source of the problem

It's always great to be offered a choice, whether it's how well done your steak is cooked or what movie you want to see. But what if you don't get your way? When you're working in Access, what if you set up a group of options, and when you make a selection, Access runs off to left field and gives you something entirely different? For example, the handy option group displays a set of mutually exclusive alternatives from which you can choose the one you want. The options can range from a list of friends' names to which form you want to work on next. The option group control is actually the frame that contains the list of options. When you select one of the options, that becomes the value of the option group.

If you are trying to add a new option to a group you created with the Option Group Wizard and the new option doesn't work in form view, you probably placed it too close to the option group border. Access then considers the new check box, option button, or toggle button a separate control (even if it does overlap the option group) rather than one of the options in the group.

The following solution shows how to solve this problem.

How to fix it

1. In the database window, select the form that contains the option group and then click the Design button.

2. Delete the option button, check box, or toggle button that doesn't work.

3. In the form design toolbox, click the icon for the control you are using for the options and move the mouse pointer over to the option group.

4. When the option group is highlighted, place the control in the group box. ▶

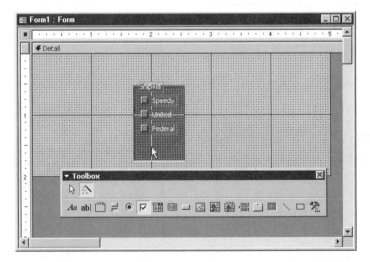

5. Use the commands on the Format menu to align the new option with the others in the group.

6. Save your changes to the form.

A different approach to options

What if you need to create a group of options that are not mutually exclusive? If you have several yes or no options that are related to the same type of information but belong to separate fields, you can create a faux option group. For example, you might want to find out what kind of books your customers like to read and you don't want to limit them to only one choice. You can add a box to the form and place the option controls in it. Then you can format the box to make it look like an option group created by the Option Group Wizard.

1. In form design view, add the independent options (check boxes, option buttons, or toggle buttons) to the form and arrange them in a group.

2. Right-click the first option control, and then click Properties on the shortcut menu.

3. In the properties dialog box, set the Control Source property for that option to the corresponding field in the table the form is based on. Repeat steps 2 and 3 for the other controls in the group.

4. In the toolbox, click the Rectangle tool and draw a rectangle around the group.

5. Right-click the rectangle, and then click Properties on the shortcut menu.

6. Set the properties of the rectangle to resemble a real option group as follows: set Back Style to Transparent, Back Color to White, Border Style to Solid, Border Color to Black, and Border Width to Hairline.

> **Tip**
> Try to avoid overlapping controls in a form or report. Access repaints the screen for each layer in the object, which can significantly slow down the display.

7. Add a label control to the form, placing it so that it overlaps the upper border of the group frame, and enter the name you want for the group of options.

8. Right-click the label, and then click Properties on the shortcut menu.

9. Change the label's Back Style property to Normal and the Back Color property to light gray.

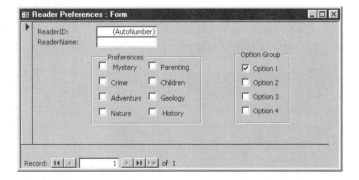

I'm having trouble creating, organizing, and sizing a tab control

Source of the problem

It seems that the more helpful a feature can be, the trickier it gets. The professional looking tab control is a shining example of this well-founded theory. Tab controls are great for grouping related information on a form that needs to display a lot of data. With tab controls you have all kinds of leeway with respect to the number of tabs to include, the size of the tab control itself, and the appearance of the tabs at the top of the pages. This flexibility is great, but it can cause frustrating problems because too much data on a single screen can be confusing.

If you are having trouble adding another tab to the control or changing the order of the tabs, you might not be selecting the right control on the form. If you're having trouble resizing the tab control to make room for another control (a command button, for example) or other information on the form, one of the tabs probably contains controls that are getting in the way. Displaying a large collection of tabs can also be tricky, especially if you want to see all the tabs at once instead of just a single row of them.

The following solutions show you how to deal with these problems.

How to fix it

1. In the database window, select the form with the tab control and click the Design button.

2. To add another tab, right-click the border of the tab control or any tab on the control and choose Insert Page from the shortcut menu. ▶

Tip

As you add tabs, the widths of the tabs are reduced. When the number of tabs exceeds the width of the control, the earlier tabs aren't displayed and scroll bars are added so that you can view all the tabs.

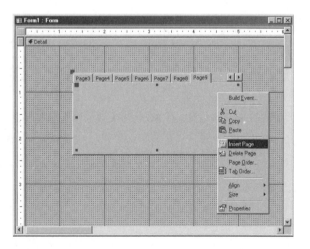

3. To see all the tabs at once, select the tab control (not one of the tab pages), click the Properties button, and set the Multi Row property to Yes. Doing this takes up more vertical space on the form, but you can see all the tab captions. ▶

Tip

To open the property sheet for the tab control, double-click one edge of the control. To open the property sheet for a specific tab, double-click the tab.

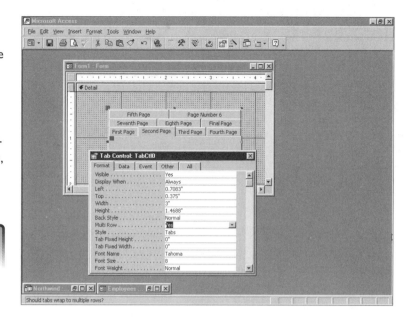

Making a tab control the right size can take some work, especially when you've added command buttons and other controls. You need to take into account their size and location when resizing the entire set of tabs.

1. To resize a tab control, look at each tab page and move or reduce the controls that exceed the page width you want to achieve.

2. If you want to specify the height or width of the tabs on the tab control, set the Tab Fixed Height or the Tab Fixed Width properties. The default 0 setting sizes the tab widths to fit the contents of the particular tab. ▶

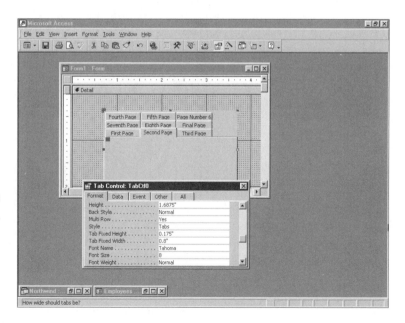

I can't make an image fit on a command button

Source of the problem

You have a picture of your favorite mountain resort or one of your firstborn that you want to use on a command button on a form. You add it to the button, but it just doesn't look right. Not only that, Access won't let you resize or position the picture while you're working on the form.

If you don't use one of the images provided by Access, you can get in trouble. And even the way you add an image to a button can result in different problems. When you use the Picture Builder to add a picture to a button, the button is automatically resized to fit the image. If you simply type the name of the picture file in the Picture property of the command button, the image is cropped to fit the size of the command button you drew.

How to fix it

1. Regardless of how you added the picture to the command button, the first step is to open the form in design view. To do this, select the form in the database window and then click the Design button. ▶

2. Double-click the command button control to open the Properties dialog box.

3. In the Picture property box, remove the file name.

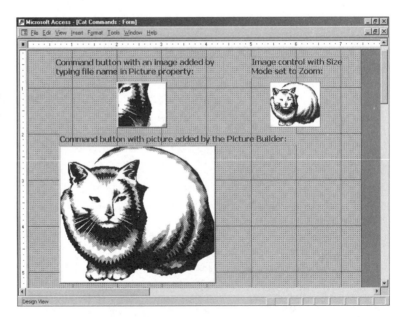

Tip

If you use a custom image on a command button, it's a good idea to add a control tip to explain what the button does.

4. Look at the Width and Height properties of the button and make note of the measurements. This will help you resize the picture to fit.

5. Open the picture file in your image program (such as Microsoft Paint, the program that comes with Microsoft Windows), and resize the button to fit the dimensions of the button. Also, you can crop the picture in the graphics program so that the important part of the image will be centered in the button.

6. Return to the form in design view, and reenter the name of the picture file in the Picture property box.

7. Switch to form view to check the picture and make sure it fits on the command button.

Pictures for every occasion

The Access Picture Builder provides over 220 images for almost any type of command button you can dream up. A lot of them are used as default images by the Command Button Wizard. For example, if you create a button with the wizard that prints the current form, the button will show a picture of a printer.

Here are just a few of the Picture Builder offerings:

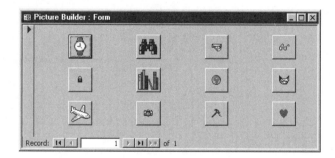

I get an error message when I click a hyperlink

Source of the problem

You expect the high-tech hyperlink to do as it's told—jump to the destination you set it to. But like your favorite pet Lab, it doesn't always obey your command.

If you get an error message when you click a hyperlink and can't reach the destination, there are several possible reasons why, aside from the hyperlink just being stubborn.

- The destination may have been renamed or deleted. Sorry, there's no real cure unless you can find out the new name.

- The destination may have been moved to another location and the link is broken.

- The destination may just be busy (assuming you have appropriate access to it).

- The destination is on your company network, but you don't have access to it. Or, the server may be down.

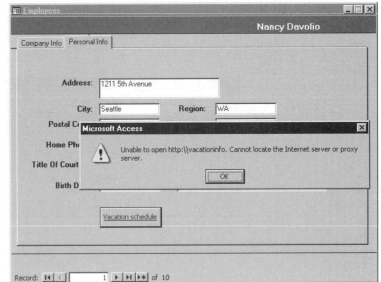

The following solution describes cures for these problems.

How to fix it

1. If the destination has been renamed or you want to link to a new location, find out the name of the destination. If the hyperlink is on your company's intranet, check with your administrator to be sure that you have access to the destination and that the network is operating.

2. Open the form in design view, and then right-click the control that includes the hyperlink.

3. Point to Hyperlink on the shortcut menu, and click Edit Hyperlink. ▶

4. Enter the correct hyperlink address.

5. Click OK in the Edit Hyperlink dialog box, switch to form view, and check the hyperlink to be sure that it works.

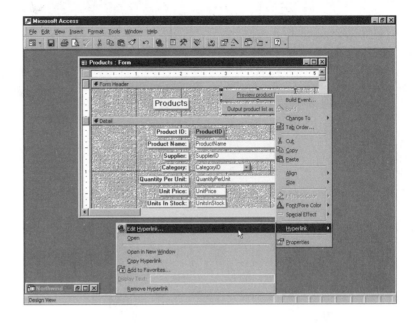

Hyperlinks to everywhere

The ability to add hyperlinks to a table or form opens up a whole new world for you, the Access user. A hyperlink can jump to a lot of different places and objects:

Tip

If the nonresponsive hyperlink is on the Internet, wait a while and try again.

● A location in another file on your hard disk

● A Web site

● A location on your local area network

● Another database object

● A location in another Office document such as a bookmark in Microsoft Word, a named range in Microsoft Excel, or a presentation in Microsoft PowerPoint

Hyperlinks that you place in a table design by adding a field and specifying the Hyperlink data type jump to a different location within each record. For example, in a table containing information about popular CDs, you can create a hyperlink field to jump to a sound clip sample from the CD.

You can assign a hyperlink to a button on a form that jumps to another location. If the hyperlink connects to a document that was created in another application, that application starts automatically.

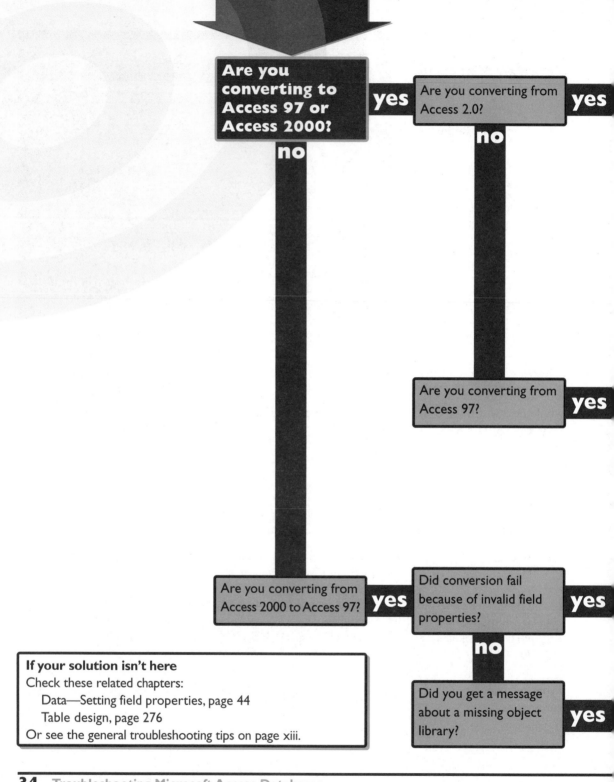

Are you converting to Access 97 or Access 2000?

yes → **Are you converting from Access 2.0?** yes

no

Are you converting from Access 97? yes

no → **Are you converting from Access 2000 to Access 97?** yes → **Did conversion fail because of invalid field properties?** yes

no

Did you get a message about a missing object library? yes

If your solution isn't here
Check these related chapters:
 Data—Setting field properties, page 44
 Table design, page 276
Or see the general troubleshooting tips on page xiii.

Do your reports in Access 2000 have the wrong margins?

yes

Quick fix

When a report is converted to Access 2000, the margins are automatically set to the minimum margin for your default printer.

1. Open the report in Access 2000.
2. On the File menu, click PageSetup.
3. Reduce the column width and spacing so the width doesn't exceed the total paper width.

no

Do you see a message about memory or indexes?

yes

Go to...
I see an error message about being out of memory or having too many indexes, page 42

no

Go to...
I'm having trouble converting an Access 2.0 database, page 36

Does a command button fail to work properly?

yes

Quick fix

The command button was created with old Visual Basic code.

1. After converting the database, delete the command button from the form.
2. Re-create the button using the Command Button Wizard.

no

Does your code fail to compile successfully?

yes

Go to...
My code won't compile, page 38

Quick fix

The Field Size property for a Number field is set to Decimal.

1. Open the table with the invalid field property in design view.
2. Select the number field, and change the Field Size property to Single or Double.

Go to...
I see a message that an object library is missing, page 40

I'm having trouble converting an Access 2.0 database

Source of the problem

It takes a quantum leap to move from Access 2.0 to Access 2000. It's like trying to put your great-grandpa on the moon. So many aspects and features have changed as Access has grown up that it would be a miracle if there were no glitches in a conversion.

Most of the problems you'll encounter converting an Access 2.0 database to Access 2000 occur under the hood. They are often caused by improvements in the Access machinery and accessories. Access tries to be as backward compatible as possible, but some innovations are just too much. Even changes to other programs have an impact on backward compatibility. For example, Microsoft Visual Basic, which you can use to automate features in an Access database, has changed with later versions. If a procedure causes an error in conversion, there might be a module and a procedure using the same name in the Access 2.0 database. In Access 2.0 this was no problem, but in Access 95 and later, procedures and modules must have different names.

If you're having trouble converting custom controls and you get a connection error, Access is trying to convert 16-bit versions of ActiveX (OLE Custom) controls to the 32-bit version. But, they are not registered in your system. If you add the 16-bit files to your system and the 32-bit versions are registered, Access will convert them to the 32-bit versions.

Here are solutions to these problems with conversions.

How to fix it

1. If you experience trouble converting your Access 2.0 database, review the names of the procedures and modules. Check for modules with the same names as procedures. If you have duplicates, rename the module or the procedure.

2. Change all references to the procedure or module you renamed, such as those in an event property in a form or a report.

If ActiveX controls are the problem, after converting the Access 2.0 database, open the Access 2000 database and follow these steps:

1. Add the file for the control to your hard disk.

2. On the Tools menu, click ActiveX Controls.

3. In the ActiveX Controls dialog box, click Register. ▶

4. In the Add ActiveX Control box, locate the path to the control you want to register.

5. Select the control, and then click OK.

6. In the ActiveX Controls dialog box, click Close.

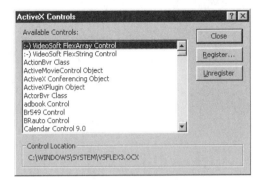

Other conversion gotchas!

When you are converting an Access 2.0 database to Access 2000, keep these two potential problems in mind. One relates to queries built in Access 97 or earlier versions that are based on date and time criteria. They can produce the wrong results because of the Y2K compliance built into Access 2000. Dates that you entered in earlier versions of Access using two-digit year values are automatically assigned a four-digit year value in Access 2000. Depending on the value, the century is assumed. The date for determining the century advances by one each year. To remedy this problem, modify the query criteria to specify the full four-digit year value.

In Access 2.0 you could use the Format property to display different values for Null and zero-length strings. After converting a database to Access 2000, you need to take a different approach. You can fix a faulty Format property that fails to tell Null values from zero-length strings by adding a new text box control to the form or report. Then, enter an expression using the IIf function together with the IsNull function in the text box's Control Source property. For example, you could use the expression =IIf(IsNull([MiddleInitial]),"NMI",[MiddleInitial]) to test for the presence or absence of text in the middle initial field. The IsNull function tests the value in the MiddleInitial field and indicates Yes if the value is blank or No if the field contains characters. Then the IIf function takes over and uses the result the IsNull function provides to display the characters NMI if the MiddleInitial field is blank or the middle initials if the field contains a value.

My code won't compile

Source of the problem

In this day and age, we've all got to have the latest model cars and the newest type of cellular phone or we just aren't with it.

Well, Access is just as fashion-conscious as the rest of us, trying to keep up with the latest trends. Each new version of Access makes use of the latest version of the Visual Basic language and syntax. The language has migrated from Access Basic in Access 2.0 to Visual Basic for Applications in Access 95 and Access 97 to full-blown Visual Basic in Access 2000. Although Microsoft works hard to achieve backward compatibility, some changes might cause compilation errors. (After all, what's the point of going modern if you have to keep all the old stuff?) These errors can interrupt or stymie database conversion.

When you try to run a database that you've converted to Access 2000, you might see an error message without any specific information about what caused the error. That's not much help, but at least you'll know you'll have to recompile the code and fix each error as it pops up.

If you're converting from Access 2.0, you may get a compile error message about syntax errors in the original version. Or you may have used a word to identify a field, control, or database object that is a reserved keyword in the later Access version. For example, if you used AddressOf, Decimal, Implements, RaiseEvent, or WithEvents in a program built with Access 2.0, your Visual Basic code won't compile in Access 2000.

Another cause for compilation errors can be failure to support older objects, methods, and properties. If you want to keep your previous version database, you must create a reference to the object library that provides a cross-reference between versions.

How to fix it

1. To recompile the code in your Access 2000 database, open any of the modules in your database in design view.

2. Click Compile <*databasename*> on the Debug menu.

3. When an error is detected, the Visual Basic Editor stops the compilation, highlights the offensive statement, and displays a dialog box with a clue as to what is wrong with the statement. The compile error shown in the figure is caused by the reference to a variable that was not defined.

The intention was to define the label name in the Dim statement as lblFix. But, in the Set statement, the variable name was misspelled. ▶

4. Click OK.

5. Correct the error, and then click the Continue toolbar button to continue reviewing the code.

6. If you had syntax errors in version 2.0 code, you need to return to the previous version database, correct the syntax errors, compile all the modules in the 2.0 database, and convert again to Access 2000.

7. If you have used a reserved word as an identifier, change the identifier so that it doesn't conflict with the Visual Basic reserved keyword.

8. To create a reference to another object library, click References in the Tools menu, select the Microsoft DAO 2.5/3.5 Compatibility Library, and click OK.

Warning

When you convert a database, you can save it with the same name or enter a new name. If you choose to use the same name, Access overwrites the old database. Unless you have created a backup file, you would be wise to use a different name.

Using references to libraries

If you want to make sure your program uses only the Access 2000 objects, methods, and properties, clear the 2.5/3.5 Compatibility Library in the References dialog box. Then, recompile all the modules in the program. The code will no longer rely on the backward compatible library. To see exactly which objects, methods, and properties are no longer included in DAO 3.6, the version Access 2000 uses, and the recommended replacements for them, open the Access 2000 Help topic, "DAO Object Library Compatibility."

I see a message that an object library is missing

Source of the problem

The libraries that Access needs to do its job aren't the same as the downtown public library where you did your homework. But they aren't all that different. Even though they don't use the Dewey decimal system to organize everything, these libraries are still precisely arranged so that Access can find what it needs quickly.

Library files, called dynamic link libraries (or DLLs) by the experts, are essential to running the Visual Basic code that's used to automate and enhance an Access database. Visual Basic can automate almost everything in an Access program. It can, for example, display a single startup screen from which you can open a form, preview a report, or log on to a Web site—anything you want.

Access 2000 stores its library files in a directory different from previous versions of Access. So, for databases converted from earlier versions, you have to give Access a road map to the location of the libraries by setting a reference. The same is true for new databases created in Access 2000 and converted to earlier versions. When you convert them to version 97, the necessary object references are often lost. If they are, you will see a message that at least one of the Access 97 object libraries is missing.

How to fix it

1. In converting the Access 2000 database to Access 97, when you see the message about missing libraries, click OK.

2. Open the database in Access 97.

3. In the database window, select any form or other object that can include a class module.

4. Click the Code button to open the Visual Basic Editor.

5. On the Tools menu, click References.

> **Tip**
> You can also open the Visual Basic Editor window by clicking Modules in the database window and then clicking New.

6. In the Available References box, clear the check boxes next to the references that are marked MISSING. Clearing the missing references forces Access to look in a different directory for the library files.

7. Check the Microsoft DAO 3.5 Object Library. ▶

8. Click OK.

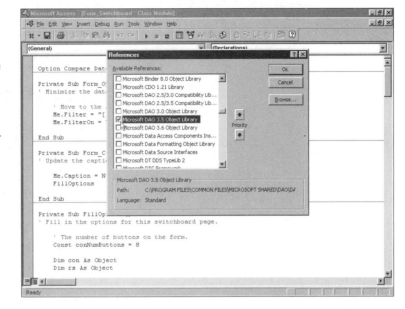

A few other 2000 to 97 issues

Any feature or functionality that is new to Access 2000 will obviously be lost when you convert a database to Access 97. For example, you will lose all links to data access pages, which are new to Access 2000.

Access 2000 uses a slightly different code system for characters—the Unicode system instead of the ANSI numbered set of 256 characters. As a result, some of the characters might not be correctly converted to version 97. If you're converting a secured database from Access 2000 to Access 97, you must have Open/Run and Open Exclusive permissions set for the database and Read Design permissions set for all the tables, queries, forms, and other objects in the database. After converting the database to Access 97, you need to open it and apply user-level security to restore system security. To set permission, click Security on the Tools menu and then click User and Group Permissions. Set the options for the database and the database options in the User And Group Permissions dialog box.

I see an error message about being out of memory or having too many indexes

Source of the problem

The version of Visual Basic used by Access 2000 is pickier than the previous versions. It won't let you have more than 1082 modules in your database. Every form and report includes a Has Module property that is set to Yes by default, whether or not any code is attached to it. Each of these blank Yeses count toward the limit. You'll only reach this limit when working with large databases. If you do try to convert a database with more than 1082 modules, Access will display a message saying you are out of memory. The obvious remedy is to dump all those forms and reports. But then you'd have to go through the trouble of re-creating them in the new version. There's a better way to solve this problem.

Also, Access 2000 has a limit on the number of indexes you can include with any single table. If you see a message that you have too many indexes, at least one of the tables in your Access 2.0 database exceeds the limit of 32. Access 2.0 automatically indexed all the linking fields involved in a table relationship—both in the primary key field table and in the foreign key table. If you have one table that is involved in a lot of relationships, you can easily exceed the 32-index limit.

Here are solutions to these problems.

How to fix it

1. If you receive an out-of-memory error, open the database you're trying to convert in the earlier version of Access.

2. Delete any unnecessary forms and reports—maybe some of the early trial versions that you abandoned in favor of later ones.

3. Try converting the database again.

If that doesn't work, you can split your application into separate databases and then perform the conversion. Follow these steps:

1. In Access 2.0, click New on the File menu to create a blank database.

2. On the File menu, click Import, and import all the tables and queries from the database you are converting to the new one.

3. Import some of the forms and reports that relate to the same activity, such as customer relations or supplier information. ▶

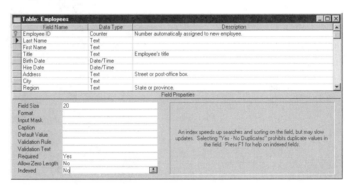

4. Create a second new blank database, and import all the tables and queries to it.

5. Import the remaining forms and reports and other objects to this database.

6. Convert both new databases to Access 2000.

7. In Access 2000, open one of the new databases.

8. On the File menu, click Get External Data and then click Import.

9. Locate the second converted database, and click Import. Select the forms, reports, and other objects in the Import Objects dialog box and click OK.

To cure the problem with excessive indexes, follow these steps:

1. Open the Access 2.0 database you're trying to convert.

2. Click the Relationships button, and look for a table that is involved in several relationships.

3. Delete some relationship lines from that table.

4. In the database window, select one of the tables that is still related to the table you worked with in step 3. Open that table in design view.

5. In the Field Properties area of the table design window, set the Indexed property for several fields to No. ▶

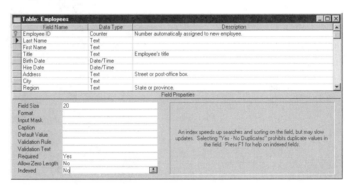

6. Close the database and convert it again. Repeat the process if your work with the first table doesn't solve the problem.

7. After you successfully convert the Access 2.0 database to Access 2000, establish the relationships and indexes again in the new database.

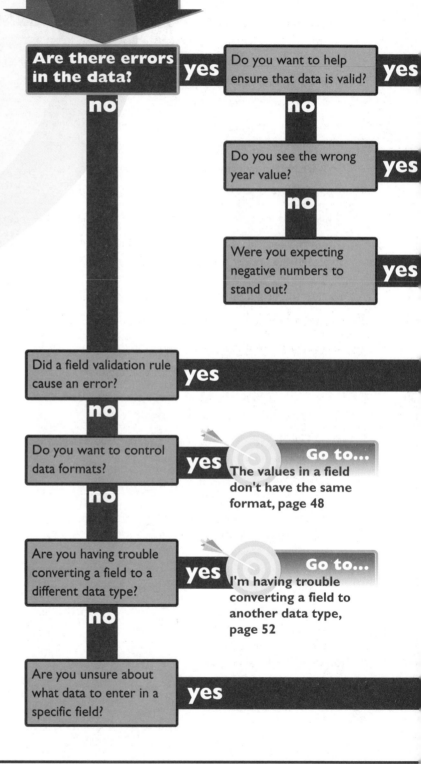

Are there errors in the data? — yes → Do you want to help ensure that data is valid? — yes

no ↓

Do you see the wrong year value? — yes

no ↓

Were you expecting negative numbers to stand out? — yes

Did a field validation rule cause an error? — yes

no ↓

Do you want to control data formats? — yes

Go to...
The values in a field don't have the same format, page 48

no ↓

Are you having trouble converting a field to a different data type? — yes

Go to...
I'm having trouble converting a field to another data type, page 52

no ↓

Are you unsure about what data to enter in a specific field? — yes

Go to...

Some data is incorrect, page 46

Quick fix

You need to set the format to show a four-digit year.

1. On the Tools menu, click Options and then click the General tab.

2. Under Use Four-Digit Year Formatting, choose This Database to limit the date format to the current database, or choose All Databases.

3. If you want the four-digit year only for a single field, change the field's Format property to mm/dd/yyyy.

Quick fix

You need to create an expression in the field's Format property.

1. Open the table in design view, and then select the field.

2. In the Format property box, enter the expression **#,##0.00[Green]; (#,##0.00)[Red]; "Zero";"Unknown"**. This expression displays positive numbers in green and negative numbers in red and enclosed in parentheses. (Blank fields display Zero or Unknown.)

Quick fix

You need to modify the validation rule.

1. Open the table in design view.

2. Select the field you set the validation rule for.

3. In the Validation Rule properties box, remove references to other fields in this or another table, controls on a form, or any user-defined functions.

4. Modify the rule so that it applies only to values in this field.

Go to...

I don't know what information to enter in a field, page 50

If your solution isn't here

Check these related chapters:

Controls—Managing data, page 12

Expressions, page 90

Table design, page 276

Or see the general troubleshooting tips on page xiii.

Some data is incorrect

Source of the problem

In spite of what some folks say, those of us who use computers are just as human as anyone else. And being human, we make just as many mistakes, especially when entering data. Most of the time, the source of incorrect data is simple human error, and that's hard to control. You might simply need to go through your data, sniff out the mistakes, and fix them. But luckily, as you enter new data, you can train Access to be diligent in its efforts to prevent errors from becoming comfortably ensconced in your database. You have two ways to help ensure the accuracy of your data:

- Create a validation rule for individual fields in a table.

- Create a validation rule that applies to a complete record in a table.

A field validation rule applies to the data entered in a single field. The rule limits the data to a range of values or to one of a few specific values. A record validation rule compares values in two separate fields in the same record. (For example, the selling price of a product must be greater than the cost to produce it.) The record validation rule is enforced when you move to another record and Access tries to save the one you just worked on.

The following solutions show how to put these rules to work.

How to fix it

To set a validation rule for a field, follow these steps:

1. In the database window, select the table with the troublesome data and click the Design button.

2. Select the field you want to apply the rule to, and then click in the Validation Rule property box in the Field Properties area. ▶

3. Enter an expression that will control the value the field can have. For example, if the date in a Date/Time field

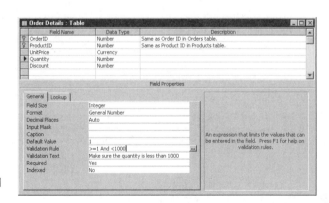

must not be later than one year from today, enter the expression **<Date()+365**. If a number (say the number of units in an order) must fall between 1 and 999, enter **>=1 AND <1000**. If you want to limit the data in the field to a short list of values, enter the items in that list, enclosing them in double quotation marks and separating them with the OR operator—for example, **"Teal" OR "Burgundy" OR "Navy"**.

Tip

If you need help with an expression, click the Build button next to the Validation Rule property box, and the Expression Builder will give you a hand.

4. Click in the Validation Text property box, and enter a message that will notify the user when there's something wrong with the value he or she typed in. ▶

5. Save the changes to the table's design.

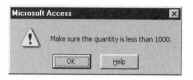

To set up a record validation rule for a table, follow these steps:

1. In the database window, select the table you want to apply the rule to and click the Design button.

2. On the toolbar, click the Properties button.

3. In the Validation Rule property box, enter the expression for the rule you want to apply—for example, **[Sales Price]>[Cost]**. ▶

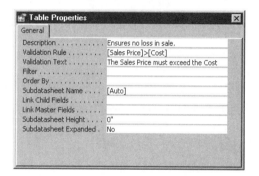

4. In the Validation Text property box, enter a message that notifies the user about the rule you've applied.

More thoughts about data validation

Tip

A table can have only one record validation rule, so if you need more than one criterion, combine them in a single expression with the AND and OR operators.

A field validation rule is enforced when you enter or edit data in that field, whether you're working in a datasheet, a form, or with an append or update query. If the rule is violated, the message you entered in the Validation Text property box appears when you move to another field. If you enter a list of values in the Validation Rule property, Access will insist that the field contain one of those values. If you want to be able to leave the field blank, you must add Null to the list even if the field's Required property is set to No. You don't need quotation marks around Null because it is a special term that Access recognizes.

If you add a validation rule after data has been entered in the field, Access offers to test the existing data against the rule. If you respond No to the offer, you can still run the test later by switching to table design view and choosing Test Validation Rules from the Edit menu.

The values in a field don't have the same format

Source of the problem

Some people enjoy seeing last names in all caps, and others get a kick out of italics. When there are many people entering and editing data in your database, their personal preferences can create a disorderly appearance. And it's possible that even you occasionally vary the data formats you use. While the data is correct, the motley display is disruptive and can confuse even the most stable of information managers.

The way to fix a haphazard display of data is to set the Format property for a field. By doing this you standardize how the data is displayed and calm any ruffled feathers. Access provides a set of standard formats for Number, Date/Time, and Yes/No fields. You can set custom formats for all types of fields except an OLE Object field. You add the formatting instructions by using special symbols. Many symbols can be used with all types of fields, while others are used only with certain types of fields.

How to fix it

To set a Format property for a text or memo field, follow these steps:

1. In the database window, select the table with the field you want to format and then click the Design button.

2. Select the field, and then click in the Format property box in the Field Properties area.

3. Using special symbols and place-holders (see the list on the next page), enter the expression you want to apply to the data. For example, the > symbol makes all the text capital letters. If you enter the formatting instruction >@, Johnny will be displayed as JOHNNY. Use the @ symbol to indicate a required character or space. The format setting @@@-@@-@@@@ will display the entry 123456789 as 123-45-6789, perfect for Social Security numbers. ▶

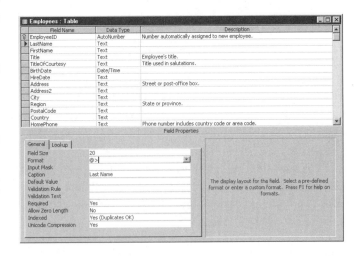

To change the default check box format for a Yes/No field, follow these steps:

1. Open the table in design view, and select the Yes/No field.

2. In the Field Properties area, click the Lookup tab.

3. From the Display Control list, select Text Box.

4. Click the General tab, and select the format you want in the Format property list. You have a choice of True/False, Yes/No, or On/Off.

5. Save the changes to the table's design.

Tip

To change the symbol that displays with foreign currency values, change the Country setting in the Regional Settings dialog box in Windows Control Panel.

Creating custom formats

Here's a table showing the symbols you use to set up text and memo field formatting.

Symbol	Effect	Example
!	Fills from left to right, forcing values in the field to be left aligned.	Text would look like this... ...not like this
"abc"	Displays the characters enclosed in quotation marks.	@"None" displays the field value, if any, or None if blank.
*	Fills the field with the character that follows.	*# displays a five-character field as ##### no matter what you enter.
\	Indicates that the character that follows is meant to be a literal instead of a special symbol.	@\! displays the field value Not here as Not here!
[color]	Displays data in color. Available colors are black, blue, green, cyan, red, magenta, yellow, and white.	@[blue] displays the field value in blue.
@	Indicates a required character or space.	@@@-@@-@@@@ displays the value 123456789 as 123-45-6789. All characters are required.
&	Indicates an optional character or space.	@@@-@@-&&&& displays the value 123456 as 123-45-6. The last four characters are not required.
>	Converts all letters to uppercase.	Tidepool is displayed as TIDEPOOL.
<	Converts all letters to lowercase.	Tidepool is displayed as tidepool.

I don't know what information to enter in a field

Source of the problem

Although you try to identify all the fields in your database with unique and informative names, there can still be some lingering doubt about exactly what is supposed to go in a field. You need a method of instructing yourself and others about what to enter in a field. One way to get the jump on consistent data entry is to create an *input mask*, which serves as a template for data entry. Fields that need a specific length (a five-digit ID number, for example) or type of data, or fields that include required characters such as slashes, commas, or hyphens, are good candidates for an input mask. When you move to the field to enter data in it, the input mask is displayed, providing guidance for the data you need to enter. The following solution shows how to curb forgetful data entry habits by using an input mask.

How to fix it

1. In the database window, select the table containing the field you want to work with and then click the Design button.

2. In the Field Properties area, click in the Input Mask property box and then click the Build (…) button at the right. This starts the Input Mask Wizard.

3. In the Input Mask Wizard, you'll see some commonly used formats to pick from. Choose the input mask you want.

4. Click in the Try It box to see how the mask will be displayed, and then enter some sample data. ▶

If you want to create a new custom input mask, follow these steps:

1. Start the Input Mask Wizard as described in steps 1 and 2 above.

2. Click the Edit List button.

Tip

The Wizard works only for text and date/time fields, but you can type a mask for any type of field. Also, you don't have to use the wizard at all; you can simply type the appropriate input mask characters in the Input Mask property box.

Input Mask Wizard

Which input mask matches how you want data to look?

To see how a selected mask works, use the Try It box.

To change the Input Mask list, click the Edit List button.

Input Mask:	Data Look:
Phone Number	(206) 555-1212
Social Security Number	531-86-7180
Zip Code	98052-6399
Extension	63215
Password	*******
Long Time	3:12:00 AM

Try It: ___-__-____

Edit List | Cancel | < Back | Next > | Finish

3. At the bottom of the dialog box, click the new record button on the record navigation bar to display a blank record.

4. For a field that contains coded parts numbers using an ABC-1234-56A format, for example, enter **>LLL-0000-00L** in the Input Mask box. ▶

5. Enter a description of the mask in the Description box and type an underscore in the Placeholder box.

6. Enter a sample of the data in the Sample Data box.

7. Click Close, and then click Finish in the Input Mask Wizard.

Customize Input Mask Wizard

Do you want to edit or add input masks for the Input Mask Wizard to display?

Description:	Product Code
Input Mask:	>LLL-0000-00L
Placeholder:	_
Sample Data:	ABC-1234-56A
Mask Type:	Text/Unbound

Help

Close

Record: 12 of 12

More about input masks

Special symbols are used to create input masks. If you want to create a custom input mask, use combinations of the following symbols.

Input mask symbol	Values you can enter	Requires an entry?	Example Input mask	Valid value
0	0–9; no + or – sign. Blanks show as 0.	Yes	00000	92118
9	Same as 0, except blanks display as a space.	No	00000-9999	92118-2450 or just 92118
#	Same as 9, except allows + and – signs.	No	#999	+456 or −456
L	Any uppercase letter.	Yes	LL???	ABcde
?	Any letter.	No	??000	ab123
A	Any letter or digit.	Yes	(999) AAA-AAAA	(619) 555-HOME
a	Any letter or digit.	No	AAA-aaaa	Big-time or Non-tox
&	Any character or a space.	Yes	(&&&)-&&&&	(1 3)-ab 2
C	Any character or a space.	No	(&&&)-CCCC	(1 3)-ab
<	Converts letters to lowercase.	N/A	<aaaa	join
>	Converts letters to uppercase.	N/A	>AAAA	JOIN
!	Fills field from left to right.	N/A	!aaaaa	Align... ...not Align

I'm having trouble converting a field to another data type

Source of the problem

No matter how careful you are defining the fields in your database, the need for information shifts. Someone is always changing something, and you have to go along with it. Your boss asks for a new report that requires date arithmetic, so a text field that contains dates most of the time must now become a Date/Time field. This sounds simple enough, but you have to be explicit with a computer program. Otherwise, it might rebel.

There are several reasons why Access might balk at your conversion:

- You're trying to convert a field to an AutoNumber.

- The data already in the field is not compatible with the type of field you want to convert to.

- You're tampering with a field that's part of a table relationship.

The following solution shows how to fix these problems:

How to fix it

If you see the message shown in the figure, you have tried to convert a field to the AutoNumber data type after you've entered one or more records. ▶

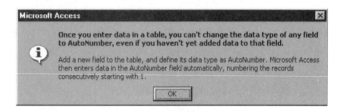

1. Click OK to dispose of the message.

2. Add a new field to the table, and select AutoNumber from the drop-down list of data types.

3. Save the changes to the table design. As the message indicates, Access will fill in the AutoNumber data all on its own.

4. If the field you were trying to convert contains relevant information, leave it as is. If you were just using the field as a primary key field with no other meaning, delete it. The new AutoNumber field will serve that purpose.

If you see the message shown in this figure, you have tried to convert a field that contains data to a different type of field. In this case, the data in the field doesn't fit the new type. Before the conversion can be successful, you'll need to revise the incompatible data. ▶

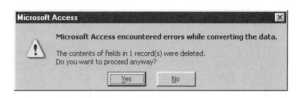

1. In the message box, click No to cancel the conversion.

2. Click the View button to switch the table to datasheet view.

3. Review the data in the field you are trying to convert, and change the records that aren't compatible with the data type you're converting.

4. Click the View button again to return the table to design view.

5. In the table design window, select the new data type for the field and then save the changes to the table design.

Tip

If you click Yes in the message, you can accept what Access gives you, have it delete the data from the records where the data doesn't match, and then reenter the data.

If you see the message shown in the figure, you tried to convert the data type of a field that is used in a relationship with a field in another table. ▶

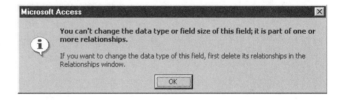

1. Click OK to close the message box.

2. On the Tools menu, click Relationships.

3. Right-click the line that runs from the field you're converting to another table or tables, and then click Delete on the shortcut menu.

4. Close the Relationships window.

5. With the table in design view, select the field you're working with. Then select the new data type from the drop-down list.

6. Save the changes to the table.

Tip

Make sure the new data type is compatible with the field that was formerly related, if you want to reestablish the relationship.

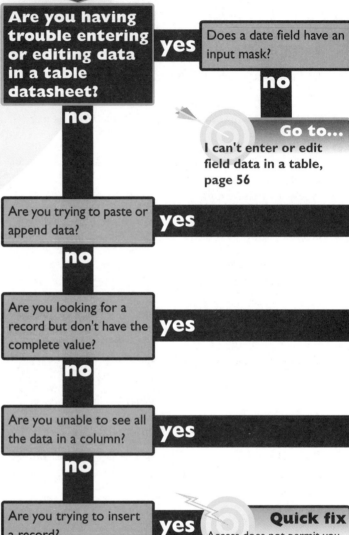

Are you having trouble entering or editing data in a table datasheet?

yes → **Does a date field have an input mask?** yes →

no ↓

no ↓

Go to...
I can't enter or edit field data in a table, page 56

Are you trying to paste or append data? yes →

no ↓

Are you looking for a record but don't have the complete value? yes →

no ↓

Are you unable to see all the data in a column? yes →

no ↓

Are you trying to insert a record? yes →

Quick fix
Access does not permit you to insert a record between other records. To put the records in the order you want, you need to sort them.

1. Open the table in datasheet view.

2. Right-click in the column you want to sort by, and then choose Sort Ascending or Sort Descending.

If your solution isn't here
Check these related chapters:
Data—Setting field properties, page 44
Datasheets—Viewing data, page 66
Filtering, page 100
Queries—Selection criteria, page 214
Or see the general troubleshooting tips on page xiii.

ing & editing data

Go to...
I can't enter dates the way I want in an input mask, page 62

Do you see an error message when you append data? **yes**

Quick fix
You have probably tried to enter a record that has the same value in a key field as an existing record.

1. Change the value in the existing record or in the record you are adding.
2. Try again.

no

Go to...
I have only part of the field value and can't find the record I want, page 64

Quick fix
The field value is too large for the column.

1. Double-click the right edge of the column header to readjust the Best Fit.
2. Or, move to the column, click Column Width on the Format menu, and then click Best Fit.

Did Access paste the data into the wrong fields? **yes**

Quick fix
Access pasted the data in the wrong field because it pastes fields into the datasheet in the same order as they appear in the original record.

1. Reorder the columns in the destination datasheet to match the order in the source (or the other way around).
2. Try again.

no

Go to...
I get error messages when I try to paste records into a datasheet, page 58

I can't enter or edit field data in a table

Source of the problem

When all you're trying to do is update the tables in your database with new or revised data, it can be a pain to have Access say you can't do it. There are several fairly simple reasons why you might not be able to edit or enter data in your table.

● The fields are of an AutoNumber data type. You can't edit these fields because Access maintains these values automatically.

● You opened the database as read-only. If you did, the New button is dimmed in the database window.

● The record or table is locked by another user.

● The field is a calculated field.

Another possible reason your value isn't accepted is that you are entering a number that exceeds the field size setting for a number field. Access might round off the number you enter to the largest value allowed. You might also be trying to enter too many characters in a text field. The default field size for a text field is 50 characters, but the field you're working with might allow fewer than 50. The following solutions show how to handle each of these problems.

How to fix it

1. If the database was opened read-only, close it and reopen it normally.

2. If you see the universal *don't do it* symbol (a circle with a diagonal slash), that's an indication that the record or table is locked by another user. Wait a while until the record or table is available again.

3. If you want to change the value in a calculated field, you need to change the value of one of the fields used in the calculation. You can't change the value in the field where the calculation is performed.

> **Tip**
> In the Open dialog box, you usually have four options when you click the Open button: Open, Open Read-Only, Open Exclusive, and Open Exclusive Read Only. (In Access 97, click the Commands And Settings button in the Open dialog box to see the options.)

If Access changed a number value you entered or if Access displayed an error message about the value not being valid, follow these steps:

1. In a number field, the Field Size property might be set to Single. Open the table in design view, and select the field you're having trouble with.

2. On the General tab of the Field Properties area, change the Field Size property to Double. Save the changes to the table design. ▶

3. Switch the table to datasheet view, and enter the value again.

4. If changing the field size doesn't fix your problem, you might have tried to enter text in a number field. With the table open in design view, check the field's data type and change it to Text if necessary.

If your problem lies with the size of a text field, follow these steps:

1. Open the table in design view, and select the field you're working with.

2. On the General tab of the Field Properties area, increase the number in the Field Size property to the maximum number of characters you expect to enter. The maximum for a text field is 255 characters. ▶

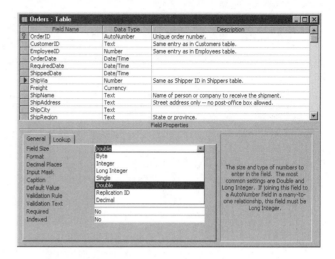

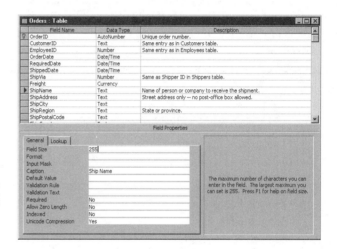

Seeing all the columns

When you are entering or editing data in a table too large to view on one screen, keeping track of which record you are working on can be difficult. Keeping one or more of the important columns on the screen while you edit can help orient you.

To do this, use the freeze column feature. Select the column or columns you want to remain visible, and then click Freeze Columns on the Format menu. As you scroll to other columns, the frozen columns remain visible at the left side of the table. When you are through editing the data, you can unfreeze the columns by clicking Unfreeze All Columns on the Format menu. Unfortunately, Access doesn't put the thawed columns back where they belong, so you will have to drag them to their previous positions.

Tip
If you need more room than 255 characters, you can change the Text data type to Memo, which has a much larger size limit.

I get error messages when I try to paste records into a datasheet

Source of the problem

Pasting records into a table sounds so easy. Just like fourth grade. Unfortunately, Access is a little pickier than your fourth grade teacher was. If Access can't paste any or all of the data you want to move or copy, you will see a message describing the problem with a clue about how to fix it, just like the messages on the homework you got back from your teacher. After explaining the problem, Access displays another message, indicating that it has saved all the records that it couldn't paste in the Paste Errors table. Reviewing the Paste Errors table is a convenient way to troubleshoot the problem you have.

Access might not be able to paste data for several reasons, including the following:

● You tried to paste text with more characters than the field you're pasting it in allows.

● The value you are trying to paste isn't compatible with the type of data the destination field can accept.

● The source field contains a value that doesn't fit with certain property settings in the destination field, such as a validation rule, an input mask, or a setting in the Required or AllowZeroLength property.

● You tried to paste records from more fields than the destination table contains.

The following solution shows how to deal with these sticky pasting problems.

How to fix it:

1. In the message box that explains the problem, click OK. ▶

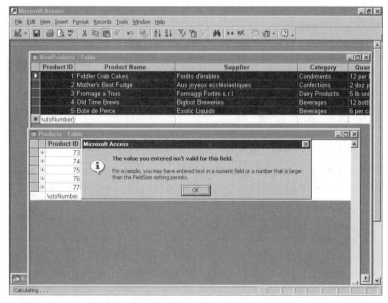

2. Click OK in the message about the Paste Errors table, and then open the Paste Errors table in datasheet view. You might need to correct the errors that caused the paste failure one by one. ▶

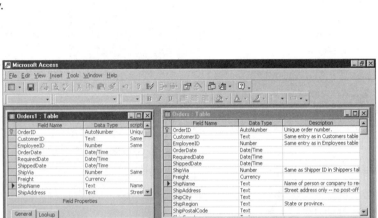

3. Open both the source and the destination table in design view.

4. On the General tabs of the Field Properties areas of the source and destination tables, compare the Field Size property settings of the problem fields. One of the fields might be too small to contain the data you are pasting. For example, text from a field that allows 255 characters won't necessarily fit into a field that allows only 40. Adjust the Field Size property setting in the appropriate table. ▶

5. Make sure the data types are compatible. For example, you can't paste text into a field with a Number data type.

6. Check the property settings of the destination fields for validation rules, input masks, and other restrictions. The data you are pasting might not follow the rules set up for the field you are pasting the data into.

7. If the problem is that you are pasting records from more fields than the destination table can handle, select fewer fields to paste.

I get error messages when I try to paste records into a datasheet

(continued from page 59)

8. After you've modified settings and field types, save any changes you've made to the tables' design.

9. Select the records in the Paste Errors table and click the Copy button on the toolbar. ▶

10. In the destination table, select the blank new record row and click Paste.

11. Delete the Paste Errors table from the database.

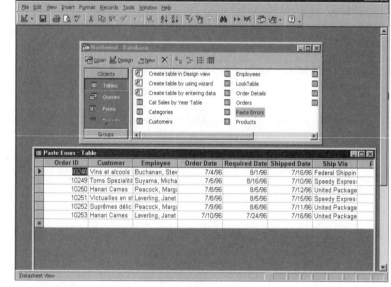

Warning

Fix the errors and complete the pasting before you attempt another paste operation. The Paste Errors table holds records only temporarily. The records in the table are overwritten with the next paste failure.

A couple of other pasting problems

There are a few other problems you might encounter when pasting records from one table to another in Access. One possibility is that the field you are trying to paste into might be in a hidden column. If so, go to the destination table in datasheet view and click Unhide Columns on the Format menu.

You might also be pasting a column name instead of data into a cell. This happens when you select data in a datasheet by clicking the left margin of the cell. You actually select the column name along with the field value. Then, when you paste the value, you are pasting only the first section of the copied text, which is the column name. Delete the column name from the destination table, and select only the data in the cell, not the complete cell. Then copy and paste it into the receiving record.

Another problem could be that you did not select a destination for the field or fields you want to paste. Or, you might have tried to cut data from or paste data into a field that is locked, unavailable, or calculated, or an AutoNumber field.

The reason for a pasting problem could be as simple as lack of permission to add or edit data in the destination database. If that's the case, reset your database permissions and try pasting the records again. You can set database permissions by clicking Security on the Tools menu. One other pasting problem might be that the primary key or unique index field of the record you are pasting is a duplicate of one already in the destination record. If that's the case, you'll need to edit the primary key value before you can successfully paste the data.

I can't enter dates the way I want in an input mask

Source of the problem

As much as you'd like to think that you can make a process as simple as entering data foolproof, we all know that errors can cunningly sneak into our data through the back door. One of the really helpful features of Access, the input mask, which tries to control what and how much data you can enter in a field, can still generate a few problems of its own.

The input mask displays fill-in spaces, often punctuated with special characters such as slashes (/), commas, and periods. An input mask often limits the number of characters you enter in a field, which can cause problems when you have a longer or shorter value to enter.

Input masks are very particular. If you often hear a beep when entering data in a field, an input mask may not match the way you are used to entering data. For example, if you enter a date as 11502 (meaning January 15, 2002), an input mask that requires six characters could display the value 11/50/2 instead of 01/15/02 because you didn't enter the first 0. And, neither the month or day can have a value of 50, so this results in an error.

You might also have trouble entering a date in a field with an input mask if the mask conflicts with the display format. For example, dates might be displayed in the format 6-June-2002, while the input mask shows __/__/__. This results in you having to enter a value that doesn't look like the values already in the field. You will hear a beep if you don't fill in all the blanks or if you try to enter the name of the month that appears in the displayed value.

Here are some solutions for these problems with input masks.

How to fix it

If you see an error message that a date value isn't appropriate for the input mask, do the following: ▶

1. Select the entire entry.

2. Press the Delete key.

3. Enter the date value following the input mask, including the leading zeros.

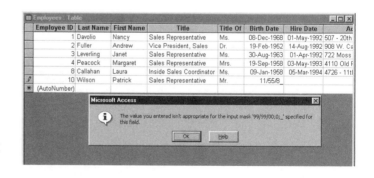

If the input mask conflicts with the format in which a date field is displayed, take these steps to correct the problem:

1. Open the table in design view, and select the field that is giving you trouble.

2. In the Field Properties area, click in the Input Mask property box and then click the Build button (…).

3. In the Input Mask Wizard dialog box, select the Medium Date mask that matches the setting in the Format property box in the table design. ▶

4. Click Finish, and save the table design.

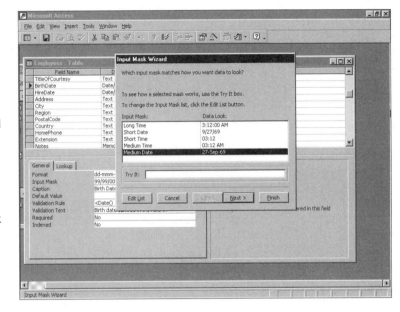

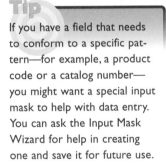

Why is a medium date format better?

To correct the problem with seeing dates in a format that's different from how you're asked to enter them, you could also change the field's Format property to Short Date. However, changing the format to Medium Date is a better solution because it eliminates any ambiguities that can result from the Short Date format. The Medium Date format shows the abbreviated month name instead of all numbers. With the Short Date format, however, if you enter 08/13/02, Access interprets it as 13-Aug-2002, but if you enter 13/08/02, the date displayed is 02-Aug-2013. If you enter a date in which both of the first two entries are less than 12, Access treats the first entry as the month and the second as the day: 10/08/02 is interpreted as 08-Oct-2002, while 08/10/02 is interpreted as 10-Aug-2002.

I have only part of the field value and can't find the record I want

Source of the problem

It's pretty easy to find everyone listed in your database with the last name of Johnson. When you try to find all the records that mention cats in a memo field, however, it can get a bit tricky. Or maybe you want to locate all the businesses on 5th or 6th Avenue so that you can bombard them with ads. If you know part of a value and that part is at the start of a field, you can simply sort on that field and track down the information you need. But difficulties arise if the part of the value you know is embedded in the field. In these cases, you have to resort to the old poker scam of wildcards, which are symbols that take the place of one or more letters or numbers.

You might have already used these special characters in place of real ones and had a problem with the values that turned up. Wildcards are usually used to search text and memo fields, but, if you are careful, you can massage them to search in date and number fields as well.

If you're not finding the right records, you might be using the wrong wildcard. If you are using more than one symbol, they might be placed in the wrong order. Another problem might be options set in the Find and Replace dialog box.

If you have tried to find data that includes one of the wildcard characters, you might not have found the records you expected. Looking for a wildcard character takes special preparation because Access thinks you are using it as a wildcard instead of it being the character you want to find. You'll have no problem looking for values that include exclamation points (!) or closing brackets (]), but other symbols need special treatment.

Here are some ways to use wildcards to your advantage.

How to fix it

If you want to find records with a certain value in a field, for example, any order for any product with "tofu" in its name, do the following:

1. Open the table in datasheet view, and place the insertion point in the column for the field you want to search.

2. On the Edit menu, click Find.

3. In the Find What box, type ***tofu***.

4. In the Match box, select Any Part Of Field.

> **Tip**
> The asterisk (*) wildcard takes the place of any number of characters and must be used as the first or last character in the Find What box.

5. Click Find Next. ▶

6. To find additional records with the same partial value, click Find Next again.

If you are looking for addresses on specific streets (in this example, 5th or 6th Avenue), you can mix wildcards with text as follows:

1. Open the table in datasheet view, and place the insertion point in the column containing the addresses.

2. On the Edit menu, click Find.

3. In the Find What box, enter ***[56]th Ave***. ▶

4. In the Match box, select Any Part Of Field.

5. Click Find Next.

Tip

The pair of square brackets ([]) enclose alternative values or a range of values. For example, using [5-9] in the expression would find addresses on 5th, 6th, 7th, 8th, or 9th Avenue.

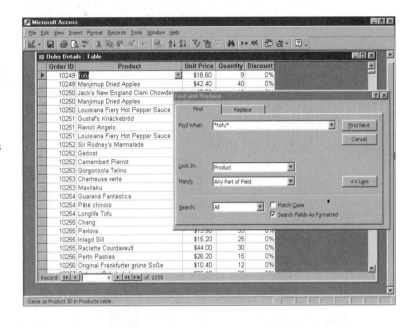

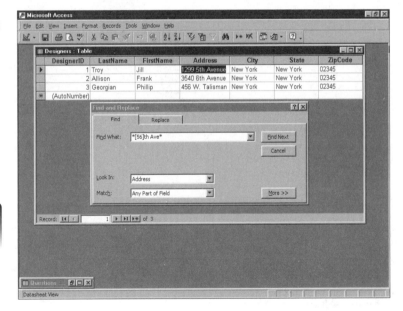

Datash

Is something wrong with your datasheet view? **yes**

no

Are you having trouble finding records? **yes**

Go to...
I can't find the records I want, page 68

no

Is something wrong with how you see data in a subdatasheet? **yes** Are you trying to insert a subdatasheet in a new query? **yes**

no

Are you trying to change the appearance of a subdatasheet? **yes**

no

If your solution isn't here
Check these related chapters:
Datasheets—Entering & editing data, page 54
Queries—Simple select, page 224
Relationships, page 236
Or see the general troubleshooting tips on page xiii.

Go to...
The size and behavior of my subdatasheet are wrong, page 76

Do you want to see all the text in a memo field?

yes

no

Does the text appear all uppercase?

yes

no

Quick fix

In forms, you can use the Zoom shortcut menu command; in a table, you need to use the keyboard.

1. Click in the memo field of the record you want to view.
2. Press Shift+F2.

Quick fix

You need to change a setting in the field's Format property.

1. Open the table in design view.
2. Select the field.
3. Remove the > symbol from the Format property expression.

Go to...

I can't change the way my datasheet displays data, page 70

Quick fix

You must save the query first.

1. Save and name the query.
2. On the Insert menu, click Subdatasheet.
3. Select the query or table on which to base the subdatasheet, and then select the linking fields.

Go to...

I can't get my subdatasheet to look the way I want, page 72

I can't find the records I want

Source of the problem

Just like car keys, Access records seem to run off and hide when you need them the most. Even using the clever search tools Access provides, you still have those days when you can't find a record that you know is there, lurking behind the scenes somewhere. When you use the Find command to locate a record, Access compares the criteria you specify to the values stored in the field. This approach sounds simple enough, but it can cause a problem when the value is displayed in a form or report in a format that's different from the one in which the value is stored in the database. Usually you use the format that a value is displayed in when you enter search criteria. Access, however, searches for records according to the format in which they are stored. There are three reasons that a stored value may not be the same as its displayed value:

- The field is a lookup field, which gets its value from another table or from a list of values for specific data. Access locates the value and stores a reference to it in the lookup field of the current table. The lookup field then displays the referenced value. When you use the displayed value to search for a record, you won't find the value in the current table because it is actually stored in the lookup table or the list.

- A date value is stored in a different format. For example, you might display a date as 15-Jan-02 while it is stored as 01/15/02. If you use the displayed format to search for the record, the search fails to find the value.

- You applied an input mask to the field after data has been entered. An input mask formats data to your specifications, so the stored values might be inconsistent and might not meet the criteria of the input mask. If you use the format designated by the input mask to search for a record, you might not find it.

Here are the solutions to these problems with finding records.

How to fix it

If the field you are searching is a lookup field or if you are searching for a date value, follow these steps:

1. In the database window, select the table, query, or form in which you are searching for records. Click the Open button.

2. On the Edit menu, click Find.

3. In the Find What box, enter the field value just the way it is displayed.

4. Click the More button to expand the Find And Replace dialog box.

5. Select the Search Fields As Formatted check box, and then click Find Next. ▶

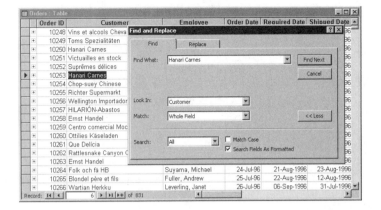

If the field has an input mask that might be creating conflicts in your search, follow these steps:

1. If the table has only a few existing records, open it in datasheet view, and modify any data in the field that is not formatted in the style designated by the input mask. You can either reenter the data or simply edit it to conform to the input mask.

2. If the table already has numerous records, open it in design view and remove the input mask from the field. You can then use the Find command to locate the information and add the input mask to the table design again, if you want.

Finding blank fields

There are two types of blank fields. A *Null value* means that the value in the field was unknown at data entry time. A *zero-length string* means there is no relevant value for that record. For example, a person without a middle initial would leave a middle initial field blank to indicate that there is no such thing, creating a zero-length string. To find records with Null values, type Null or Is Null in the Find What box in the Find And Replace dialog box. If you need to locate records with zero-length strings, type a pair of quotation marks ("") with no space between them. Be sure to clear the Search Field As Formatted option in the Find and Replace dialog box. Also be sure to check Whole Field in the Match box.

I can't change the way my datasheet displays data

Source of the problem

Although you have probably created some handsome forms for viewing your data, there's no doubt that sometimes you'll just want to take a look at a simple datasheet. Still, as simple as viewing a datasheet might seem, it can cause problems. Some of the columns might be missing, or one column might be the wrong width. You might need to change the check box that represents a Yes/No field to something else. In Access 2000, if you don't see the subdatasheet of related data, you might have set the table's Subdatasheet Name property to None, which prevents Access from automatically creating subdatasheets from related tables. Or maybe you have the opposite problem: subdatasheets are always displayed, whether you want them to be or not.

The following solutions give you clues about how to solve these datasheet mysteries.

How to fix it

If you are having trouble with columns in your datasheet, follow these steps:

1. In the database window, select the query or table you are working with and then click the Open button.

2. If any columns are missing from the datasheet view, click Unhide Columns on the Format menu. In the Unhide Columns dialog box, check all of the columns you want to see.

3. If you want to change column width to fit the contents of a column, double-click the column divider at the right side of the column.

> **Tip**
>
> Double-clicking a column to change its width only works for data that is already in the column. If you enter a longer value later, the column does not adjust to fit it. You have to adjust the width again.

If you want to change the display of Yes/No values in a datasheet, follow these steps:

1. In the database window, select the table you are working with and then click the Design button.

2. Select the Yes/No field in the upper pane.

3. In the Field Properties pane, click the Lookup tab.

4. In the Display Control property box, change the setting to Text Box.

5. Click the General tab, and choose the Format property you want for the Yes/No field. ▶

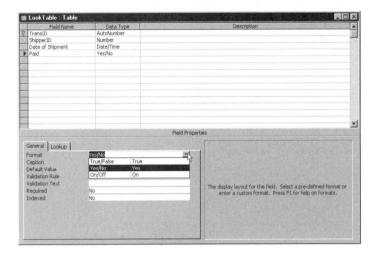

If you are working in Access 2000 and don't see a subdatasheet (or the plus sign) in your main datasheet, follow these steps:

1. In the database window, select the table you're working with and then click the Design button.

2. On the toolbar, click the Properties button.

3. Set the Subdatasheet Name property of the table to Auto. ▶

If you don't want to see the subdatasheet, follow these steps:

1. Open the table or query in datasheet view.

2. On the Format menu, click Subdatasheets and then click Remove.

Tip

You can also set the Subdatasheet Name property to the name of any other related table or query in your database.

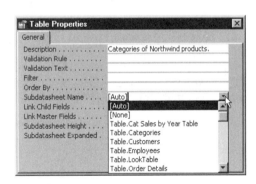

Making datasheets look the same

You can change the default appearance for all datasheet views—for tables or queries—in your database. On the Tools menu, click Options and then click the Datasheet tab. Here you can elect to show or hide the horizontal and vertical gridlines and change their color and weight. You can also determine how cells will appear. For example, you might want the cells sunken or raised, or you might want to vary their background color. You can also change the font style, weight, and size. Once you set the default datasheet formatting, you can still change individual datasheet views.

I can't get my subdatasheet to look the way I want

Source of the problem

Just because subdatasheets are new to Access 2000, you don't have to go along with whatever they want to show you. You are the boss, and you can coax these helpful views of data to look the way you want. These are some of common problems you might have encountered with viewing data in subdatasheets:

- The subdatasheet always shows the same records from the related table or query, instead of only the records related to the active record in the datasheet. The Link Child Fields and Link Master Fields properties are probably not correct. Subdatasheets can be linked to a datasheet by the fields that form the relationship between the tables or by any other pair of fields that contain matching data.

- You expanded a few subdatasheets and expected to see them expanded again the next time you opened the table. However, Access didn't save the view you were using when you closed the table or query datasheet. Unfortunately, it's all or nothing—all subdatasheets expanded or all collapsed. There's no half and half.

- You can't find the foreign key field or matching field or fields in the subdatasheet. Access doesn't expect that you want to see duplicate field values when you view a subdatasheet. But you can fix this, at least temporarily.

- You want to eliminate the subdatasheet completely from the datasheet view. Doing this does not remove the related data from the database.

The following solutions explain how to deal with these problems.

How to fix it

If you see the same records in the subdatasheet no matter which record is active in the main datasheet, follow these steps:

1. In the database window, select the table or query that contains the subdatasheet and click the Open button.

2. On the Insert menu, click Subdatasheet.

---

3. In the Insert Subdatasheet dialog box, choose the table or query that contains the data you want to display in the subdatasheet.

4. From the Link Master Fields list, choose a field from the main datasheet that matches a field in the subdatasheet.

5. In the Link Child Fields box, choose the matching field in the subdatasheet. ▶

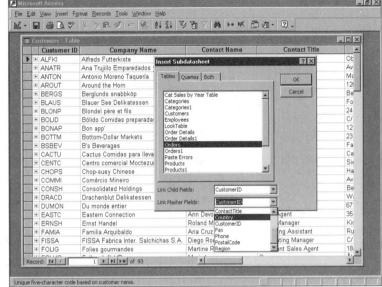

6. If you want to specify more than one matching field between the subdatasheet and main datasheet, enter additional field names in the Link Child Fields and Link Master Fields boxes. Separate the field names with semicolons.

To change the Subdatasheet Expanded property, follow these steps:

1. Open the table or query containing the subdatasheet in datasheet view.

2. On the Format menu, click Subdatasheet and then click Expand All or Collapse All. ▶

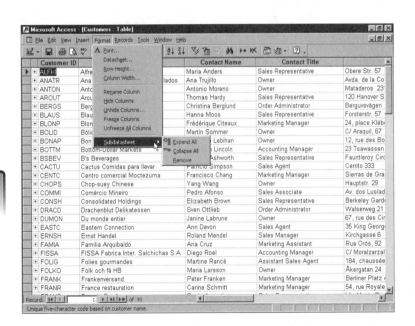

Tip

If you want a more permanent effect, open the table or query in design view and set the Subdatasheet Expanded property to Yes in the property sheet.

I can't get my subdatasheet to look the way I want

(continued from page 73)

To show the matching fields in the subdatasheet—including those that are hidden—follow these steps:

1. Open the query or table that contains the subdatasheet in datasheet view.

2. If the subdatasheet is not displayed, click the plus sign to expand it.

3. Click in the subdatasheet.

4. On the Format menu, click Unhide Columns.

5. In the Unhide Columns dialog box, verify that all the columns you want to see are selected. Select any columns that have been hidden that you want to display. ▶

6. In the Unhide Columns dialog box, click Close.

If you want to remove the subdatasheet from the datasheet view, follow these steps:

1. Open the table or query that contains the subdatasheet in datasheet view.

2. On the Format menu, click Subdatasheet and then click Remove.

3. If you don't want a datasheet to have a subdatasheet at all, open the table or query in design view and change the Subdatasheet Name property to None. ▶

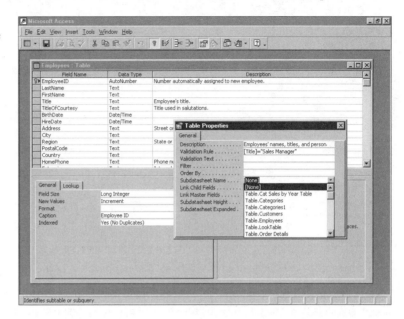

What about displaying subdatasheets?

Hiding or displaying columns in a subdatasheet has no effect on the underlying data, only on the display of the data.

The fields you use to link a subdatasheet with a datasheet don't have to have the same names, but the fields must contain the same kind of data (for example, both fields must include numbers) and be of a compatible data type and field size. The most commonly used matching fields are the fields that form the relationship between the tables. You can use any fields that you expect to contain the same values. There would be no point in linking a datasheet to a subdatasheet by a field you know will never match.

The size and behavior of my subdatasheet are wrong

Source of the problem

Microsoft had a great idea when it decided to include subdatasheets with Access 2000. You no longer have to design a form or report to see related data. You can now view related data in the table or query datasheet. If you are having trouble making the subdatasheet behave the way you want, you have a couple of options:

- Do you want all the subdatasheets expanded or collapsed when you open the table or query in datasheet view? Having all the subdatasheets collapsed is the default behavior.

- Do you want to limit the number of records that appear when you expand the subdatasheet? The default setting is "0," which expands each subdatasheet to fit the number of related records it contains. This can often take up a lot of space on your screen.

The following solution explains how to solve problems with the subdatasheet environment.

How to fix it

To change the default setting so that all subdatasheets are expanded when you open the table or query in datasheet view, follow these steps:

1. In the database window, select the table or query and then click the Design button.

2. On the View menu, click Properties.

3. In the Table Properties dialog box, set the Subdatasheet Expanded property to Yes. ▶

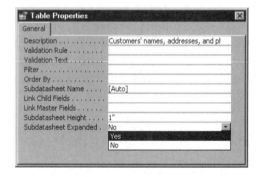

To set the height of an expanded subdatasheet and limit the number of records you'll see, follow these steps:

1. In the database window, select the table or query and then click the Design button.

2. On the View menu, click Properties.

3. In the Table Properties dialog box, set the Subdatasheet Height property to the height (in inches) you want the subdatasheet to be. ▶

4. Save the changes to the table.

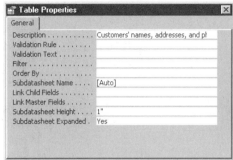

More about subdatasheet behavior

Here are some special hints about subdatasheets.

If you want to expand all the subdatasheets only once in a while, point to Subdatasheets on the Format menu and click Expand All. When you close the datasheet, reply No when asked if you want to save changes. This way, the property change is not saved, and the next time you open the datasheet, the subdatasheets will not be expanded.

If there are more records to display than will fit the height of the subdatasheet, a vertical scroll bar is added to the subdatasheet. If the records in the subdatasheet do not fill the specified height, the subdatasheet expansion shrinks to fit. This way, no display area is wasted.

When you are navigating in a subdatasheet, the navigation buttons at the bottom of the datasheet window refer to records in the active subdatasheet. This helps you tell how many records are in a subdatasheet with a specified height display.

You can nest subdatasheets within one another to give an added dimension to viewing related data. Each subdatasheet can have only one subdatasheet nested within it, but you can nest as many as eight levels from the original datasheet.

If you want to use a subdatasheet in a form, add a subform control to the form design and set the Source Object property to the table that contains the data you want to see. Make sure the Link Child Fields and Link Master Fields properties are set to the linking fields in the form and the table. Double-click the form selector button (at the top-right corner) for the subform control and change its Default View property to Datasheet. When you view the form, you'll see the subdatasheet with the data that relates to the current record in the main form.

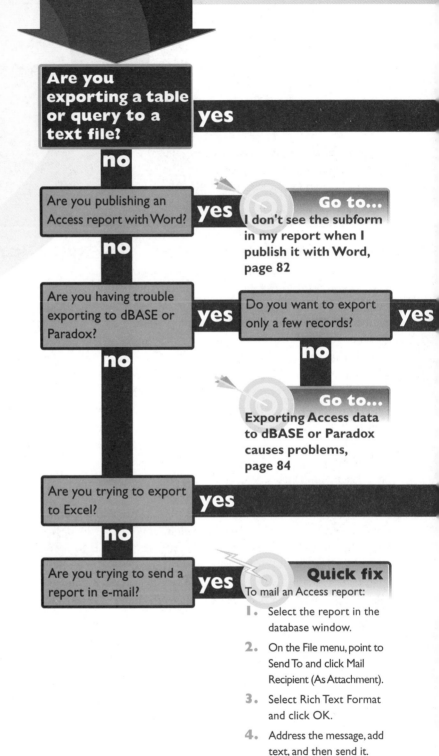

Are you exporting a table or query to a text file?

yes

no

Are you publishing an Access report with Word?

yes

Go to...
I don't see the subform in my report when I publish it with Word, page 82

no

Are you having trouble exporting to dBASE or Paradox?

yes

Do you want to export only a few records?

yes

no

Go to...
Exporting Access data to dBASE or Paradox causes problems, page 84

no

Are you trying to export to Excel?

yes

no

Are you trying to send a report in e-mail?

yes

Quick fix

To mail an Access report:

1. Select the report in the database window.

2. On the File menu, point to Send To and click Mail Recipient (As Attachment).

3. Select Rich Text Format and click OK.

4. Address the message, add text, and then send it.

Exporting

Do number and date values look wrong after exporting?

yes → **Go to...**
Numbers don't look right after I export them to a text file, page 80

no ↓

Do you want all values enclosed in quotation marks?

yes → **Quick fix**
Delimited text files use quotation marks as special characters.

1. Create a query based on the table you want to export.

2. Instead of adding the field names to the grid, enter an expression that concatenates the ASCII character for quotation marks with the field value. For example, **LName: Chr(34) & [Last Name] & Chr(34)**.

3. Save the query.

4. Export the query to the text file.

Quick fix
All the records in a table are exported.

1. Create a query with only the field data you want to export.

2. Add criteria to the query to limit the records.

3. Save and export the query.

Did Access create an Export Errors table?

yes → **Go to...**
I get errors when I export a table to Excel, page 86

no ↓

Go to...
Excel doesn't show the totals in the report I exported, page 88

If your solution isn't here
Check these related chapters:
   Importing and linking, page 138
Or see the general troubleshooting tips on page xiii.

Numbers don't look right after I export them to a text file

Source of the problem

You've designed a table with all sorts of number and currency fields. Now, when you try to put the table in a text format, things go crazy. Maybe some of the formatting you defined in the table doesn't carry over to the text file.

One of the problems you might see is the number and currency values aligning at the left instead of at the right. If you think about this, it makes sense. After all, you're converting the numbers to text, and text usually starts on the left. But that doesn't make the number values look any better in the text file. You really want at least the decimal points to line up.

Another problem you might have experienced when exporting numbers to a text file is the truncation of numbers to two decimal places. Maybe the Export Text Wizard thinks that all numbers are currency and that you need only two decimal places.

The following solutions describe ways to solve these problems when you're exporting Access data to a text file.

How to fix it

If your problem is number alignment and truncated decimal places, do the following: ▶

1. In the database window, click Queries and then click New.

2. In the New Query dialog box, click Design View and then click OK.

3. In the Show Table dialog box, choose the name of the table you want to export, click Add, and then click Close.

4. From the list of field names, drag the fields you want to export to the query grid, except for the number field you're having trouble with.

5. In the first blank column in the query grid, add an expression to format the number field—for example, **Sales: Format([ItemsSold],"00000.0000")**. Sales is the name that will appear in the column heading. ItemsSold is the field name from the table. The Format function defines the format for the value. This expression places five digits both before and after the decimal point. ▶

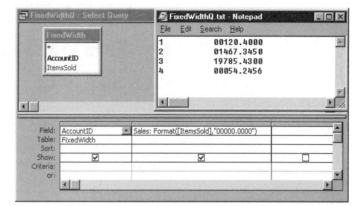

6. Save and close the query.

7. In the database window, select the query you just created and then click Export (Save As/ Export in Access 97) on the File menu.

8. In the Export Query To dialog box, select Text Files from the Save As Type list and then click Save. (If you're using Access 97, first select To An External File Or Database in the Save As dialog box.)

9. In the Export Text Wizard, select the Fixed-Width option and then click Finish.

The trouble with exporting dates

Exporting dates to a text file can cause problems too. When you export a table or query that includes a date field, the equivalent in the text file can go overboard and include a time format as well as the date. If you don't want to see the time value (and hardly anyone needs the exact time in a typical database), you don't need to show the 0:00:00 that indicates no time value. A query can save the day once again.

Start a new query (following steps 1 through 4 of the previous solution). In the Field row for the date field you want to format, enter an expression such as **Birthdate2: Format([Birthdate], "mm/dd/yy")**, where Birthdate2 is the name of the expression, Birthdate is the field name, and the "mm/dd/yy" format displays the date values as 1/15/99, for example, with no time values. Save and close the query.

In the database window, select the query you just created and then click Export (Save As/ Export in Access 97) on the File menu. In the Export Query To dialog box, select Text Files from the Save As Type list and then click Save. (If you're using Access 97, first select To An External File Or Database in the Save As dialog box.) In the Export Text Wizard dialog box, select Delimited and then click Finish.

I don't see the subform in my report when I publish it with Word

Source of the problem

You're about to use Microsoft Word to publish the monthly report that you spent the last week creating in Access. One of the great things about Microsoft Office is the cooperation among its colleagues. For example, Word will take an Access report and turn it into a professional looking document with the Publish It With MS Word Office Link command. But now when you call upon Word, you see a cryptic message about not being able to process any subforms. The data in the subform looked great in print preview in Access, but Word can't seem to swallow it.

You go ahead with the export, and the result in Word contains the data from each record in the main report followed by a page break for each record that should appear in the subform. If you had clicked No in the message box, the report would still have been exported, but you would see only the data from the main report with a single page break after each record.

The cause of this problem is that Word can't publish subforms in a report, it can only publish subreports. (You can publish an Access form with Word, but any subforms are ignored. You also don't get a warning as you do when you publish a report.)

The following solution shows you the steps you need to take to correct this problem.

How to fix it

If you see this message when you try to publish the report with Word (in Access 97, the message says it can't process any *subreports* rather than subforms), do the following: ▶

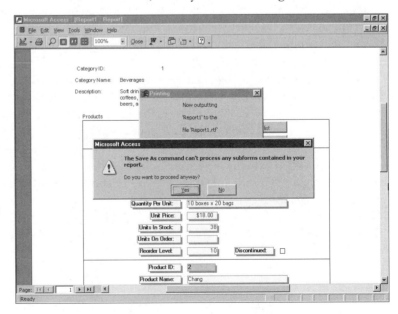

1. In the message box, click No. The report is still exported, but the export takes less time than it does if you click Yes.

2. Close the report in Word and return to Access.

3. In Access, close the report print preview window.

4. In the database window, click Forms and then select the subform.

5. If you're working in Access 2000, on the File menu, click Save As. In the As box in the Save As dialog box, select Report and then click OK. ▶

   If you're working in Access 97, right-click the name of the subform in the database window and then click Save As Report on the shortcut menu. Then enter a name in the Save As dialog box and click OK.

6. Open the main report in design view.

7. Select the subform control, and then click the Properties button on the toolbar.

8. On the Data tab, in the Source Object property box, select the name of the subform you saved as a report. ▶

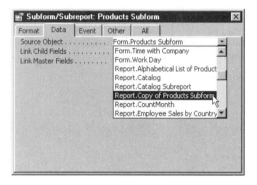

9. Save and close the report design.

Now you're ready to export the report again to the Word Publisher:

1. In the database window, select the report.

2. On the Tools menu, point to Office Links and then click Publish It With MS Word.

3. Click Yes to replace the previous report with this new one.

Tip

When you use the Publish It With MS Word Office Link command, you can export tables, queries, forms, and reports. Using the Merge It With MS Word Office Link command, you can export only tables and queries because tables and queries contain the data. Forms and reports are merely designs.

Exporting Access data to dBASE or Paradox causes problems

Source of the problem

"You've seen one database, you've seen them all." Unfortunately, it doesn't quite work that way. Database management systems that use their own file formats and table structures can differ from what you're used to with Access. Access tries hard to be friendly and understanding when sending data to Paradox or dBASE, but you can still run into problems.

One of the major differences between Access and dBASE is the length of field names allowed. dBASE limits field names to 10 characters, including spaces. If you're exporting an Access table or a query that has fields with names longer than 10 characters, the field names are truncated to 10 characters. If two fields use the identical first 10 characters, you can end up with duplicate field names. This causes an error message, and the table or query is not exported. Paradox allows 25 characters in field names, so exporting to Paradox is not likely to present a problem with field names.

Table names in both dBASE and Paradox are restricted to 8 characters, but with no spaces. There's no such restriction in Access. This means that the names of tables and queries you export from Access might be clipped, and these shortened names might not convey enough information about the data in the table.

The following solution describes how to correct these problems.

How to fix it

If you see the error message shown in the figure, do the following: ▶

1. Click OK to clear the message.

2. In the Access database window, select the table you're trying to export and then click Copy on the Edit menu.

3. On the Edit menu, click Paste.

4. In the Paste Table As dialog box, enter a name for the copy of the table.

5. Select Structure And Data, and then click OK.

6. Open the copy of the table in design view. Rename any fields with names that contain more than 10 characters. In the new names, try to use no more than 10 characters, including spaces. If you need more than 10 characters in the field names, be sure the first 10 characters are unique to a field.

7. Save and close the table.

8. In the database window, select the new table and try to export it again.

If you're having trouble with field names in a query you're exporting, try the following:

1. In Access, open the query in design view.

2. In the Field row, enter an expression such as **AliasName: MyFieldNameAgain** in place of the redundant fields. ▶

3. Save the query and try exporting again.

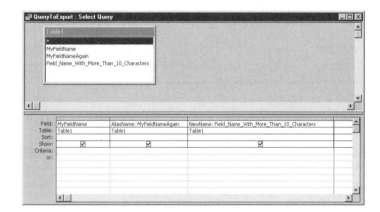

If you end up with confusing table names in dBASE, do the following:

1. Open the table in dBASE and save it with a different name.

2. You could also make a copy of the table in Access and rename the table with a shorter, more informative name before exporting it to dBASE.

What if the format I want isn't on the Save As Type list?

If you need to export an Access table to a format (such as Microsoft Works) that isn't in the list of available types, you can export it part way to a format that you can then export the rest of the way. To export a table or query to Works, select dBASE IV in the Save As Type box in the Export Table (or Query) As dialog box. In the File Name box, enter a name containing no more than eight characters, and then click Save. (In Access 97, click Export.) Open dBASE and export the table or query to Works keeping the same short name.

Using the same technique, you can export a table or query to QuattroPro by funneling it through Lotus 1-2-3.

I get errors when I export a table to Excel

Source of the problem

It seems like a pretty simple job, sending a datasheet from Access to Microsoft Excel. Both programs look at data in neatly arranged rows and columns, after all. So how come you got errors when you performed the export process?

A couple of things might have gone wrong, usually because of the data you're exporting and not the process itself. For example, Excel doesn't recognize dates prior to 1/1/1900. If your table contains a date earlier than that, you will get a Date Out of Range export error and the field will be left blank in the Excel worksheet. Another problem you might have encountered is with memo fields that contain a lot of text. Excel limits its worksheet cells to 255 characters. Any character over that number in your Access memo field is chopped off.

When you export Access data to Excel, you can choose to save the formatting. If you don't select this option, Access creates an Export Errors table. Access adds a record to the table for each error that occurs in the export. The record describes the type of error and indicates the field in which it occurred as well as the row number.

If you do use the Save Formatted option in the Export dialog box, no Export Errors table is created in Access. With this option, cells with that ancient date value are filled with pound signs (#), and you won't lose any characters from a lengthy memo field.

The following solution presents the means to correct these problems.

How to fix it

If you see an Export Errors table in Access after you have exported a table to Excel, do the following:

1. In the Access database window, click the Export Errors table and then click Open. The figure shows an Export Errors table. ▶

2. Print the table, or simply note the location and type of the errors recorded in the table.

3. Start Excel (or switch to Excel if it's already running), and open the Excel workbook that contains the data you exported.

Error	Field	Row
Date Out Of Range	BirthDate	2
Field Truncation	Notes	2
Field Truncation	Notes	5
Field Truncation	Notes	6
Field Truncation	Notes	7

Employees_ExportErrors1 : Table

Record: 1 of 5

4. Move to the row numbers indicated in the Export Errors table and correct the data. Most often, you'll be correcting a Date Out of Range error. If this is the case, click in the blank date field and enter the correct date. ▶

5. If the cell contains nothing but pound signs, select them and enter the correct date.

6. To complete truncated memo field text, click in the cell of the row that contains the Field Truncation error.

7. Click in the formula bar and complete the memo text. ▶

8. Save the workbook.

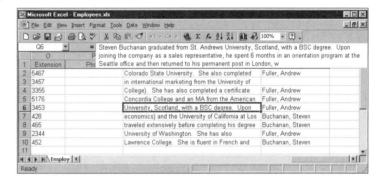

Watch where you're putting the data

If you're exporting an Access table or query to an existing Excel file, be careful not to overwrite the data in the spreadsheet. To avoid this, always save the exported file to the Microsoft Excel 5-7 or Microsoft Excel 97-2000 format. These formats use a different workbook structure than earlier versions of Excel. The structure includes a number of worksheets, and when you export an Access file to one of these formats, the data is placed in the first empty worksheet.

Tip

When you click in a cell filled with pound signs, you see a negative number in the formula bar. For example, if the field in the Access table contains the date 3/15/1876, you will see –8690 in the formula bar.

Tip

Number formatting is a little different in Excel than in Access, so when you export your table, you might see a warning that some of the formatting could be lost when you choose Save Formatted.

Excel doesn't show the totals in the report I exported

Source of the problem

One of the really neat benefits of working with Microsoft Office is the smooth way you can move data, forms, and reports from one Office program to another. You get so used to the easy interaction between Office mates, it comes as a rude surprise when things don't behave perfectly.

For example, you've used Access to finish the year-end report of sales, with totals by salesperson and country, and you want to ship it to the accounting department for final tuning. The accounting department uses Excel, so you export the report to Excel for them. Luckily you open the report in Excel before giving Accounting the go-ahead, because the summary totals you put in the group footer for each salesperson don't show up.

The following steps show you how to create the Excel version of the Access report complete with all the totals.

How to fix it

If this figure looks like the result when you export your report to Excel, do the following:

1. In the Access database window, select the report and click Preview.

2. On the File menu, click Export. (If you are working in Access 97, click Save As/Export.)

3. In the Save As Type box, choose Rich Text Format and then click Save.

(If you are working in Access 97, in the Save As dialog box, select To An External File Or Database, click OK, and then choose Rich Text Format in the Save Report dialog box. Click Export.)

4. Close Access and start Microsoft Word.

5. On the File menu in Word, click Open and locate the RTF file you just created. Click Open.

6. On the Edit menu, click Select All.

7. On the Edit menu, click Copy.

8. Start Excel, and open a new workbook or display an empty worksheet in an existing workbook.

9. On the Edit menu, click Paste. The report should appear, complete with all the totals. ▶

10. Name and save the new Excel worksheet.

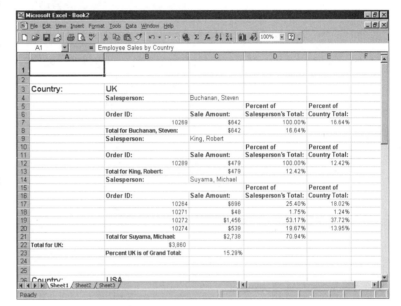

Tip

The same problem occurs when you use the Analyze It With MS Excel Office Link to output the report to Excel.

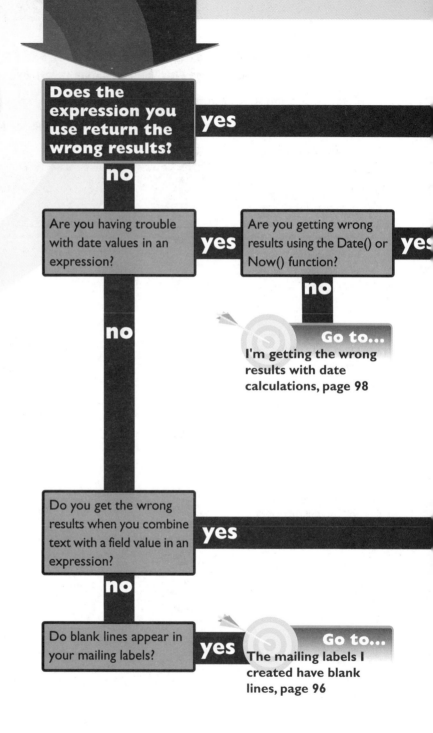

Does the expression you use return the wrong results? yes

no

Are you having trouble with date values in an expression? yes

Are you getting wrong results using the Date() or Now() function? yes

no

no

Go to...
I'm getting the wrong results with date calculations, page 98

Do you get the wrong results when you combine text with a field value in an expression? yes

no

Do blank lines appear in your mailing labels? yes

Go to...
The mailing labels I created have blank lines, page 96

Expressions

Do you see *#Error* in a text box or calculated control?

yes →

Go to...
The expression I used displays *#Error*, page 92

no ↓

Does your calculated field divide two numbers but return no decimal places?

yes →

Quick fix

You need to set the Decimal Places property.

1. Return to the design view, right-click on the control, and then click Properties.

2. Set the Decimal Places property to the number of places you want to see in the result.

3. If you have used an arithmetic operator, make sure you have used the forward slash (/). The backward slash means integer division.

Quick fix

Date() gets its value from the computer's date. Now() gets date and time data from the computer's clock.

1. Click the Start button and point to Settings. Then click Control Panel.

2. Double-click Date/Time.

3. Set the correct date and time, and then click OK.

4. You may need to correct date and time values already stored.

Go to...
The text I combined with a field value isn't displayed, page 94

If your solution isn't here

Check these related chapters:

Data—Setting field properties, page 44

Filtering, page 100

Queries—Selection criteria, page 214

Or see the general troubleshooting tips on page xiii.

The expression I used displays #Error

Source of the problem

When you ask a simple question in a foreign language and receive an unexpected answer, it's pretty puzzling. It's a lot like your surprise when Access evaluates an expression you used and displays *#Error*. Depending on what you are trying to do, the source of the strange outcome can be pinned on any number of things, such as the following:

- You're referring incorrectly to a form or a report in the expression.

- You're referring incorrectly to a control on a form or report, or even to a property of a control.

- You're not referring to table fields correctly.

- You're using the name of a control in an expression in the control, creating a circular reference.

- You're trying to use the Sum() function to add up values from a calculated field in a different control. Expressions using the functions Sum(), Avg(), Count(), and others can include field names but not control names.

The following solution explains how to correct each of these problems.

How to fix it

1. In the database window, select the form or report you're working with and click the Design button.

2. Right-click on the control displaying *#Error*, and then click Properties on the shortcut menu.

3. Click the Data tab, and check the expression you are using. An expression that refers to a form, report, or other database object, or to a control or property in the expression, must use the full identifier—complete with brackets, single or double quotation marks, periods, or exclama-

tion marks. For example, to refer to the value of the Total control on the OrderDetails form, use the following expression: **=Forms![OrderDetails]![Total]**. ▶

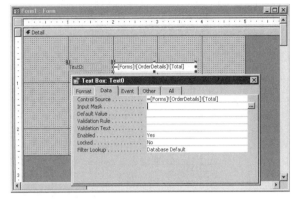

4. If you refer to a table field in the expression, edit the expression to remove the table identifier. That's because of a bug in the Access Expression Builder, which causes an error if the table identifier is included. (See "Using table names in the Expression Builder" below.)

5. Check the control's Name property to be sure it is different from the name of the field that you are using in the expression. If the Name property is the same as the field name, rename the control.

6. If you see *#Error* in one calculated control, see if that control is using one of the aggregate functions, such as Sum(), Avg(), or Count().

7. If the expression using the function includes the name of a control that is part of a calculation itself, delete the name of the control from the expression and replace it with the entire expression from the Control Source property of the control. ▶

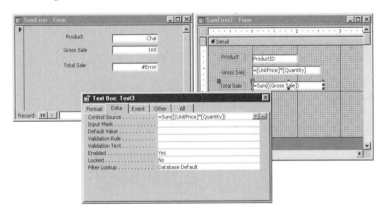

Using table names in the Expression Builder

When you add fields from a table to an expression using the Expression Builder, it adds the table name to the identifier. The expression [Order Details]![UnitPrice], for example, refers to the UnitPrice field from the Order Details table. Unfortunately, adding the table name results in the error signal *#Name?* in the text box. The *#Name?* error signal usually happens when the field named in the Control Source property is no longer available or its name has been misspelled. The easiest way to avoid this problem is to edit the expression to remove the table identifier.

The text I combined with a field value isn't displayed

Source of the problem

After listening to all the database gurus and splitting up your information into tiny field-size pieces, now you need to add some text to a field to enhance the information it displays. Sounds simple enough, but when you try to combine field values with text, it somehow doesn't work the way you expect. The problem probably lies in how you've marked the text you want to display. Combining field values with text in an expression is called *concatenating*. To combine these elements in an expression, you use the concatenation symbol (&). Access interprets *literal values* (such as the text you want to add) exactly as you write them. Numbers, strings of characters, or dates, for example, appear in expressions something like this: "San Diego", 155, or #15-Jan-02#. Notice that character strings are enclosed in double quotation marks, and that dates are enclosed in the pound sign (#), the date delimiter. If you are using literal values, your error might have occurred because a delimiter is incorrect or missing.

The following solution explains how to correct these common problems.

How to fix it

1. In the database window, select the form or report you are working with and click the Design button.

2. Right-click the control you want to add text to, and then click Properties on the shortcut menu.

3. In the Control Source property box containing the problem expression, make sure you have not left out the required brackets, date delimiters, or single or double quotation marks that are required by the literal value. ▶

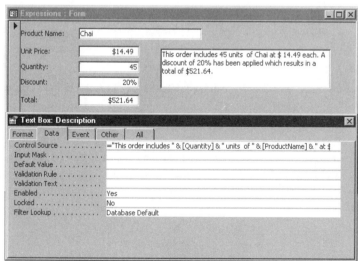

4. Check to make sure the delimiters you used to enclose literal values appear in pairs. ▶

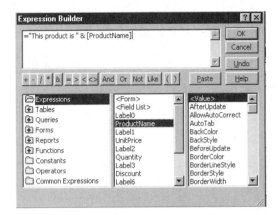

If you want to know more about using field names in an expression

When you use a field name in an expression, such as when you build a record validation rule or create a calculated field in a form, the field name is the *identifier*. An identifier must comply with certain rules or you'll get unexpected results from your expression.

Enclose field names in square brackets (for example, [UnitPrice]) to let Access know that the field name is one you dreamed up, not one of the Access keywords.

If the field in an expression is from a table in the database that's different from the table you're working in, you must also provide a *qualifier* to clearly indicate the name of that table or query. In the expression, separate the qualifier from the identifier with an exclamation mark (the "bang" operator). This tells Access that you thought up the name that follows. For example, Customer![CustomerName] refers to the CustomerName field in the Customer table.

When you use a table name (or the name of another Access object for that matter), you don't have to enclose it in brackets unless it contains a space or a character that has a special meaning to Access, such as an underscore.

Warning

Some Access applications use vertical bars as delimiters instead of double quotation marks and the concatenation symbol (&). This approach is not a good idea because it can produce unexpected results in some circumstances.

If you want more help with expressions:

You can use the Expression Builder to help you add functions to an expression. Click the Build (...) button in a property box to start it.

In the lower left pane of the Expression Builder dialog box, you can double-click the plus sign next to Functions to expand the list to include Built-In Functions and the name of the database you're using if it contains any functions. When you click Built-In Functions, a list of function categories appears in the center pane. Select the category for the function you want and then paste it into the expression. When you click a function name, the syntax you need to enter for the function appears at the bottom of the dialog box so you can see what additional information you need to add.

The mailing labels I created have blank lines

Source of the problem

You have taken great care to include all possible items in your customer mailing address report. A few customers have a second address line that indicates their particular building number or office suite, but not all of your customers are so metropolitan. You've designed your labels to accommodate those few, but you get blank lines in the labels for the others. That doesn't look professional. You want to leave out the blank lines when you print the labels for the complete address list.

What you need to do is combine fields in an expression in a way that Access will skip over the fields that are blank. Here's how to do that.

How to fix it

1. Open the form or report you use to print labels in design view.

2. Add a new text box control to the detail section of the form or report, and name it something like Full Address.

3. Right-click on the text box control, and then click Properties on the shortcut menu.

4. In the Control Source property for the control, enter an expression such as **IIf(IsNull([Address2]),"",[Address2] & Chr(13) & Chr(10))**. If the Address2 field is blank, this expression returns a zero-length string—in other words, no text. If the field contains data that should be in a separate row (a building or suite number, for example), the expression returns the field value. The field value is followed by a carriage return created by the *Chr(13)* in the expression, and a line feed created by *Chr(10)*.

5. You can add IIf() function statements to the expression to accommodate other fields in the full address. For example, some addresses might include a person's title while others don't. ▶

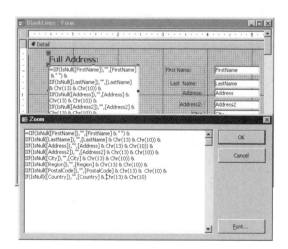

6. Set the text box control's Can Grow and Can Shrink properties to Yes so that the control will resize vertically depending on how many lines appear in the address. ▶

Tip

This solution can be useful when you want to import an address list to another application.

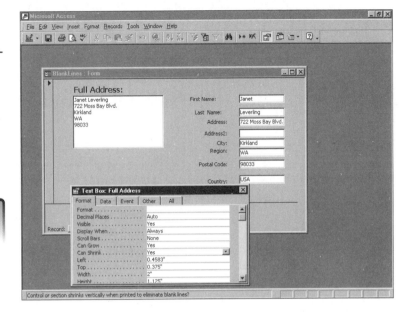

Using expressions to handle blank fields

Access provides three handy functions for dealing with blank fields. You can use them in expressions in queries or in the Control Source property of a control on a form or report.

The IsNull function answers yes or no to the question "Is the field blank?" For example, the expression IsNull([Address2]) returns Yes if there is no secondary address and No if the field contains a value.

When you combine the IsNull function with the IIf function (IIf stands for Immediate If; you can also think of the IIf function as the test function), you can specify what Access should do if the field is blank. The format of the IIf function is IIf(*condition, true, false*). For *condition*, you enter the information you want to test; for example, is the MiddleInitial field in an employee's record blank? For *true*, you specify the outcome you want if the condition is true; for *false*, you specify the outcome if the condition is false. With a combination of IIf and IsNull, you can create an expression to control the results of working with blank fields. For example, the expression IIf(IsNull([MiddleInitial]),"NMI",[MiddleInitial]) displays the letters NMI if the MiddleInitial field is blank. The expression displays the value of the MiddleInitial field if it is not blank.

The third useful function is the Nz function. You use this function to return a specific value if the field is blank. For example, the expression Nz([Address2],"None") returns the value of the Address2 field if there is one or the word "None" if the field is blank. Notice that you must enclose the text string None in double quotation marks in the expression, but you won't see the quotation marks when None is displayed.

I'm getting the wrong results with date calculations

Source of the problem

It's hard enough to remember the date of your next dental checkup or your mother's birthday. Working with dates and times in an expression can be a real challenge. Dates look so much like simple numbers that Access can confuse the two if you aren't careful and give you some bizarre results.

If you are including a date in an expression and don't get the results you expect, you might have forgotten to enclose the date with the date delimiter symbol (#). Access will have interpreted the date to be a number, and you might see an error message that you are trying to divide by zero or see a long decimal number as the result of your expression. When you place a date in an expression in a query, Access automatically adds the delimiters. But when you add a date to an expression in the Control Source property for a text box or a list box on a form, for example, you're on your own.

You might also get into trouble when you try to calculate the span of time between two dates. When you subtract one date from another, the result you see is the number of days between the two. This is not always what you want or expect.

The following steps show you how to overcome these obstacles.

How to fix it

If you get an error message about dividing by zero or see a long decimal number as the result of your expression, do the following:

1. Open the form or report in design view, and select the control containing the expression.

2. On the toolbar, click the Properties button and locate the problem date in the Control Source property box.

3. Insert the pound sign delimiter (#) before and after the date. ▶

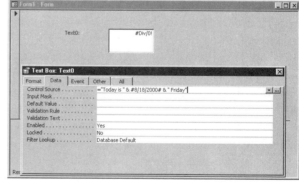

4. Enter zeros that Access removed from two-digit month, day, or year values. The date is now in the format that Access requires.

5. Save the form or report.

If you are having trouble calculating the time between two dates, do the following:

1. Open the form or report in form view, and select the control containing the expression. Notice that the Time With Company field in this example doesn't show the correct data. ▶

2. On the toolbar, click the Properties button and then click in the Control Source property box.

3. Enter an expression such as **=DateDiff("yyyy",[*FieldName*],Date()) & " years"**. This expression calculates the number of years between today's date (which is calculated using the Date() function) and the date in the field you include in *FieldName*. If you want to see the number of months between the dates, use *m* rather than *yyyy*; to see the number of calendar weeks, use *ww*; and for the number of work weeks use *w*. Use *d* for the number of days. ▶

4. Save the form or report.

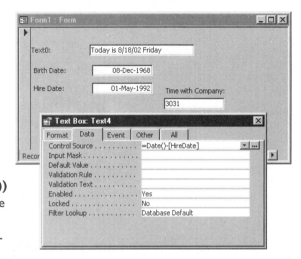

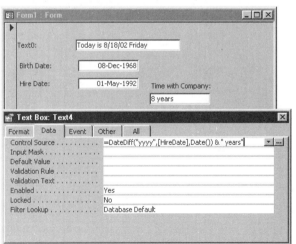

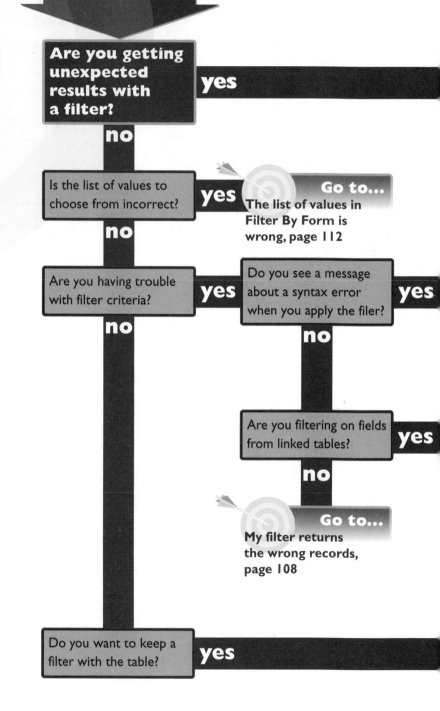

Are you getting unexpected results with a filter?

yes

no

Is the list of values to choose from incorrect?

yes

Go to...
The list of values in Filter By Form is wrong, page 112

no

Are you having trouble with filter criteria?

yes

Do you see a message about a syntax error when you apply the filer?

yes

no

Are you filtering on fields from linked tables?

yes

no

Go to...
My filter returns the wrong records, page 108

no

Do you want to keep a filter with the table?

yes

Filtering

Does the filter return too few records? **yes** → **Go to...** My filter doesn't return all the records I want, page 102

no

Does the filter return too many records? **yes** → Did you filter the subdatasheet? **yes** → **Quick fix** The filter you built for the subdatasheet applies only to the subdatasheet.

1. Create a separate filter for the datasheet.

no

Go to... My filter returns too many records, page 106

Quick fix The value you picked from the drop-down list in Filter By Form probably contained a comma.

1. To correct the syntax error, enclose the value in quotation marks.

Quick fix Values for fields from linked tables that you use in sort criteria are case-senstive. Make sure they match the field values exactly.

Go to... The filter I created isn't saved with my table, page 110

If your solution isn't here
Check these related chapters:
- Datasheets—Viewing data, page 66
- Expressions, page 90
- Queries—Selection criteria, page 214

Or see the general troubleshooting tips on page xiii.

My filter doesn't return all the records I want

Source of the problem

You sent out a fancy questionnaire to your customers and got an impressive response. But when you filter your database to tally the results, you see disappointingly few records. Something is wrong here! The source of the problem, as well as the solution, depends on how you filtered the records in the table, query, or form.

- If you used Filter By Form, you might have entered criteria using the *And* operator, which returns fewer records than the *Or* operator.

- If you used Filter By Selection, you might have selected the wrong value. Or, you might be filtering records in a combo box whose values come from a value list instead of from the table itself. When you filter on the value in a combo box, Access looks in the first column in the list for matches to the value. If the first column in the list is not the one bound to a field, Access won't find a match.

- If you are using the Filter For command, you might have applied more than one filter or the wrong filter criteria.

- If you are taking advantage of the Advanced Filter/Sort command, you have probably specified too many criteria, which limits the number of records returned by the filter.

The following solutions offer ways to cure these problems.

How to fix it

If you used Filter By Form, follow these steps:

1. At the bottom of the Filter By Form window, click the Or tab and add alternative sort criteria. (Entering criteria in the same row of the Look For tab implies the *And* operator.) The additional sort criteria should increase the number of records returned when you apply the filter.

2. If step 1 doesn't work, delete any value or expression that might limit the number of values too much. For example, an expression that combines two values with the *And* operator so that both conditions must be met reduces the number of values returned. The expression can be on the Look For tab or on an Or tab in the Filter By Form window. The filter shown in the figure will return only three records from the Northwind sample database Orders table. Removing one of the values from the filter or moving it to the Or tab—it doesn't matter which—increases the number of records returned by the filter to 133. ▶

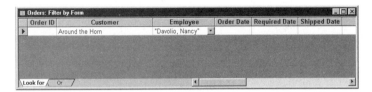

If you are filtering on a value displayed in a combo box that gets its values from a value list, follow these steps:

1. Check to be sure that the value you see is in the first column in the list.

2. If it is not, change the combo box so that the bound column (the one that contains the values that are stored in the field) appears first. To do that, first open the form in design view.

3. Double-click the combo box control.

4. In the Row Source property box, change the value list so that the bound column is the first column in the value list. ▶

5. Change the Bound Column property to 1, the number of the column.

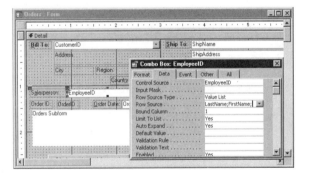

> **Tip**
>
> You can also simply enter the actual field values from the table or query in the Row Source property box, separated by semicolons. (For example, Small, Medium, and Large for a field that records the size of apparel.) If you do this, be sure the Row Source Type property is set to Value List.

My filter doesn't return all the records I want

(continued from page 103)

If a filter you set up with the Filter For command is already applied to the records, do the following:

1. Remove the filter by clicking the Remove Filter button.

2. Right-click in the datasheet column or form control, enter a different value or expression in the Filter For box on the shortcut menu, and press Enter. ▶

3. If that doesn't work, point to the Filter command on the Records menu and click Advanced Filter/Sort.

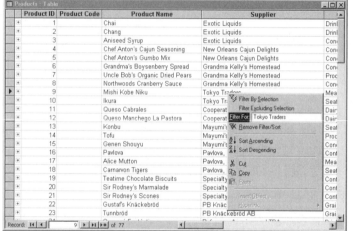

4. Look at the grid in the Advanced Filter/Sort window. If you have specified more than one expression or value, each one will show up in the grid.

5. Check for incorrect criteria expressions. For example, you might have combined mutually exclusive values with the *And* operator.

If you already used Advanced Filter/Sort to create the filter, follow these steps to change the filtering criteria:

1. On the Records menu, click Filter and then click Advanced Filter/Sort.

2. Delete some of the criteria you've entered.

3. You can also move some of the criteria to the Or row instead of placing criteria in the same row, which creates *And* combinations.

4. If that fails to return the number of records you expect, change some expressions from *And* to *Or* in the Criteria row combinations. The filter shown in the figure returns only four records. All records must contain *Davolio, Nancy* in the Employee Name field, but they may have either of the company names. If you move one of the criteria to the Or row, the filter returns 142 records. ▶

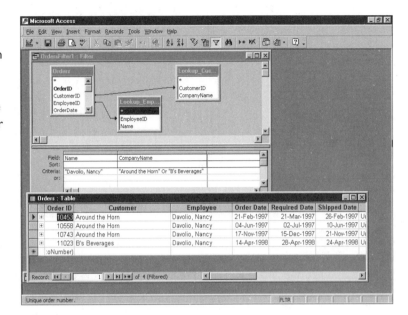

What's in the Filter By Form list?

The window that opens when you click the Filter By Form button displays controls that you can use to select or enter values with which to filter the underlying data. Access reads records in the data and finds unique values for each field. It then places these values in a combo box or list box for the control. You can then select the value you want to use as a filter.

If the recordset contains thousands of records, you can set the Don't Display Lists Where More Than This Number Of Records Read option to a reasonable number. If the recordset contains more records than that, Access doesn't fill the box with the actual field values—only two values: Is Null and Is Not Null. To set this option, click Options on the Tools menu and then click the Edit/Final tab.

My filter returns too many records

Source of the problem

You are trying to find a few good records, and you get snow-balled with more than you can handle. You need to figure out how to be pickier without shutting the door completely. When a filter returns too many records, the cause of the problem depends on the type of filter you applied to the table, query, or form.

- If you are using Filter By Form, you need to adjust the values or expressions you're using so that fewer records are returned.

- If you are using Filter by Selection, you can apply a filter to only one value at a time, but you can apply additional filters, one after the other, to narrow down the selection.

- If you are using Filter Excluding Selection, you may have selected values in more than one row. Access interprets that as an instruction to exclude records with the first or the second value, but not records with both values. What you need to do is exclude records with the first value and then exclude records with the second value.

- If you are using the Filter For command, you can apply a filter repeatedly until you have just the set of records you want. You can filter on the same field using a different value or filter on a different field.

The following solutions show you how to fix these problems.

How to fix it

To fix the problem of too many records if you're using Filter By Form, follow these steps:

1. Display the datasheet you want to filter.

2. On the Records menu, click Filter and then click Filter By Form.

3. On the Look For tab, enter a value or expression or pick a value from the drop-down lists in the grid.

4. If you have added values or expressions on the Or tab, which expands the search, remove one or more of them. Otherwise, include them on the Look For tab, which makes them *And* criteria.

If you need to further limit the number of records returned by a Filter By Selection operation, you need to select more than one value.

1. Open the datasheet you're trying to filter, select the field you want to filter on first, and then click the Filter By Selection button on the toolbar.

2. Select the next field you want to filter on, and then click the Filter By Selection button again. Your second choice further filters the records returned by the first filter.

To fix the problem if you're using Filter Excluding Selection, apply the filters separately as follows:

1. Select the first value you want to exclude, right-click, and then click Filter Excluding Selection on the shortcut menu. ▶

2. Select the second value, and repeat step 1 to apply the filter.

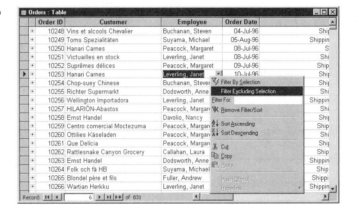

If filtering by more than one field with Filter Excluding Selection doesn't work, follow these steps:

1. With the datasheet open and the filters applied, point to Filter on the Records menu and click Advanced Filter/Sort.

2. Change the *Or* operator in the Criteria row to *And*.

3. Click the Apply Filter button.

With the Filter For shortcut menu command, do the following:

1. Right-click the datasheet in the field you want to filter.

2. In the Filter For box in the shortcut menu, enter the value you want to filter on and then press Enter. ▶

3. Repeat the filter to add another value. Each time you add a value, you further limit the number of records.

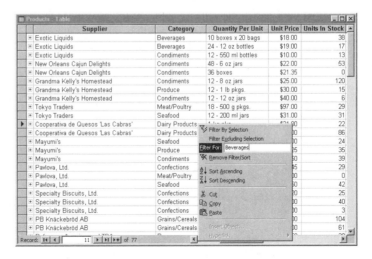

My filter returns the wrong records

Source of the problem

It doesn't help at all if you are looking in your database for all the owners of sport utility vehicles and turn up with a list of cat lovers. Just hope that you catch the mistake before sending out your notices of free brake inspections.

One reason for the wrong results could be that you are using the wrong field or fields in the filter. You might also have entered the wrong value or criteria. Another possibility is that you used the wrong operator in the filter expression.

If you are using an expression to filter the records and the value starts with the word *is*, that's at least part of your problem. *Is* is a reserved word in Access and can be used only in an expression that compares values with Null or Not Null. So, if you enter *is** as the filter expression, you get an error message.

If the records filter the way you want but the sort order is not what you expected, you might have arranged the fields to sort by in the wrong sequence in the filter design grid.

The following solution shows you how to solve these problems.

How to fix it

1. If you have entered expressions in the Filter By Form or Advanced Filter/Sort window, make sure you are using the right operator. When to use *Or* and when to use *And* can be tricky. Use *Or* when you want to include records with either value in the field, such as Condiments or Beverages. Use *And* when you want records that include both values in two different fields, such as Condiments (Category) and Exotic Liquids (Supplier).

2. If your filter uses multiple criteria, make sure you've placed the criteria in the correct row. Putting the criteria in the same row implies the *And* operator. Using separate rows combines the criteria with the *Or* operator.

3. If your expression starts with the word *is* and you type **Is***, you will see an error message. ▶

4. Click OK, and enclose the whole string in quotation marks, including any wildcard character (*) you have added.

5. Open the Filter By Form window and check to make sure the filter expression reads *Like "is*"*.

6. If the sort order is not what you expected, rearrange the fields in the Filter By Form design grid.

7. Place the first level sort field in the leftmost column with lower priority sort fields to the right. For example, sort first by Last Name. Then for records with the same value for Last Name, sort by First Name.

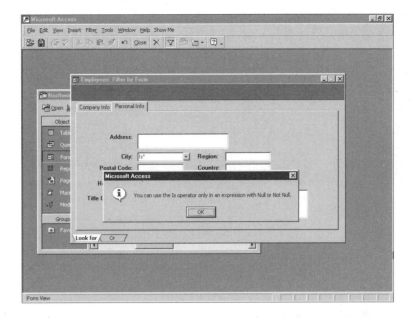

Which filter to use?

Which filter you use depends on what you want to do.

If you want to search for records that meet more than one criterion at once, you can use any of the five types of filters: Filter By Selection, Filter By Form, Filter For, Filter Excluding Selection, or Advanced Filter/Sort. They will all apply conditions with the *And* operator.

If you use Filter By Selection, you have to apply each condition separately. The order doesn't matter; all the conditions must be met by the values to be returned by the filter. With the other methods, you can combine all the conditions in one operation.

If you want to combine conditions with the *Or* operator or enter criteria expressions, you must use Filter By Form, Filter For, or Advanced Filter/Sort.

If you also want the records sorted in concert with the filtering process, you have only one choice: Advanced Filter/Sort. You can, however, still sort records after they've been returned by the filter. All you have to do is click one of the Sort buttons on the toolbar.

The filter I created isn't saved with my table

Source of the problem

After you have spent hours—several minutes anyway—creating a filter to isolate the records you want, why can't you call it up again at a later date? Only the last filter you built is saved with a table, and only then if you answer "Yes" when asked whether you want to save the changes to the table. When you open the table again, you can reapply that filter.

But the filter you created last week, before you made several changes to the table, is long gone. Microsoft knew this could create a problem and thoughtfully added a way to save the filter as a query. If you save a filter as a query, you can reapply the filter you saved.

How to fix it

1. Open the table with the records you want to filter.

2. Create the filter you need with Filter By Form or Advanced Filter/Sort.

3. Click the Save As Query toolbar button. ▶

4. Enter a name for the query, and then click OK.

When you need to apply the query to the table, open the table and follow these steps.

1. If you used Filter By Form to create the filter, click the Filter By Form button; if you used the Advanced Filter/Sort command to create the filer, click Filter on the Records menu and then click Advanced Filter/Sort.

2. Click the Load From Query toolbar button. ▶

3. In the Applicable Filter dialog box, select the query you want to use. ▶

4. Click OK.

5. Click the Apply Filter button.

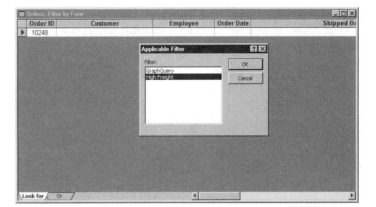

Queries make good filters

Queries are saved as database objects on their own and can be called upon to serve as filters at any time. There are, however, a few requirements the query must follow in order to qualify as a filter.

The query must be a simple select query (it can't be an action query or a crosstab query) that's based on the same table or query that underlies the datasheet or form you're filtering. It also can't include fields from any other tables or queries. You can't filter with queries that have records grouped by field values or queries that compute aggregate values such as Sum, Count, Avg, Max, or Min.

The list of values in Filter By Form is wrong

Source of the problem

Value lists are very helpful—just pick a value from the list Access displays. That's much easier than having to remember (and spell correctly) the value you want to use as a filter. But sometimes the drop-down list is blank, or worse yet, you see only the ubiquitous Is Null and Is Not Null options to choose from.

If the list is blank, you may have set the option that displays value lists only for indexed fields. Having Access display only indexed fields saves time, but it can be confusing. If you have just the two Null options, the setting for the maximum number of records might be too low. Another reason you don't see the values you want could be that the field you're looking at is a memo field, an OLE Object field, or a hyperlink field that can be filtered only on whether they are blank or not. Not much you can do about that.

In other cases, a value list is so long it seems to take days to find the value you want, even if you have tried to limit the number of unique values in the list. The field is probably a lookup field that doesn't even listen to such limitations. If that's the case, you can change the Row Source property of the field so that it limits the list.

How to fix it

If the list is blank because the field is not indexed, you can remove that restriction. Follow these steps:

1. On the Tools menu, click Options and then click the Edit/Find tab.

2. In the area labeled Show List Of Values In, select the option Local Nonindexed Fields.

Tip
To find out whether a field is indexed or not, open the table that contains the field in design view. Note whether the Indexed property for that field is set to Yes or No.

To increase the number of records to read to find the unique values, follow these steps:

1. On the Tools menu, click Options and then click the Edit/Find tab.

2. Increase the number in the setting for Don't Display Lists Where More Than This Number Of Records Read. ▶

If the field is a lookup field, follow these steps:

1. Open the table in design view, select the field, and click the Lookup tab in the Field Properties area.

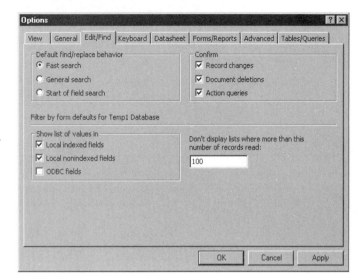

2. Click the Build (...) button next to the Row Source property box.

3. In the upper pane of the Query Builder window, right-click and choose Properties from the shortcut menu.

4. Change the Top Values property from All to the number of values you want in the list. ▶

5. Click Yes to apply the change.

6. Click Yes when asked whether you want to save changes to the table design.

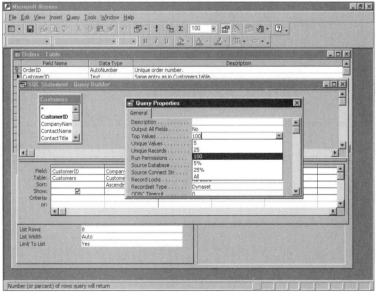

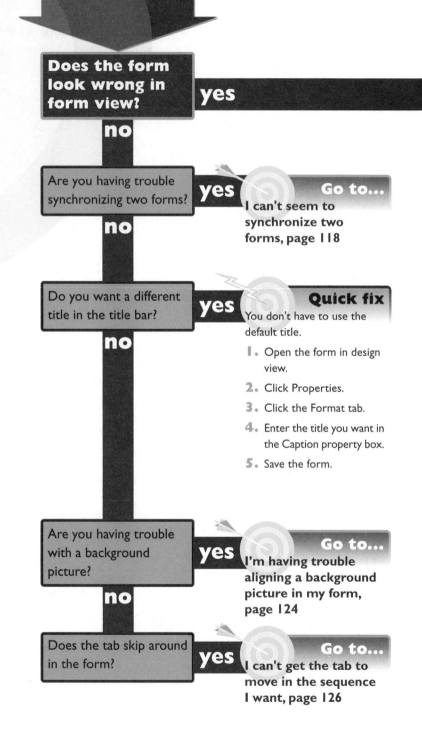

Does the form look wrong in form view?

yes

no

Are you having trouble synchronizing two forms?

yes

Go to...

I can't seem to synchronize two forms, page 118

no

Do you want a different title in the title bar?

yes

Quick fix

You don't have to use the default title.

1. Open the form in design view.
2. Click Properties.
3. Click the Format tab.
4. Enter the title you want in the Caption property box.
5. Save the form.

no

Are you having trouble with a background picture?

yes

Go to...

I'm having trouble aligning a background picture in my form, page 124

no

Does the tab skip around in the form?

yes

Go to...

I can't get the tab to move in the sequence I want, page 126

Is the form the wrong size, or does it display incomplete records?

yes → **Go to...** My form is the wrong size and doesn't display complete records, page 116

no ↓

Do you see an icon where there should be an object?

yes → **Quick fix**
You probably chose to display the picture as an icon when you converted it.

1. Open the form in design view.
2. Click the icon.
3. Point to the appropriate Object command (for example, Chart Object) on the Edit menu and click Convert.
4. Clear the Display As Icon box in the Convert dialog box.
5. Click OK in the Convert dialog box, and then save the form.

no ↓

Are you having trouble aligning text boxes?

yes → **Go to...** I can't get my text boxes and labels to line up right, page 120

no ↓

Quick fix
If you want the form to look less like a data entry form, do the following:

1. Open the form in design view, and click the Properties button on the toolbar.
2. On the Format tab, set the Scroll Bars property to Neither, and set the Record Selectors, Navigation Buttons, and Dividing Lines properties to No.
3. Save the form.

If your solution isn't here
Check these related chapters:
Controls—Managing data, page 12
Controls—Placing & formatting, page 24
Forms—Entering data, page 128
Or see the general troubleshooting tips on page xiii.

My form is the wrong size and doesn't display complete records

Source of the problem

We usually think of a form as an object fixed in size and appearance, like the IRS Form 1040. Access forms, however, can be nonconformists, and sometimes they do whatever they want. If you're having trouble keeping a form at the size you want (for example, you want it to be the same size when you open it as it was when you saved it), it's helpful to know how a form and the form window relate. A form has its own height and width, and these dimensions don't necessarily match those of the window in which you view it. (One benefit of these independent dimensions is that the form looks the same when you print it no matter how it looks in the form window.) But you can display the form in the window at the size you want. If a form doesn't retain changes you made to its size, you probably resized the window rather than the form. The problem could also be blamed on the form's Auto Resize property, which sizes the form to display a complete record.

You might want the form to display complete records when it opens. To do so, you set the Auto Resize property to Yes. If the form still shows partial records when there is room on the screen for a complete record, you might have switched to form view from design view rather than opening the form in form view from the database window.

The following solution shows you some ways to solve these problems.

How to fix it

If you're trying to resize the form and the form window, do the following:

1. In the database window, select the form and click the Design button.

2. Drag the right border of the form (not the window) to the width you want. ▶

3. Drag the bottom edge of the form so that the form's at the height you want.

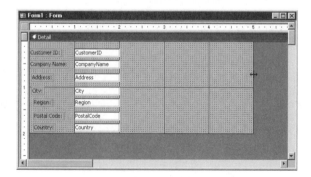

4. On the toolbar, click the Properties button.

5. In the properties dialog box, click the Format tab.

6. Set the Auto Resize property of the form to No.

7. Click the View button.

8. If the form window is maximized, click the Restore button on the title bar.

9. On the Window menu, click Size To Fit Form. ▶

10. Save the form.

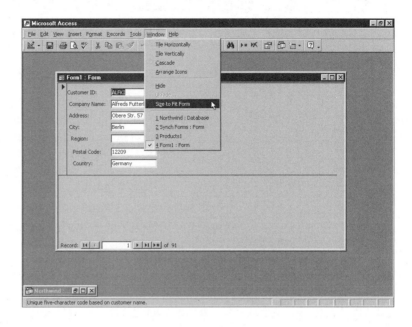

The Size To Fit Form command behaves differently depending on the setting of the form's Default View property. If Default View is set to Single Form, the form window is cropped to fit one record. But if a single record is too large for the screen, the window expands to display as much of the record as possible.

If the Default View property is set to Continuous Forms, Access crops any partial record showing at the bottom of the screen. If the window can hold only one record, Access expands the form window to display as much of the record as possible.

If a form you've created doesn't resize automatically to display complete records when you open it, do the following:

1. In the database window, select the form and open it in design view.

2. On the toolbar, click the Properties button and then click the Format tab.

3. Set the Auto Resize property to Yes.

4. Click the View button to switch to form view.

5. Save and close the form.

When you open the form in form view, always open it from the database window. If you open it first in design view and then switch to form view, the form window won't resize.

I can't seem to synchronize two forms

Source of the problem

When you design a form for data entry or retrieval, you want to keep it as simple as possible. A form that looks too busy can be distracting. Still, there are times when you'd like to have a little more information about the record you see in a form. So you create a separate form to display the related records. Trouble is, you don't see information in the second form that is related to the record in the first form. The likely cause of this trouble is that the forms are not linked by fields that contain matching data.

The following solution shows you how to fix this problem and synchronize the view of related information in two forms.

How to fix it

If you have already created the forms and want to link and synchronize them, do the following:

1. Open the main form in design view.

2. In the toolbox, make sure the Control Wizards button is selected and then click the Command Button tool.

3. Click in the form where you want to place the button. The Command Button Wizard starts.

4. In the Categories box, click Form Operations. In the Actions box, click Open Form. Click Next.

5. Choose the form that shows the data related to the record in the original form, and then click Next.

6. Select the option Open The Form And Find Specific Data To Display, and then click Next. ▶

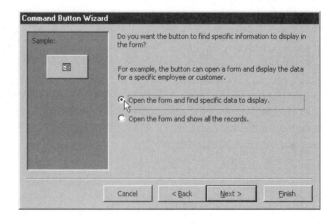

7. In the lists displaying the fields from each form, select the matching fields, and then click the <-> button. Click Next. ▶

8. Enter text or choose an image to place on the button. Click Finish. The figure shows the Products form linked to the Categories form. You open the synchronized form by clicking the command button labeled Products1. ▶

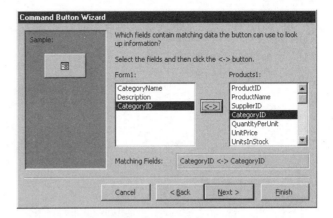

Synchronizing forms from scratch

If you haven't yet created the forms you want to synchronize, you can use the Form Wizard to create two related forms.

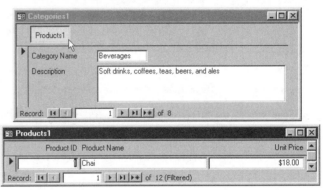

In the database window, click Forms and then click New. In the New Form dialog box, select Form Wizard. Click OK. (You don't need to select a table or query from the drop-down list in this step.)

From the list of tables and queries, select the one you want to base the main form on and add the fields you want to include on the form. Then, select the table or query on which you want to base the related form and add the fields you want to include. Click Next.

In the next Form Wizard dialog box, click the Linked Forms option and then click Next.

In the next two sections of the Wizard, change the style of the forms and rename the forms if you want. Click Finish. When the main form opens, click the button that opens the linked form.

I can't get my text boxes and labels to line up right

Source of the problem

Most of the time you probably don't care that much about precision when you're placing controls on a form. But at times, it's really important that controls such as text boxes and their labels are positioned well. Precise placement gives your form a professional appearance and is handy for keeping the data on the form accessible and easy to work with. Several factors are at play in placing and aligning text boxes and their labels on a form.

- Do some controls move when you don't expect them to? When you drew a rectangle to select controls, you might have included more controls than you wanted.

- Another problem you might encounter is trying to move one or more text box controls to a precise location. The form grid can help, but it might not be the complete solution.

- Trying to align the labels one way and the text boxes another might create a problem.

- If you're having trouble with the spacing among a group of controls, you might have selected a control outside the row or column you're trying to adjust. Or you might have turned off the Snap To Grid option, which often results in uneven placement.

The following solutions show you some ways to cure these problems.

How to fix it

If text boxes move with a group of controls but you don't want them to, do the following:

1. If you selected the controls by dragging the selection arrow in a ruler, hold down Shift and click the text box or label you don't want to move. ▶

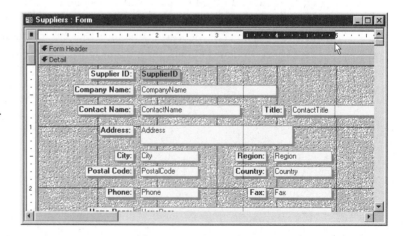

2. If you selected the controls by drawing a rectangle around the controls in the form's design view, hold down Shift and click the ones you don't want to move.

3. If you just want to move the labels and leave the text boxes alone, hold down Shift while you click on just the labels.

If you're having trouble moving selected text box controls to the right place, try the following:

1. Click the moving handle on one of the text boxes, and drag it to the position you want.

2. To keep the selected text boxes horizontally or vertically aligned when you move them, hold down Shift while you drag the controls.

3. If you need to move the controls a short distance, hold down Shift and click one of the arrow keys. The selected controls move in the direction of the arrow one-fourth of a grid unit with each click.

Tip

Using the arrow keys to move the controls temporarily turns off the Snap To Grid feature.

If you're trying to align text box controls to the left and align their attached labels to the right, follow these steps:

1. Hold down the Shift key, and select each of the text boxes.

2. On the Format menu, click Align and then click Left. ▶

3. Hold down the Shift key, and select each of the labels.

4. On the Format menu, click Align and then click Right.

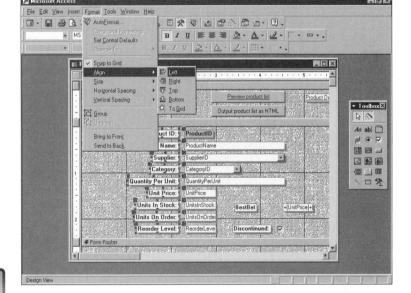

Tip

The Align buttons on the Formatting (Form/Report) toolbar apply to the text within the text box and label controls, not to the alignment of the controls themselves.

I can't get my text boxes and labels to line up right

(continued from page 121)

If you're having trouble changing the spacing between selected text boxes, try these steps:

1. Select the column of text boxes, including their labels. If you accidentally include a control that is not part of the column, hold down Shift and click on the control to remove it from the selection.

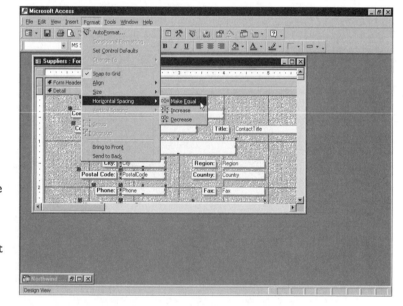

2. On the Format menu, click Horizontal Spacing and then click Make Equal. ▶

3. If you want to add space between the text boxes, click Horizontal Spacing on the Format menu and then click Increase. This command keeps the top control in place and widens the space between the remaining controls uniformly by one grid interval.

4. To keep the top control in place and decrease the horizontal spacing between the controls, click the Horizontal Space command and then click Decrease.

Tip

If you are not satisfied with the size of the grid in the form design window, you can change it by changing the Grid X and Grid Y properties of the form. By default, the horizontal grid (Grid X) is set to 10 dots per inch, and the vertical grid (Grid Y) is set to 12 dots per inch. (The unit of measure depends on the Regional Settings in Windows Control Panel.)

Putting labels above the text boxes

If you don't want the default labels on the left and level with text boxes, you can change the standard placement of the label by changing the settings of the Label X and Label Y properties for text box controls. To change the settings, click the Text Box control in the toolbox and then click the Properties button.

Label X determines the horizontal distance from the label text to the upper-left corner of the text box. A negative Label X places the label text to the left of the text box, and a positive setting places it to the right of the upper-left corner of the text box. Label Y specifies the vertical distance from the upper-left corner of the text box. A setting of 0 aligns the label horizontally with the text box. A negative Label Y setting places the label above the text box, and a positive setting places it below. Combining a positive setting in the Label X property with a negative setting in the Label Y property places the label above the text box.

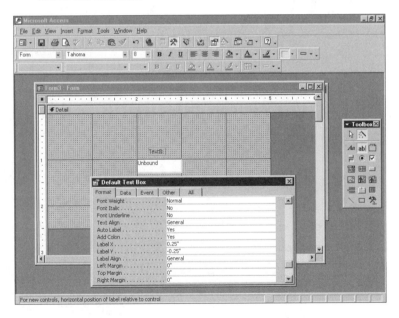

I'm having trouble aligning a background picture in my form

Source of the problem

Subliminal messages floating in the background on a form can create a welcoming atmosphere. They might even soften the blow when you reach the bottom line.

Background pictures are different from the images and other objects that you can add to forms and reports. They have some special property settings that may seem elusive. If you're having trouble aligning a background picture and making it fill the form, you might not be using the appropriate Picture Size Mode property setting.

If you're trying to repeat the picture across the whole form (which Access refers to as tiling the image), you don't have to embed several copies of the picture file. The form has a tiling property to help you arrange the pictures.

The following solutions help you solve some of the background picture problems.

How to fix it

To have the background picture fill the whole form, follow these steps:

1. In the database window, select the form and click the Design button.

2. Click the Properties button on the toolbar.

3. Click the Format tab.

4. In the Picture Size Mode property box, select Zoom. ▶

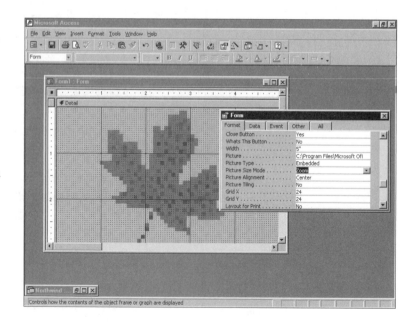

If you want to create a wallpaper effect, you can use the Picture Tiling property:

1. Follow steps 1 through 3 on the previous page.

2. In the Picture Size Mode property box, select Clip. ▶

3. Set the Picture Alignment property to Center.

4. Set the Picture Tiling property to Yes.

5. Click the View button to see how the form looks in form view.

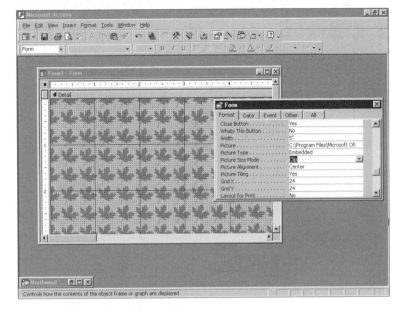

Setting the picture alignment

Aligning a picture can be a little challenging. If the picture is not tiled, settings for the Picture Alignment property such as Top Left, Top Right, Center, and Bottom Left are self-explanatory. The setting that needs explanation is Form Center. This setting centers the picture horizontally in relation to the width of the form and vertically in relation to the height of the entire form. If the picture is tiled, the Picture Alignment setting determines where the tiling will begin—at the top left, center, top right, and so on.

I can't get the tab to move in the sequence I want

Source of the problem

You've seen horses in a pasture—nibbling a little grass here, taking a couple of steps and nibbling a few more blades there. It seems that there's no reasonable pattern involved in the grazing. Sometimes, when you start to enter data in a new form, tabbing from control to control, you find yourself jumping all around on the screen instead of progressing in a logical manner.

The culprit is probably the tab order—the sequential list of controls that determines the path of the cursor through the maze of controls on the form. The tab order is first determined by the order in which you add the controls to the form. But often, after you create the form, you move controls around and add more controls. Using the Tab key to move from control to control on a form under these circumstances can give the form the behavior of the grazing horse. It's definitely not taking you where you want to go.

Access offers ways to set the tab order just the way you want. However, be warned that when you change the tab order in a form, the order of the columns in the form's datasheet view will be changed to match.

Another problem you might have encountered is that you can't get to a control at all by pressing Tab.

The following solutions give you ways to fix these problems.

How to fix it

To change the tab order of controls on your form, do the following:

1. Open the form in design view.

2. On the View menu, click Tab Order.

3. In the Tab Order dialog box, click the selector button beside the name of the control you want to reposition in the tab order and then drag the control name up or down until it is where you want it. ▶

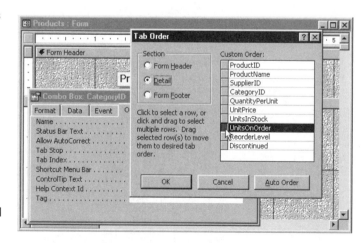

4. Switch to form view and press Tab repeatedly to move through the controls.

5. Return to design view and repeat these steps for the other controls until you have the tab order you want.

Tip

The Auto Order button in the Tab Order dialog box sets the tab order based on the physical layout of controls on the form—from left to right, and top to bottom. If this is the way you want to move through the controls, click Auto Order instead of moving the controls by hand.

Tip

The controls are listed in the Tab Order dialog box by their Name property. If you don't recognize the one you want to move, close the Tab Order dialog box, double-click the control, and then look at its Name property.

6. Save the form.

If a control is skipped in the tab order or if you want to skip it when you tab through the controls on a form, do the following:

1. Open the form in design view, and then click the Properties button on the toolbar.

2. Select the control, and click the Other tab in the properties dialog box.

3. Set the Tab Stop property to Yes to include the control in the tab order; set the Tab Stop property to No to omit the control. ▶

4. Save the form.

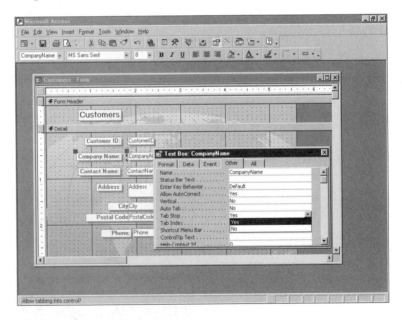

Clues about other tab order properties

The Tab Index property is a number indicating the control's position in the tab order. The first control to receive focus when the form opens in form view has a Tab Index of 0. The Auto Tab property works with fields that have input masks. When the Auto Tab property is set to Yes, the cursor moves to the next control in the tab order when the last character permitted in the input mask is entered.

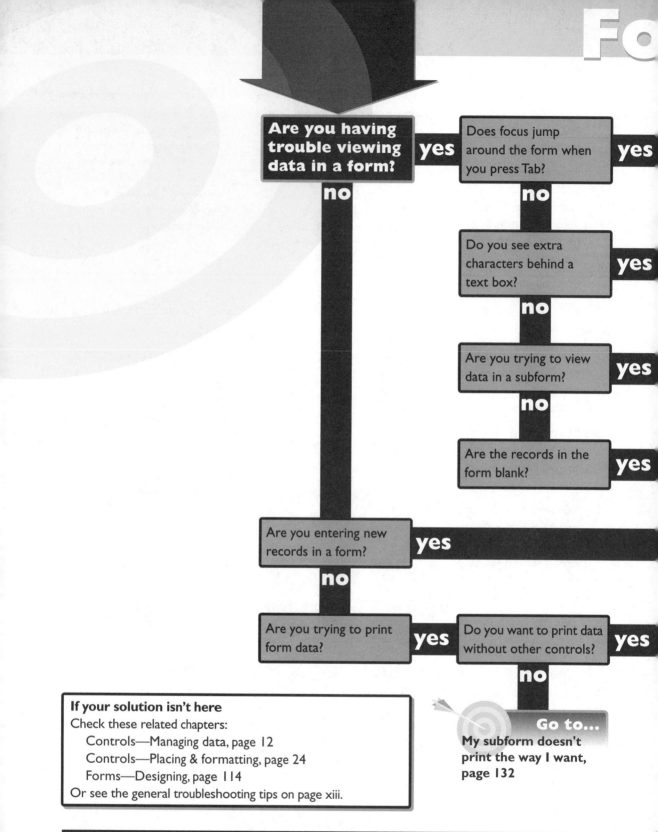

Fo

Are you having trouble viewing data in a form? **yes** → Does focus jump around the form when you press Tab? **yes**

no

Do you see extra characters behind a text box? **yes**

no

Are you trying to view data in a subform? **yes**

no

Are the records in the form blank? **yes**

Are you entering new records in a form? **yes**

no

Are you trying to print form data? **yes** → Do you want to print data without other controls? **yes**

no

If your solution isn't here
Check these related chapters:
   Controls—Managing data, page 12
   Controls—Placing & formatting, page 24
   Forms—Designing, page 114
Or see the general troubleshooting tips on page xiii.

Go to...
My subform doesn't print the way I want, page 132

Quick fix

The tab order is determined by the order in which you add controls to the form.

1. Open the form in design view.
2. Click Tab Order on the View menu.
3. Click the field you want to change in the tab order.
4. Drag the field by the selector box to a new position.
5. Click OK and save the form.

Quick fix

There is probably a vagrant label behind the text box control.

1. Open the form in design view.
2. Select the text box control.
3. Click Send To Back on the Format menu.
4. Select the extra label control and press Delete.

Go to...

My subform doesn't show the data I expected, page 136

Go to...

My form is blank where there should be data, page 134

Are you having trouble typing data in a multiline text box?

yes

Quick fix

You might be pressing Enter, which moves you to the next control instead of the next line in the text box.

1. For a temporary solution, press Ctrl+Enter.
2. For a permanent solution, open the form in design view.
3. Right-click the text box, and then click Properties.
4. Set the text box's Enter Key Behavior property to New Line In Field.
5. Save the form.

no

Quick fix

You can specify when you want the command button to show.

1. Open the form in design view.
2. Right-click the command button, and then click Properties.
3. Set the Display When property to Screen Only.
4. Repeat for other buttons and save the form.

Go to...

I'm having trouble entering records in my combo box or list box, page 130

I'm having trouble entering records in my combo box or list box

Source of the problem

Data entry forms are supposed to make life easier, not stubbornly decline to accept the data you try to enter. This is especially true for controls that are designed to speed things up, such as combo boxes and list boxes. When you click in a combo box, a list of acceptable values is displayed from which you can pick the one you want. List boxes display the values without you having to click the arrow. Sometimes you have to choose from the list, but other times you can enter whatever you want.

If you're having trouble entering data in a specific control, you might have one of the following problems:

- If the control is a combo box, there might be a problem with the Row Source, Control Source, or Bound Column property. The Row Source property tells Access where to get the values to display in the list. The Control Source property tells Access where to store the value you select from the list or manually enter in the control. The Bound Column property indicates which column of data in the list is to be stored in Control Source. If any of these properties are improperly set, you will see an error or an incorrect value will be entered.

- If you are trying to enter a value that's not listed in the combo box or list box, the Limit To List property might be set to Yes.

The following solution shows you how to solve these problems.

How to fix it

1. In the database window, select the form containing the combo box or list box, and then click the Design button.

2. Select the combo box or list box control, and then click the Properties button on the toolbar.

3. In the Control Source property box, make sure that the field indicated is the one in which you want to store the value you select in the list. Make sure the name of the field is accurate and spelled correctly.

4. Review the information in the Row Source property box. It should be an SQL statement (as shown in the figure), the name of a lookup table, or an actual list of values. The Row Source Type property setting indicates where the values come from: Table/Query, Value List, or Field List. ▶

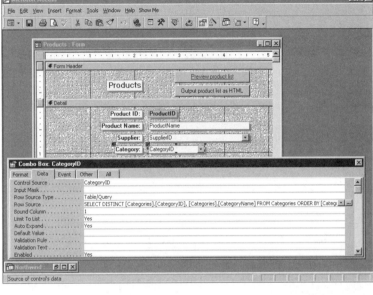

5. In the Bound Column property box, enter the number of the column from the Row Source that contains the value you want stored.

6. If you want to be able to enter a value not in the list, change the Limit To List property to No. Note that if the column displayed in the combo box is not the bound column, the Limit To List property is set to Yes.

Tip

In the figure above, an SQL statement creates a query with two fields, both from the Categories table: CategoryID (column 1) and CategoryName (column 2). The category name is displayed, but the value from CategoryID (column 1) is stored in the control.

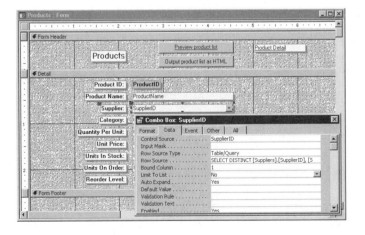

My subform doesn't print the way I want

Source of the problem

Granted, forms are more for online work than for printed documents, but there are still times when you want to print a form and you want it to look right. Even when you set all the printer options and lay out the form the way it ought to look, there are things that can go wrong. Some problems you might have encountered include the following:

- Your subform is definitely included in the form's design, but it doesn't appear in Print Preview. The reason is probably that there are no records in the subform that are related to the current record in the main form. It is also possible that the Data Entry property for the subform is set to Yes, which would show an empty record in the subform.

- When you print a form that includes a subform, not all the records in the subform that are related to the current record in the main form are printed. Or, when there are no records in the subform and you want to save space, the subform prints anyway.

The following solutions explain how to solve these problems.

How to fix it

If the subform appears empty in form view or in Print Preview and you know there are related records, follow these steps:

1. In the database window, select the subform and then click the Design button.

2. On the toolbar, click the Properties button.

3. In the properties dialog box, click the Data tab and change the Data Entry property to No. ▶

4. Save the subform.

5. Look at the form in form view or Print Preview and check the subform to be sure it is no longer empty.

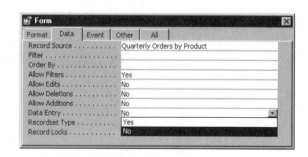

If you want all the records in the subform to print with the record in the main form, follow these steps:

1. In the database window, select the subform and then click the Design button.

2. On the toolbar, click the Properties button.

3. On the form, click the Detail section indicator.

4. On the Format tab, set the Can Grow property to Yes. ▶

5. If you want to suppress printing the subform because it's empty, set the Can Shrink property to Yes.

6. Save the subform.

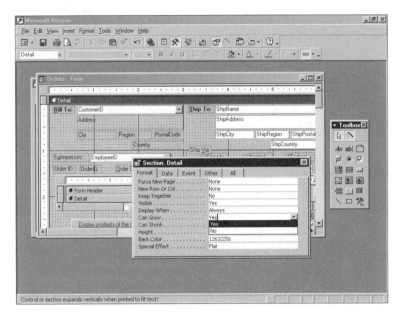

Problems with printer fonts

Another problem you might encounter when you print a form is that the printer you use prints the text in a crazy font—one you've never seen before, much less know the name of. Chances are the printer doesn't have the font you used and substituted one similar to it. For example, if you format a form with Adobe PostScript fonts and send the document to a LaserJet printer, you may see unexpected results because LaserJet printers don't use PostScript fonts. If possible, try to print the form using the printer you used when making the settings for the form. Also, try to use fonts that are universally accepted and processed the same by all printers, such as TrueType fonts.

After you select the printer options and set up the page to fit the form when it prints, all those settings are saved with the form. You don't have to worry about them unless you make changes to the form's layout or change printers.

My form is blank where there should be data

Source of the problem

It's bad enough when you see the wrong data or a weird error message instead of your familiar data. But when the form is blank, it's hard to know where to turn. Sometimes only one or two fields are blank; on other occasions the whole form is blank. Here are some of the reasons for this apparent lack of cooperation:

- The form might not be bound to a table or query. Remember, a form has to get its data from somewhere. You can create an unbound form, of course, but you wouldn't expect to see data in it.

- The query the form is based on doesn't return any records. You might have added criteria to the query that are so stringent that no records comply with it. You might also have used conflicting criteria, such as a combination of mutually exclusive conditions with the *And* operator.

- The form is in Data Entry mode. If the Data Entry property is set to Yes, a new blank form appears when you open the form rather than existing records.

The following solutions show you how to get around these problems.

How to fix it

1. In the database window, select the form and then click the Design button.

2. Click the Properties button on the toolbar.

3. In the properties dialog box, confirm that the Record Source property for the form is set to one of your tables or queries. ▶

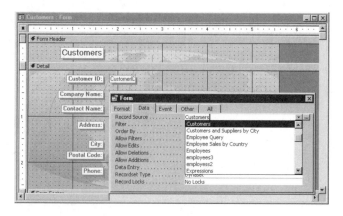

4. If it is, make sure the name of the table or query is spelled right.

5. If it's not, click the arrow next to the Record Source property and select the table or query that contains the records you want to work with in this form.

If the form is bound to a query but it isn't displaying any data, check the criteria the query is using:

1. Close the form, select the query in the database window, and then click the Design button.

2. In the query design grid, remove the first expression in the Criteria row.

3. Click the Datasheet View button to see whether the query now returns the records you want.

4. If the query still doesn't return the records you want, delete the other criteria expressions one by one, switching to datasheet view each time to check whether the correct records are displayed.

5. Once you get the right combination of criteria, save and close the query.

6. Open the form in form view. The proper records should now appear.

If the form is completely blank, follow these steps:

1. Open the form in form view, and then click the Apply/Remove Filter button to turn off the data entry mode temporarily.

2. Click the View button to switch to design view.

3. Click the Properties button on the toolbar, and then click the Data tab.

4. Set the Data Entry property to No. ▶

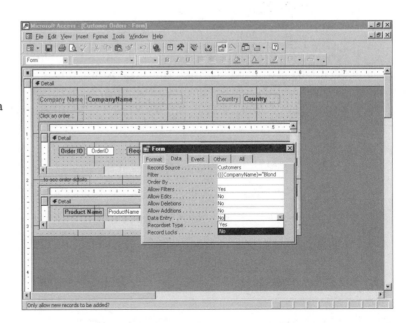

My subform doesn't show the data I expected

Source of the problem

Subforms can be tricky. They present a whole new set of problems when you least expect them. Some of the more common problems with displaying data in a subform are the following:

- When you open the form containing the subform in form view, the subform displays all the records from the query or table it is based on instead of just the ones related to the current record in the main form. In this case, you may have used control names instead of field names to link the form and the subform.

- When the form starts to open, you see an unexpected parameter prompt. The problem might be that the fields linking the main form and the subform aren't identified correctly.

- When you try to limit the datasheet view of the subform to a single record, Access shows you as many records as will fit in the subform.

When working with subforms, keep in mind that the subform object is saved as a separate form in the database, while the subform control is part of the main form. The object and the control have different sets of properties.

The following solutions show you some ways to solve these problems.

How to fix it

If you see all the records in the subform instead of the shorter list you expected, do the following:

1. In the database window, select the main form and click the Design button.

2. Right-click a border of the subform control, and then click Properties on the shortcut menu.

3. On the Data tab, look at the names in the Link Child Fields and Link Master Fields property boxes. They should be the names that link the record source for the subform (Child) to the record source for the main form (Master).

4. If the fields don't match, click the Build button to open the Subform Field Linker dialog box and choose different fields. Click OK.

> **Tip**
>
> Click the Suggest button in the Subform Field Linker dialog box to see the suggested linking fields.

If you see an unexpected parameter prompt, follow these steps: ▶

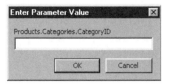

1. In the database window, select the form and click the Design button.

2. Select the subform control, and then click the Properties button on the toolbar.

3. Remove the table names from the Link Child Fields and Link Master Fields property boxes. For example, if you see **Categories.CategoryID** in the property box, delete the table name (in this example, Categories), including the period.

4. Save the subform.

To see a single record in the subform, do the following:

1. In the database window, select the subform and then click the Design button.

2. Click the Properties button on the toolbar.

3. On the Format tab, change the setting in the Default View property box to Single Form.

4. Set the Views Allowed property to Form.

5. Set the Navigation Buttons property to Yes so that you can move through the records in the subform.

6. Set the Dividing Lines property to No to get rid of the line below the record data.

7. Save the subform, and open the main form in form view. ▶

Tip
Each subform is saved as a separate form in the database. You have two ways to open the subform in design view. You can open it from the database window by clicking the Design button or, in Access 2000 if the main form is already open, double-click the subform selector (the square in the upper left corner of the subform). After making changes and saving them, you return to the main form design view.

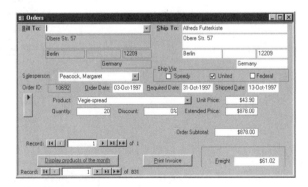

Do you get a message that Access can't find the linked file? yes

no

Are you trying to interface with another database? yes

no

Do you see *#Error!* in a linked Excel spreadsheet? yes

Quick fix

Someone has closed the spreadsheet in Excel.

1. Close the linked Excel table in Access.

2. Reopen the table to re-establish the link with the Excel spreadsheet.

no

Are you trying to import a spreadsheet or text file? yes

Go to...

I get errors when I import a spreadsheet or text file to my Access database, page 146

no

Do you get errors when you append a spreadsheet or text file? yes

Go to...

I get errors when I try to append a spreadsheet or text file to an Access table, page 148

If your solution isn't here

Check these related chapters:

Queries—Action, page 184

Or see the general troubleshooting tips on page xiii.

Quick fix

The file that contains the table might have been moved or renamed.

1. Open the database that contains links to tables.

2. Point to Database Utilities on the Tools menu, and click Linked Table Manager. (In Access 97, click Add-Ins on the Tools menu.)

3. Select the check box for the tables whose links you want refreshed.

4. Click OK.

5. If you're on a network, make sure you haven't lost your connection.

Does a filter return the wrong records from a linked table?

yes

no

Quick fix

The values in the criteria are case-sensitive.

1. Open the underlying table.

2. Check for uppercase and lowercase field values.

3. Correct the mismatches.

Have you linked to other database tables?

yes

no

Go to...

I can't open or update a linked table, page 140

Have you imported tables from other databases?

yes

no

Go to...

I'm having trouble with an imported table, page 144

Quick fix

If you can't import data from Microsoft Works or another format that Access doesn't support, do the following:

1. Open the file in the host application.

2. Save the file in dBASE IV format.

3. Open Access, point to Get External Data on the File menu, and click Import.

4. Select the file and click Import.

I can't open or update a linked table

Source of the problem

When you're working with cohorts who aren't "with it" enough to be using Access as their master information storage resource, you might have to bend a little and make the best of the situation. While Microsoft works hard to make Access compatible with most other popular database programs, problems can still arise, especially when you need to link to tables in other databases. You want the people who run those databases to enter and manage the data, while you want access to the latest info. Sometimes, you might also want to make changes of your own in the linked tables.

If you can't open a table you've linked to in dBASE, Microsoft Visual FoxPro, or Paradox, the table or one of its associated files, such as an index file, might have been moved or deleted. A dBASE or FoxPro table needs an index file (a file with an extension of .idx, .cdx, .ndx, or .mdx), and Paradox needs a .px index file. Another reason you might not be able to open the file is that the information file (one with the extension .inf) that Access created when you linked to the table has been moved or deleted.

Files associated with a memo field are also essential to a linked table in Visual FoxPro, Paradox, or dBASE. Memo values are kept in a separate file, and if the file has been moved or deleted, you can't open the table. FoxPro and dBASE memos are stored in a .dbt file; Paradox memos are stored in an .mb file.

If you updated the dBASE or FoxPro table in its native habitat, you might not have updated the corresponding index file. If that's the case, you won't be able to open the table in Access until the index file is updated in the other program. When you update a linked table in Access, the index file is automatically updated so you don't need to worry.

If you can open the table but you can't update its values, either the table file or one of the index or memo files might be set to read-only. You must be able to update all the associated files, including the information file that Access creates, as well as the table. In addition, a Paradox table must have a primary key set if you want to update it with Access.

You also must have the Borland Database Engine (version 4.x or higher) installed to be able to update a linked table in dBase or Paradox. Without it, you can import a file to an Access database, but when you link to it, it will be linked as read-only.

The following solutions show how to set up your links so you can open and update those tables.

How to fix it

To link or restore missing index or memo files, do the following. These steps also re-create the Access information file:

1. Open the database you're working with in Access. In the database window, right-click the linked table (an arrow icon indicates a linked table) and then click Delete on the shortcut menu.

2. In the message box that appears, click Yes to delete the link to the table in the other program. Repeat these steps for each of the linked tables you're having trouble with.

3. On the File menu, point to Get External Data and then click Link Tables.

4. In the Link dialog box, select the file type you want to link to (dBase or Paradox, for example) in the Files Of Type box.

5. Locate the file you want, and then double-click its icon.

6. If the file is a dBASE file and there are index or memo files in the same folder, the next dialog box shows the index (.ndx or .mdx) and memo (.dbt) files. Double-click each file that belongs with the table you chose in step 4. (Usually these files have the same name as the table file, with the extension for an index or a memo file.) ▶

7. Click Close. If none of the files match the table you're linking to, click Cancel. If you don't select an index file before closing the dialog box, Access selects it for you—either one that matches the table name or the file most recently created or modified.

8. If the file is a Paradox file, make sure the index (.px) file and any memo (.mb) files that belong to the table you're linking to are in the same folder as the table file.

Tip

If you let Access pick the dBASE index file, it might pick one with the Display First Duplicate Key Only setting turned on. In this case, some of the data might seem to be missing when you open the table in Access. To fix this, delete the linked table and link to the table again, selecting a different index file.

I can't open or update a linked table

(continued from page 141)

If a linked table has been updated in dBASE or Visual FoxPro, do the following:

1. Open the database in the host program and update the index file associated with the table you want to link to from Access.

To solve the problem with files that are opened read-only, follow these steps:

1. Open Windows Explorer, and display the folder that contains the tables you want to link to your Access database.

2. Right-click the file name, and then click Properties on the shortcut menu.

3. Click the General tab. Clear the Read-only check box, and then click OK. ▶

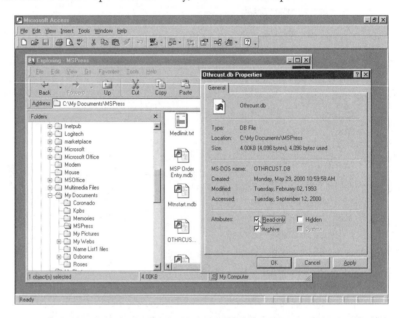

An essential linking tool

If the tables you want to link to are in a database created with one of the new versions of dBASE or Paradox (dBASE 7 or Paradox 8), you will need to install the Borland Database Engine (BDE), version 4.*x* or later (the current version is 5.1.1) to link tables to your Access database. You can link to tables in databases created in earlier versions—dBASE III, IV, and 5.0 and Paradox 3.*x*, 4.*x*, and 5.0 without BDE—but the tables will be read-only. You can get BDE by installing Paradox 8.0 or dBASE 7. You can also download it from the Borland Web site at *www.borland.com*.

Linked doesn't have to mean carbon copy

If you don't like the look of linked tables, you can change some of the field properties that affect how the data appears in Access. None of these changes are made to the source table. For example, you can change a field's Format property to display a different date or number format. In a number field, you can change the Decimal Places property to display the number of decimal places you want to appear. Changing or adding an input mask can help with data entry in a form. If you want to see a different name in a datasheet or form, you can add a name to the Caption property.

To set these properties, select the table in the database window in Access and click the Design button. The properties are listed in the Field Properties area of the window.

If you want to change other field properties to make data entry easier and more accurate, you can create a form and set validation rules, validation text, and default values for the controls on the form. These changes do not affect the source table. (See "Data—Setting field properties," on page 44, for information about validation rules.)

You can also rename the linked table to take advantage of the longer table names allowed by Access (up to 64 characters, including spaces). Again, this has no effect on the source table; it simply changes the name Access uses.

Should you import or link?

Whether you should import or link to tables outside your database depends on what you're trying to do. There are pros and cons on both sides, but here are some guidelines for deciding which to do.

You should import a table if:

- The file is small and doesn't change often.
- You don't need to share current data with others.
- You're replacing the old application and don't need the old format.
- You want the best in performance with the copy in Access format.

You should choose to link to the file if:

- The file is quite large (over 1 gigabyte).
- The data is changed frequently.
- You're splitting the database and placing the data on a network server.

I'm having trouble with an imported table

Source of the problem

When you import a table from another database program (instead of linking to it), you can usually treat the newcomer pretty much the same as one of your Access tables. You're almost waving a magic wand and declaring, "You are now an Access table!" In some cases, however, you can run into a few problems because the table you're importing might contain types of data that differ from the types Access recognizes. The table might also have slightly different requirements, such as versions of input masks or validation rules.

When a table is imported, Access tries to convert the data types in that table to equivalent Access data types, but that doesn't always work. For example, the Paradox Graphic, Binary, and Formatted Memo data types have no equivalent in Access. If you want these types of data in an Access table, you need to enter the items in the appropriate format (such as the OLE Object field type) after importing the source table.

The Name AutoCorrect feature in Access 2000 doesn't work automatically yet for imported tables. Access doesn't automatically create a name map for imported tables like it does for tables created in Access. The name map traces changes in field, query, table, form, and report names and passes them on to other database objects that refer to them. Even though this feature doesn't work automatically, you can work around it for now.

You might be trying to append the data in an imported table to a table in Access. Doing this doesn't work unless all the column headings match the field names in the Access table. You might need to use a two-step process to do this.

The following solutions describe how to cure these problems.

How to fix it

If there are data types in a Paradox table that don't match Access field data types, do the following:

1. In Paradox, open the table and convert any Formatted Memo fields to Memo.

2. Save the Paradox table, and then import the table again to Access.

3. In Access, select the table in the database window and then click Design.

4. If the Paradox table had a Paradox Graphic field (used to store image files), add an OLE Object field to the table design in Access.

5. If the Paradox table included a Binary field (used to store other file types), add another OLE Object field to the table design in Access.

6. Click the View button to switch to datasheet view.

7. Locate the files corresponding to the objects and insert them into the imported table.

To turn on the Name AutoCorrect feature for imported tables in Access 2000, do the following:

1. In the database window, click Options on the Tools menu.

2. Click the General tab.

3. Select both the Track Name AutoCorrect Info and Perform Name AutoCorrect check boxes. Click OK. ▶

4. In the Access database window, select the imported table, click the Design button, and then click the Save button on the toolbar. Saving the table creates the name map Access will use.

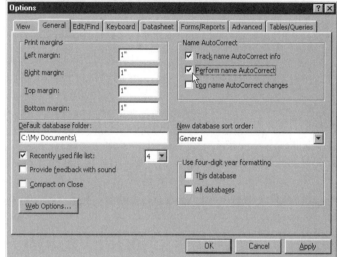

If you're having trouble appending imported data directly to a table, try this:

1. Import the table into your Access database as a new table.

2. Create an append query based on the imported table.

3. In the query grid, add just the fields you want to append to the existing Access table. (See "Queries—Action," on page 180, for information about append queries.)

4. Run the append query.

5. Save the Access table and delete the imported table.

Tip

The names of tables you have imported don't always give you a clue about what is stored in the table. Some applications limit field and table names to eight characters with no spaces. You can rename the tables in Access so they have a much more informative title. Renaming the imported table has no effect on the original table.

I get errors when I import a spreadsheet or text file to my Access database

Source of the problem

It probably doesn't surprise you that importing files from different programs can cause errors. What should surprise you is that so few big problems occur. And when they do, Access warns you that some of the information won't be imported. Access also keeps track of certain types of common errors in a table called Import Errors so you can deal with them one at a time.

If, when importing a file, you told the Import Wizard that the first row of information in that file contained column headings (which Access uses as field names), the column headings might not be valid for an Access field name. There could be a blank column heading, for example. In this case, Access displays a message and automatically assigns a valid field name such as Field1.

Access creates the table to receive an imported spreadsheet with enough fields to hold the first row of values from the spreadsheet. If later rows of the spreadsheet contain more fields than the first, Access adds a field name such as Field*nn*, representing the number of the last column. An extra field delimiter in a text file can also cause this error.

Sometimes data in a spreadsheet or text file can't be stored in a field in an Access table because of the data type that Access has assigned to that field when it imports the information. Access assigns a data type to the field based on the data in the first row that's imported. You might have included a text value in a later row for a field where Access expects only numbers. Another cause for this type of error is a row in the text file or spreadsheet that contains summary data or extraneous characters that don't follow the type and size assigned to the field.

The following solutions show how to fix these problems.

How to fix it

If Access has created an Import Errors table, you will see the message shown in the figure to the right. To correct the import errors, do the following: ▶

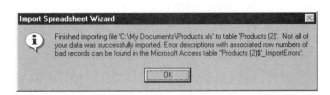

1. In the database window, select the imported table and then click Open.

2. In the database window, select the Import Errors table and then click Open.

3. On the Window menu, click Tile Horizontally so you can see both tables at once. ▶

4. In the Import Errors table, review the errors and then correct the data in the imported table.

5. After correcting the data, save the imported table and delete the Import Errors table.

If you see strange generic field names (such Field1 or Field13), do the following:

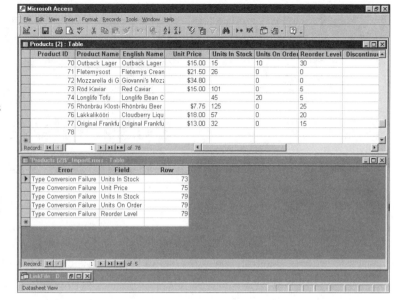

1. Select the imported table in the database window, and then click Design.

2. If the fields contain valid data, rename the fields with useful names, replacing the generic names Access provided.

3. Save the table.

4. If the generic fields are the result of having too many fields in a row in the spreadsheet or text file, open the file you're trying to import and delete the extra fields so that every row has the same number of columns.

5. Import the file into Access again, and replace the original imported table.

If you think the field data type is correct but the data can't be stored in it, try this:

1. Open the text file or spreadsheet.

2. Edit the data to correct the errors. For example, remove text from a number field or delete extraneous characters.

3. If you're importing only part of a worksheet, name the range of cells and import that range, instead of the whole worksheet, using the Access Import Wizard.

4. Save the file.

5. Return to Access and import the file again.

Tip
An easy way to import an Excel worksheet is to copy it to the Windows clipboard and then paste it into an Access database. This creates a new table with the Excel data. It helps if you have included the column headings. Access will use them as the field names.

I get errors when I try to append a spreadsheet or text file to an Access table

Source of the problem

You've found some really great information in a Microsoft Excel spreadsheet that needs to be added to a table in your Access database. Of course, you could spend all night typing it in, but there is a better way. Just tack the data in the spreadsheet onto the data that's already in the table. Sounds like a piece of cake, right? But, as with importing data from other databases, things can sometimes go wrong. For example, it's possible that one or more rows in the file you want to append contain more fields than the first row of the destination table does. See "I get errors when I import a spreadsheet or text file to my Access database" on page 146 for answers to this kind of problem.

You might also have encountered some other problems when you tried to append spreadsheet or text files.

- The field names in the spreadsheet or text file don't match those in the destination table. If you indicated that the first row contains the field names, they must match.

- The data you're appending might not be the right data type for the receiving field. For example, the table field has a Number data type and the incoming data is text. Or, the data in a numeric field might be too large for the field size specified for the destination field. If the Field Size property in the Access field is set to Byte, for example, the field can't hold a number larger than 255.

- The appended spreadsheet or text file might contain duplicate values in the field you designated as the primary key or a uniquely indexed field for the destination table.

The following solutions show you the steps to take to correct these problems.

How to fix it

If you see a message that the file was not imported, the fields probably don't match. ▶

1. Open the table you are appending records to in design view.

2. Change the field names to match the headings in the spreadsheet or text file you are appending.

3. If some fields are missing, add them to the table design.

4. Save the table.

5. Import the spreadsheet or text file again to append the records.

If the message indicates that Access couldn't append all the data, do the following:

1. Note in the message that Access displays how many records are missing data and how many records were lost. ▶

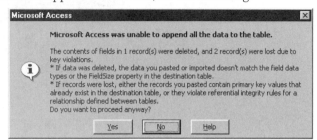

2. If there are only a few errors and you'd like to deal with them manually, click Yes.

3. Open the table you appended the records to in datasheet view.

4. Click the column that might have caused the data type or size mismatch problem, and then click Sort Ascending. Any blank fields will move to the top of the window.

5. Enter the values from the spreadsheet or text file into the blank fields in the table.

6. Repeat steps 4 and 5 for other fields that might have caused errors.

7. If the records that were lost are not duplicates of records already in the table, manually enter the lost records, being careful to assign unique values to the key fields.

If there are too many errors to correct manually, do the following:

1. Click No to clear the message.

2. Click Cancel to abandon the append operation.

3. Open the table you're appending records to in design view.

4. Select the primary key field, and then click the Primary Key toolbar button to remove the primary key designation.

5. Save and close the table.

6. Append the spreadsheet or text file again.

7. Open the table you appended the records to in datasheet view and edit the field you want as the primary key so that all records have unique values.

8. While you're at it, edit the blank fields as necessary with valid data type values.

9. Return the table to design view, set the primary key field again, and save the table.

Tip
You might have to return to the source spreadsheet or text file to find out what the value should be.

Tip
If you're appending data to a table that's related to another table, you might also experience errors caused by violating referential integrity. For example, you might experience an error if you're attempting to add records to a child table that have no related record in the parent table.

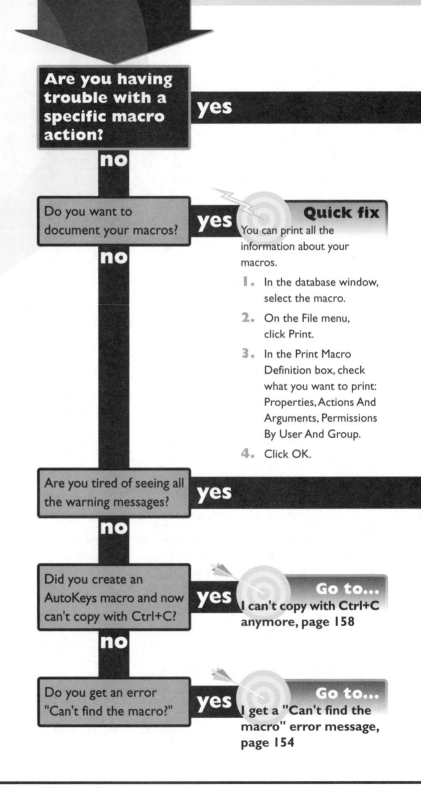

Are you having trouble with a specific macro action?

yes

no

Do you want to document your macros?

yes

no

Quick fix

You can print all the information about your macros.

1. In the database window, select the macro.
2. On the File menu, click Print.
3. In the Print Macro Definition box, check what you want to print: Properties, Actions And Arguments, Permissions By User And Group.
4. Click OK.

Are you tired of seeing all the warning messages?

yes

no

Did you create an AutoKeys macro and now can't copy with Ctrl+C?

yes

Go to...
I can't copy with Ctrl+C anymore, page 158

no

Do you get an error "Can't find the macro?"

yes

Go to...
I get a "Can't find the macro" error message, page 154

Is the SendKeys action giving you trouble?

yes

no

Are you having trouble creating multiline messages with the MsgBox action?

yes

no

Does the SetValue macro action not work when it's supposed to?

yes

Go to...
I can't put a multiline message in a message box, page 152

Go to...
My SetValue macro runs at the wrong time, page 156

Quick fix

You are trying to send keystrokes to a dialog box but they're not getting there. The action that displays the dialog box suspends the SendKeys macro, waiting for a response from the user.

1. In the database window, select the macro and click Design.
2. Rearrange the order of the macro's actions, moving the SendKeys action before the action displaying the dialog box.
3. Set the MsgBox Wait argument to No.
4. Save the macro.

Quick fix

You need to turn off the warnings at the start of the macro and turn them back on at the end.

1. Open the macro in design view.
2. Add a SetWarnings action at the beginning of the macro.
3. Set the Warnings On argument to No.
4. Add another SetWarnings action at the end of the macro and set the Warnings On argument to Yes.

If your solution isn't here
Check these related chapters:
Expressions, page 90
Or see the general troubleshooting tips on page xiii.

I can't put a multiline message in a message box

Source of the problem

Sometimes a short phrase such as "Need a tune-up" doesn't quite convey enough information to get a message across. You need more information to help you or someone else make the right decision. Of course, the right decision may depend on whether you are repairing cars or selling them.

If you're having trouble creating a multiline message with the MsgBox macro action, you might not have entered the text correctly. When you enter a longish message, the message box expands and might exceed the width of your screen. You need to use a special character (the @ sign) to break up the message into multiple lines.

The following solutions show you two ways to enter multiple-line messages in a message box. You'll also learn how to display the @ symbol in a message for cases when you need to show it in the message box rather than use it as a special character.

How to fix it

If you are trying to display more than one line in a message box (similar to the built-in error messages that Access displays), follow these steps:

1. In the database window, click Macros and then click New.

2. In the Action column, select MsgBox from the drop-down list.

3. In the Action Arguments section at the bottom of the window, click in the Message argument box and type the first line of the message you want to display. ▶

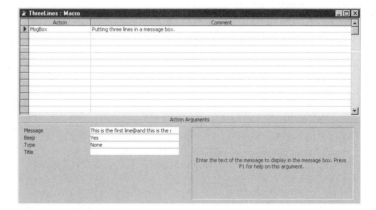

4. Enter the @ character, and then type the second line.

5. Enter another @ character, and then type the third line of the message.

6. Click the Save button, and then name the new macro.

7. Click the Run button on the toolbar. ▶

Tip

When you create a multiline message, the first line appears in bold at the top of the message box. The other lines appear in normal text below the first line. You can enter up to 255 characters in the message box.

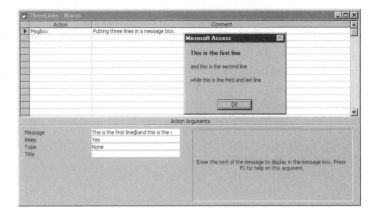

Another way to create a multiline message is to use an expression that includes the carriage return and line feed characters (indicated by the symbols Chr(13) and Chr(10)), which will move the text to the next line. Follow these steps:

1. Open the macro in design view.

2. In the Action column, select MsgBox from the drop-down list.

3. In the Message argument box, enter an expression, such as **="This is the first line" & Chr(13) & Chr(10) & "and this is the second" & Chr(13) & Chr(10) & "and this is the third line."**

4. Save the macro, and then click the Run button.

Warning

If you don't precede the expression with an equals sign, you'll see the whole expression in the message box, including the quotation marks, the Chr functions, and the & symbols.

If you want the @ character to appear in the message (very handy if you want to display an e-mail address), you need to enter an expression such as the following, which uses the Chr function with the character code for @:

1. Open the macro in design view.

2. Enter an expression such as **="You can send me e-mail at vandersenZ"& Chr(64) &"aol.com"**

3. Save the macro and click the Run button. ▶

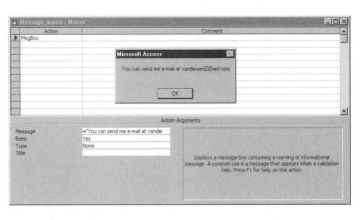

Tip

You can use Chr(64) only once in the message. If you use it twice, the message is broken into three lines.

I get a "Can't find the macro" error message

Source of the problem

Access seems so helpless when it displays a message saying that it can't find a macro. You know that no macro was supposed to run when you opened a form or moved to a control. Why is Access looking for one, and why didn't Access tell you the name of the macro it was looking for?

If no macro name appears in the message, someone (we won't name names or point fingers) might have inadvertently typed a space or two in one of the event property boxes for a form or a control. If the property box isn't totally blank, Access sniffs around for a macro to run.

If the message does show the name of the missing macro, the macro name might not match the macro selected in the form. The following solutions tell you how to cure these problems.

How to fix it

If the error message doesn't contain the name of a macro, follow these steps:

1. Open the form in form view. You'll see the "Can't find macro" error message box.

2. Click OK to clear the message, and then click View to switch to design view. ▶

3. Click Properties, and then click the Event tab.

4. If the error message appeared when you opened the form, click in the On Load event property box.

5. If the property box is blank but the insertion point is not at the left end of the property box, press Backspace until the insertion point is at the far left. This removes any spaces.

6. Repeat steps 4 and 5 for the On Open and On Current event properties. ▶

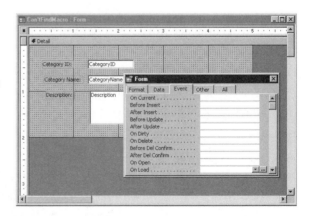

7. If the message appeared when you saved the current record in the form, check the Before Update and After Update event properties and remove any spaces from the blank boxes.

8. If the message appeared when you moved to a control or changed the data in a control, click that control.

9. In the properties dialog box for the control, click the Event tab and remove any spaces from the On Got Focus, Before Update, and After Update event properties.

10. Click View to switch to form view.

11. If the message still appears, go through each event property box that is blank and press Backspace.

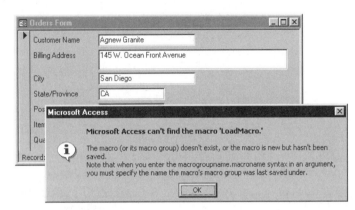

If the message contains the name of the missing macro, that's some comfort, but you still have a problem. Try the following remedy:

1. In the database window, select the macro attached to the form and click the Design button.

2. Compare the name of the macro with the name that was displayed in the error message.

3. If the names are different, click Save As on the File menu and save the macro with the name that appeared in the message.

4. If you want to keep the current macro name, open the form in design view and click Properties.

5. Move to the property box for the event that caused the problem and change the name of the macro in the property box to match the name of the existing macro.

A word about grouped macros

Grouping macros is a good way to keep macros that apply to the same form or report together where you can find them. However, if an event is attached to one of the macros in a macro group and you have moved the macro to a different group or renamed the group without updating the name in the event property box, you will get the "Can't find the macro" error message. Remember, to refer to a macro in a macro group, use the identifier **MyNewMacroGroup.mymacro**.

My SetValue macro runs at the wrong time

Source of the problem

In a database program like Access (which is often called an event-driven system), nothing happens until something else happens. If that doesn't make sense, think about not going to the refrigerator until a commercial comes on. Macros can automate some of your tedious tasks, but they have to be told when to perform; in other words, macros need to know which event should make them run. Sometimes macros don't go on when they're scheduled.

If you're having problems with the timing of a SetValue macro, you might have attached it to the wrong event. For example, you might have attached it to a form event such as On Load or On Open, in which case the macro runs when you open the form in form view.

Your intent might have been to have the macro run when you entered or updated the information in a specific field. For example, you have used the SetValue macro to add 30 days to the date you enter in the Billing Date field and place the result in the Reminder Date field. But when you enter the Billing Date, the Reminder Date is not entered as planned.

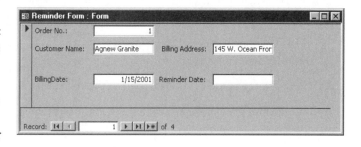

However, the next time you open the form, the date is there. Clearly the macro is doing its thing, but it's doing it at the wrong time.

The following solution shows you how to solve this problem.

How to fix it

1. Open the form containing the macro in design view, and then click the Properties button.

2. In the properties dialog box, click the Event tab.

3. Remove the name of the macro from the On Load or On Open property box.

4. Click the control that you want to have run the macro.

5. On the Event tab, click the down arrow in the After Update event property, and select the macro you want to run from the list. ▶

6. Click View to return to form view.

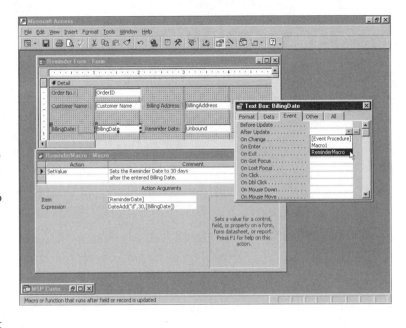

SetValue is a useful tool

You can use the SetValue macro action not only to set the value of a field or a control. You can also use it to set properties in a control, form, or report. The SetValue action is easy to use because it has only two arguments: the item that is the focus of the action and the expression that contains the value you want to set for the item.

But be warned! The expression you use with the SetValue action is a little different from the one you would set as a control source. When you use an expression in the Control Source property in a control on a form or report, you must precede it with an equals sign. But when you use an expression in the Expression argument of the SetValue action, you must not use an equals sign. If you do, you'll get unexpected results such as a wrong date.

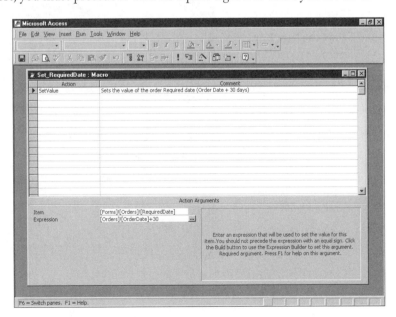

I can't copy with Ctrl+C anymore

Source of the problem

You have probably found that keyboard shortcuts are a quick and handy way to get something done, especially if you are mouse-squeamish. Instead of rolling the pointer around the screen and clicking on something, you can simply press a couple of keys.

Access allows you to create a special macro group called AutoKeys that lets you assign your own action or group of actions to a single key or key combination. You can create as many AutoKey macros as you need and add them to the AutoKeys macro group.

Unfortunately, if you use a key combination that Access has already spoken for, you will replace that action with your own. If you can't copy with the key combination Ctrl+C anymore, this key combination has probably been used in an AutoKeys macro named ^C. (The caret symbol (^) represents the Ctrl key.)

The following solution shows you how to fix this.

How to fix it

1. In the database window, click Macros.

2. Select the AutoKeys macro group and click the Design button.

3. Locate the macro named ^C, and rename it, assigning a key combination that's not used by Access. ▶

4. Save and close the AutoKeys macro.

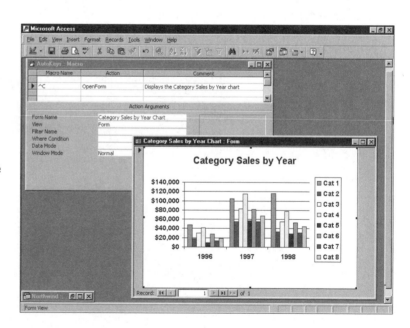

Some useful shortcut key combinations

The following list gives you an idea of the kinds of key combinations you can use as macros in the AutoKeys macro group. Ctrl is represented by the caret symbol (^) and Shift is represented by a plus sign (+).

Key Combination	Example Macro Names
Ctrl+any letter or number	^B, ^2
Any function key	{F2}
Ctrl+any function key	^{F2}
Shift+any function key	+{F2}
INS	{INSERT}
DEL	{DELETE} or {DEL}

You can also combine Ctrl or Shift with INS and DEL.

Neat things you can do with macros

You can create macros that will jump to attention, doing what you want when you want. Once you build the macro with the right actions, conditions, and arguments, you can attach it to an event, such as clicking a button, and your wish is now the macro's command. Here are just a few of the things you can do with macros:

- Display a message box.

- Specify a validation rule to help keep data errors out of your database. Create a macro that will run under conditions that would produce invalid data and display an error message with the MsgBox action.

- Set field and control values under specific conditions by using the SetValue action.

- Set form, report, or control properties with the SetValue action.

- Synchronize the data in two forms with the OpenForm action.

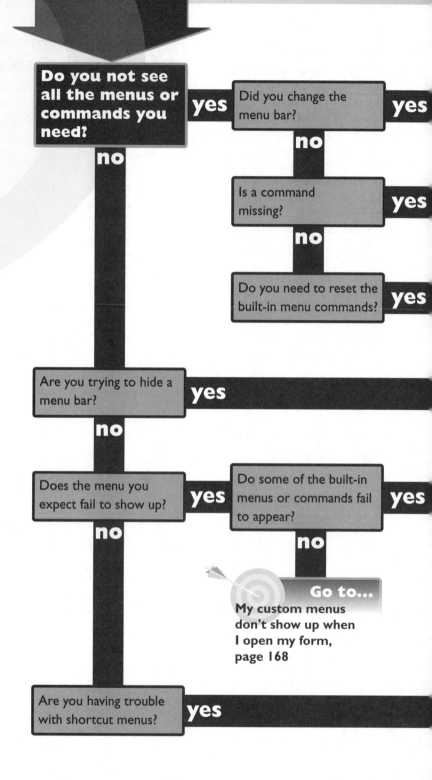

Do you not see all the menus or commands you need?

yes → Did you change the menu bar? **yes**

no ↓

Is a command missing? **yes**

no ↓

Do you need to reset the built-in menu commands? **yes**

no ↓

Are you trying to hide a menu bar? **yes**

no ↓

Does the menu you expect fail to show up? **yes** → Do some of the built-in menus or commands fail to appear? **yes**

no ↓

Go to...

My custom menus don't show up when I open my form, page 168

Are you having trouble with shortcut menus? **yes**

Go to...
I can't restore my built-in menu bars, page 162

Quick fix
You have removed it from the menu bar.

1. Right-click the menu bar and click Customize.
2. Select the menu bar on the Toolbars tab.
3. Click the Properties button.
4. Click Restore Defaults.
5. Click Yes.
6. Click Close twice.

Go to...
I can't reset my built-in menus, page 164

Quick fix
The menu property prohibits hiding.

1. Right-click the menu bar and click Customize.
2. Choose the menu bar you want to hide on the Toolbars tab.
3. Click the Properties button.
4. Select the Allow Showing/Hiding check box.
5. Click Close twice.

Go to...
Some of the built-in menus or commands aren't displayed, page 166

Go to...
My shortcut menus aren't right, page 170

If your solution isn't here
Check these related chapters:
Toolbars, page 286
Or see the general troubleshooting tips on page xiii.

I can't restore my built-in menu bars

Source of the problem

When you begin to make little changes in Access menus and then make a few more, the menus can wander a long way from where they started. Someone might have had a hand in this migration, modifying your menus for you. If that's the case, you might not even recall what the menus used to look like, let alone what they can do for you.

Before we get to fixing the problem, let's take a look at a couple of definitions. When we talk about a *menu bar*, we're referring to a group of menus that usually appears in a bar across the top of the screen. *Menus,* on the other hand, are the individual labels shown on the menu bar. *Menu commands* are the actions you select from after clicking a menu. Most menu commands are also available on toolbars.

If you or someone else has changed a menu bar and you no longer need those changes, you have two remedies to consider:

- Reset the original structure of the entire menu bar, with all its menus and submenus.

- Restore the default properties and other settings for the menu bar that were in effect when you first started Access—settings such as allowing docking and moving, resizing, and showing and hiding menus.

When you reset the entire menu bar, all the commands revert to their original behavior, appearance, and arrangement. The menu bar looks just like it did when you first installed Access. All the menus are in the same order on the menu bar, and all the commands do what they did before the changes. When you restore the default properties and settings, the default screen location, size, and options, such as Allow Showing/Hiding, are restored.

The following solutions show you some ways to fix these problems.

How to fix it

To reset a menu bar to its original structure, follow this steps:

1. On the View menu, point to Toolbars and then click Customize.

2. Click the Toolbars tab and highlight the name of the menu bar you want to reset from the Toolbars list.

3. Click Reset, and then click OK to confirm the change. ▶

4. Click Close in the Customize dialog box.

If you want to restore the default properties and settings of a menu bar, do the following:

1. On the View menu, point to Toolbars and then click Customize.

2. Click the Toolbars tab, and then click the Properties button.

3. From the Selected Toolbar list, select the name of the menu bar you want to restore.

4. Click Restore Defaults and then click Yes to confirm the action. ▶

5. When you're finished, click Close in the Toolbar Properties dialog box and then close the Customize dialog box.

Tip

After you open the Toolbar Properties dialog box, you can make changes to several menu bars without returning to the Customize dialog box to select the next one. Simply select the next victim from the Selected Toolbar list and make your changes.

Do's and don'ts about restoring and resetting menus

You might have noticed in the figure showing the Toolbar Properties dialog box that some of the properties are dimmed, which indicates that they are not available for changing. The Toolbar Name, Type, and Show On Toolbars Menu options can't be changed in a built-in menu.

In addition, the Restore Defaults button becomes available only after you have made a change to the original built-in menu. It is never available, however, for custom menu bars, and neither is the Reset button in the Customize dialog box. Makes sense, doesn't it?

I can't reset my built-in menus

Source of the problem

When you created your own personal menu bars, you probably took a shortcut and used some of the built-in menus, such as View or Records as a starting point. Of course, these menus weren't exactly the way you wanted, so you added a few touches of your own. (Maybe you added a new command here or took another off there.) Now you want those menus back the way they were.

It's easy to reset the default settings for a built-in menu, whether the menu is part of a built-in menu bar or part of a menu bar you created yourself. Maybe what you didn't realize is that if you make changes to a built-in menu such as the View menu, the change affects that menu in every menu bar on which that menu appears. Understanding your penchant for customization, Access makes it quite easy to undo the changes and return the menu to normal.

The following solution shows how to reset built-in menus.

How to fix it

1. Display the menu bar that contains the built-in menu you want to restore. If the menu bar is attached to a form or report, open the form or report.

2. Right-click the menu bar, and then choose Customize from the shortcut menu. The Customize dialog box will appear.

3. In the menu bar, right-click the menu you want to restore, and then click Reset on the shortcut menu. ▶

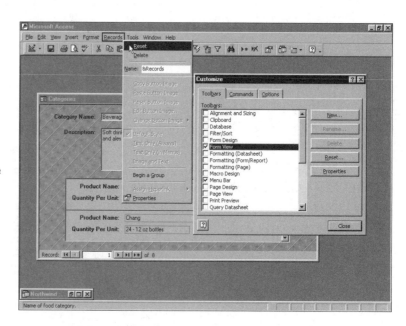

4. Click Close in the Customize dialog box, or keep it open for more resetting.

Are some menus or commands missing?

If you are working with Access 2000 and you want to see all the menu commands without having to expand the list, you need to clear two options in the Customize dialog box. On the View menu, point to Toolbars and then click Customize. Click the Options tab, and clear both the Menus Show Recently Used Commands First check box and the Show Full Menus After A Short Delay check box. But watch out—these options affect all the Microsoft Office 2000 programs!

If some of the built-in menus don't appear anymore on the screen when they are supposed to, some of the settings might have been changed in the Startup dialog box. In Access, click Startup on the Tools menu, and take a look at the options that are selected. If the Allow Full Menus check box isn't selected, you might not see all the menus in their default views.

If you don't see all the menus that are supposed to be on the menu bar, they might have been removed from that menu bar. Don't panic—they're still available from the Customize dialog box, and you can easily restore them to their rightful place on the built-in menu bar.

Tip

Notice that in the shortcut menu, most of the settings are not available for the built-in menu Records because the settings apply only to toolbar button appearance.

Tip

When you restore a menu, it is restored in all views that normally include that menu, so don't be surprised to see the change in other menu bars.

Some of the built-in menus or commands aren't displayed

Source of the problem

It's confusing when you look at the menu bar you've been using for ages and sense something is missing. Maybe one of the menus is gone or one of the commands on a menu no longer appears when you click the menu.

There are a few reasons for problems such as these. You (or someone else) might have changed the startup settings to keep the menus or shortcut menus from appearing.

Personalized menus are new to Access 2000. Only those menu commands you use often or that Access expects you to use often are displayed on the menu bar. If you see a down arrow at the bottom of the menu, the command you're looking for might be in the expanded menu. You can expand the menu each time you use it, or you can change the display option for menus so that menus appear every time in their full, expanded manner.

Another reason you don't see a menu is that it might have been moved to another menu bar. You can easily move it back or add another copy of the menu to the original menu bar.

The following solutions show how to deal with these problems.

How to fix it

To change the startup settings so that your full menus appear, follow these steps:

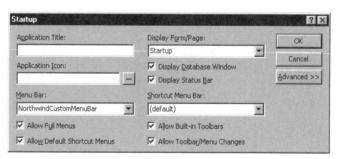

1. On the Tools menu, click Startup.

2. Select the Allow Full Menus check box to restore a complete set of built-in menus. ▶

3. Select the Allow Default Short-cut Menus check box to restore the shortcut menus related to different views.

4. Click OK.

5. Close the database, and then reopen it to activate the changes.

Tip

If you're reluctant to change the startup options but still want to see all the built-in commands, hold down the Shift key when you open the database.

If you are working with Access 2000 and want to see all the menu commands without expanding the list, do the following:

1. On the View menu, point to Toolbars and then click Customize.

2. Click the Options tab.

3. Clear the Menus Show Recently Used Commands First check box and the Show Full Menus After A Short Delay check box.

4. Click Close.

To add a missing menu to a built-in menu bar, follow these steps:

1. Display the menu bar you want to add the menu to.

2. On the View menu, point to Toolbars and then click Customize.

3. Click the Commands tab, and then click Built-in Menus in the Categories list.

4. Locate the missing menu name, and drag it to the menu bar.

5. Drop the item when you see the dark I-beam. ▶

6. Click Close.

The built-in Menu Bar is persistent

The dominant built-in menu bar named Menu Bar can't be removed from the display by clearing the check box in the Customize dialog box. If you try to clear it, a beep sounds, the audible slap on the wrist. The only way to remove it from view is to change one of its properties. In the Customize dialog box, select Menu Bar on the Toolbars tab and click Properties. In the Toolbar Properties dialog box, select the Allow Showing/Hiding check box and then click Close. Then you can use the Customize dialog box to show or hide the menu bar.

Tip

If you add a menu such as the Tools menu to a built-in menu bar that appears in more than one view, that menu will appear in the menu bar in all the views. Most of the commands in the added menu are carried over, depending on the context of the new menu bar.

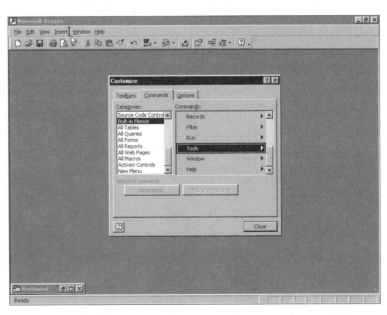

My custom menus don't show up when I open my form

Source of the problem

You have created a neat data entry form with so many custom features that even your dog could enter data without a mistake. Well, maybe your cat. You built a custom menu bar with just the menus and commands that you needed to use the form efficiently. You left out all the commands that could cause trouble, such as Design and Delete. You also created some quick shortcut menus to use with some of the controls on the form. The shortcut menus contain just the actions you need and nothing more—for example, allowing only sorting and filtering records based on the data in a control. Now, when you open the form to enter data, the same old vanilla menu bar shows up instead of your custom one, and when you right-click a control, there's no shortcut menu either.

The most common source of these problems is that you have not told Access that the custom menu bar and the shortcut menus belong to the form and its controls. The menus are considered properties of the form and its controls, and you need to set these properties like you do others.

It can be just as unsettling when you try to open a form and are greeted by an error message saying something about a missing macro. What Access is trying to tell you is that it can't find the menu bar you said belongs to the form. You might have deleted or renamed the menu bar or misspelled it in the property box.

The following solutions give you some ways to correct these problems.

How to fix it

If you have built a custom menu bar for a form, do the following:

1. Open the form in design view.

2. Click the Properties button on the toolbar, and then click the Other tab.

3. In the Menu Bar property box, click the down arrow and select the name of your custom menu bar from the list. ▶

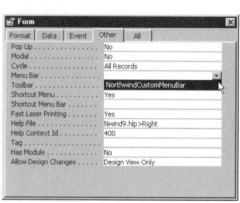

4. Click the View button to switch to form view to verify that the custom menu has replaced the standard menu bar.

If you don't see a shortcut menu that you created for one of the controls on a form, follow these steps:

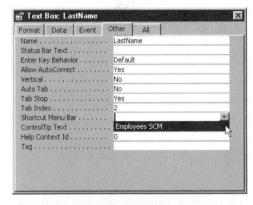

1. Open the form in design view, and then click the control.

2. Click the Properties button on the toolbar, and then click the Other tab.

3. In the Shortcut Menu Bar property, click the down arrow and select the menu name from the list. ▶

4. Switch to form view, and right-click the control you just added the shortcut menu to. ▶

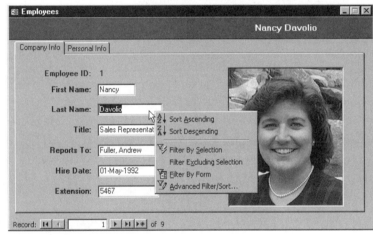

5. If you still don't see the shortcut menu you designed, click the View button to return the form to design view.

6. Double-click the form selector (the small gray square where the rulers meet in the upper left corner). The form's properties dialog box appears.

7. Click the Other tab, and change the Shortcut Menu property to Yes.

If you see an error message indicating Access can't find a macro, try the following steps: ▶

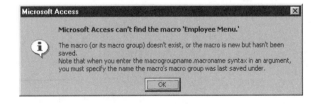

1. Click OK to clear the message.

2. Open the form in design view, and then click the Properties button.

3. On the Other tab, delete the menu bar name from the Menu Bar property or choose a different name from the drop-down list.

4. Save the form and switch to form view.

My shortcut menus aren't right

Source of the problem

The beauty of shortcut menus is that they're convenient and precise. When you need to do something now and you're where you need to do it, just right-click and the commands you need are there. But the shortcut menus that you see when you right-click in Access are not immune from modification. You or someone else might have modified them, so now they aren't as useful as you want them to be.

Access provides an easy, pain-free way to restore and reset shortcut menus. In fact, you can restore the original structure and properties for all built-in shortcut menus all at once. You can even restore any changes you made to shortcut menus. You can fix all the shortcut menus that appear in a single view with a single click.

How to fix it

To reset all the shortcut menus to their original structure, do the following:

1. On the View menu, point to Toolbars and then click Customize.

2. In the Customize dialog box, click the Toolbars tab and then select Shortcut Menus from the Toolbars list. ▶

3. Click Reset.

4. Click OK to confirm the action.

5. Click Close in the Customize dialog box.

To restore specific shortcut menus, do the following:

1. On the View menu, point to Toolbars and then click Customize.

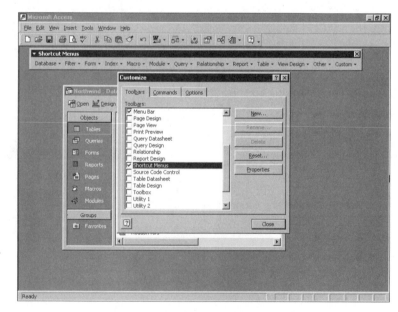

2. In the Customize dialog box, click the Toolbars tab and then select Shortcut Menus from the Toolbars list.

3. A menu bar showing the shortcut menus for different views will appear. ▶

4. To reset all the shortcut menus for a particular view, click the name of the view on the Shortcut Menus menu bar and then click the Reset button in the Customize dialog box.

5. If you want to reset a specific shortcut menu in a view, click the down arrow next to the view name.

6. From the list that appears, select the shortcut menu you want to reset. The list of shortcut menus is organized by location and function. For example, to reset the shortcut menu that appears ▶ when you right-click in the query design grid, click Design View Grid.

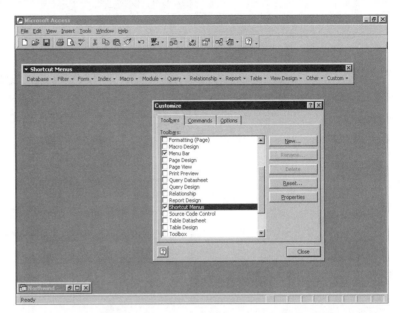

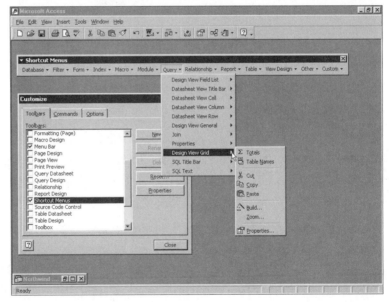

7. Click the Reset button in the Customize dialog box.

8. Click OK to confirm the change, and then click Close in the Customize dialog box.

Tip

If you want to restore a single command in the shortcut menu, click the right arrow next to the shortcut menu name, select the command, and then click the Reset button.

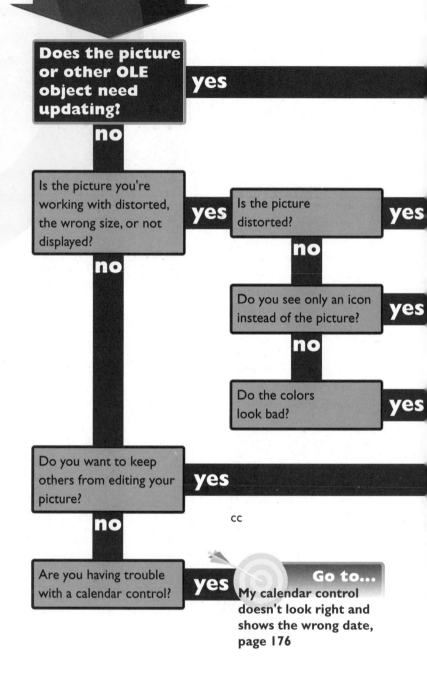

Pictu

Does the picture or other OLE object need updating?

yes

no

Is the picture you're working with distorted, the wrong size, or not displayed?

yes — Is the picture distorted?

yes

no

Do you see only an icon instead of the picture?

yes

no

Do the colors look bad?

yes

no

Do you want to keep others from editing your picture?

yes

cc

no

Are you having trouble with a calendar control?

yes

Go to...
My calendar control doesn't look right and shows the wrong date, page 176

Are you having trouble opening the object?

yes

Go to...
I can't open an OLE object, page 174

no

Are you having trouble editing the object?

yes

Go to...
I can't edit my OLE object, page 180

Go to...
The picture is distorted and doesn't fit the frame, page 182

Go to...
I see an icon where I put a picture, page 178

Quick fix
The picture was probably created on a computer that has more colors.

1. Open the form or report in design view and click the Properties button.

2. Set the Palette Source property to the one used to create the picture, if it's available.

Quick fix
Others can edit the picture in an unbound object frame unless you change it to an image.

1. Open the form in design view.

2. Select the picture.

3. Point to Change To on the Format menu and click Image.

4. Click OK to confirm the change.

Note: Don't do this with a video object or you will see only the first frame.

If your solution isn't here
Check these related chapters:
    Controls—Placing & formatting, page 24
    Forms—Designing, page 114
Or see the general troubleshooting tips on page xiii.

I can't open an OLE object

Source of the problem

You've spruced up your form with an image of your newly decorated storefront. Now you want to make some changes to the image, but Access won't open it when you double-click it. Instead you get one of those obscure messages that supposedly explains the problem in clear terms that we all can understand.

In Access terms, an image is an *OLE object*. What the message is really trying to tell you is that Access can't open the image file (in other words, the object) for some reason. Whether the object is linked or embedded, you need to have the program that created the object installed on your computer to be able to open and edit it. If you are working in a database with multiple users, a problem can occur with a linked object when someone else already has the object open for exclusive use in its source program. The object will be tied up until the other user closes it.

Even if you have the program that created the object properly installed and no one else has access to the file, there are several possible reasons for the failure of Access to open the object. The reason depends on whether the object is linked to the original file or embedded in your form or report. You could have one of the following problems:

> **Tip**
>
> For more information about linking and embedding objects, see page 181.

- If the object is linked, the source file may have been moved or renamed. Access won't be able to find the file because it is following the old path. An object such as an employee's picture might be bound to a field in the underlying table. On the other hand, an object such as your company logo or a background picture might be unbound in a form or report. If the object is bound to a field, it changes with each record and each record needs a separate file.

- The error message might mention that you don't have enough memory to run the source program. This can happen if you have several programs running at once.

- If the source program is installed and running, there may be a dialog box open in the program, waiting for a response. This freezes up the program. The object won't open until the program is active again.

The following solutions show you how to solve these problems and get on with your work.

How to fix it

To reconnect the link to an object whose source file has been moved or renamed, do the following:

1. Click OK to clear the message. ▶

2. If the object is not bound to a field, open the form or report in design view and click on the object. If the object is bound to a field, open the form in form view, locate the record that contains the object, and then click the object.

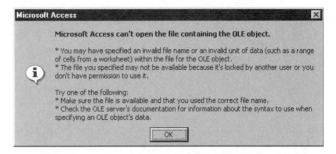

3. On the Edit menu, click OLE/DDE Links.

4. Look at the original path and name in the Links dialog box. ▶

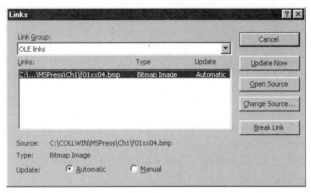

5. If the object has been moved or renamed, click the link and then click the Change Source button.

6. Locate and select the file that's been moved or renamed, and then click Open.

7. In the Links dialog box, click Close. The link is restored.

8. Save the form or report.

If the error message indicates that you haven't enough memory to open the source application, try the following:

1. Click a button on the Windows task bar to move to another program that's running. Choose a program that isn't directly involved with your current activity.

2. Close the program.

3. Repeat steps 1 and 2 to close other programs that aren't required.

4. Try opening the object again.

If the source program is already running, do the following:

1. On the Windows task bar, click the button for the program that created the object.

2. Close all open dialog boxes.

3. On the task bar, click the icon to return to Access.

4. Double-click the object to open it in the source program.

Tip

When you change the link to a bound object, you're updating the link only for the current record. Move to another record and repeat the process to reconnect the link as necessary.

My calendar control doesn't look right and shows the wrong date

Source of the problem

You discovered the neat ActiveX calendar control that you can use to dramatize a schedule of appointments. But much to your dismay, the calendar doesn't match your way of scheduling meetings and other appointments and, what's worse, it displays an incorrect date.

The problem with the calendar's schedule display has to do with how some of the calendar's properties are set up. You might want a different first day of the week than the calendar displays, for example, or you might need to reduce the size of the labels. Changing the settings of the calendar's properties will correct these problems.

If your problem is an incorrect date, you might have set the calendar's Control Source property to the wrong date field or not set it at all. If you don't set the Control Source property to a field, the calendar uses the current system date.

Here are solutions to fix these problems.

How to fix it

To change the appearance of the calendar control, do the following:

1. Open the form in design view, and then click the calendar control.

2. Click the Properties button on the toolbar, and then click the Other tab.

3. Click in the Custom property box, and then click the Build button (…).

4. In the Calendar Properties box, make the changes you want. For example, choose Monday as the first day of the week or clear the Vertical Grid check box to remove the lines running between

the days of the week. You can also clear the Month/Year Selectors check box to remove the drop-down lists from the calendar title.

5. Click Apply after each change to see its effect on the appearance of the calendar. ▶

6. In the Calendar Properties box, click OK and then save the form.

To solve the problem of the wrong date showing in a calendar control, follow these steps:

1. Open the form in form view, and then click the calendar control.

2. Click the Properties button on the toolbar, and then click the Data tab.

3. In the Control Source property box, select the date field you want the calendar to display. ▶

4. Save the form, and then switch to form view.

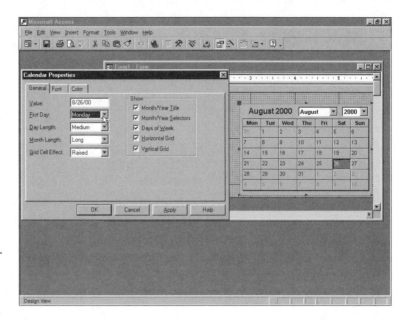

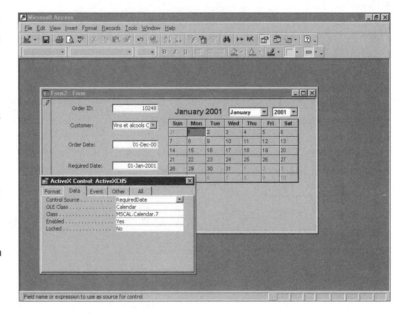

I see an icon where I put a picture

Source of the problem

They say a picture is worth a thousand words. But if the picture turns out to be a little icon without much information, it isn't worth much at all.

When you use the Insert menu to add an image to a form or report, you have the option to display a small icon instead of the whole picture. This option saves you the time it takes to display the whole picture. Doing this is helpful while you design the form or report, but if you forget that you have left that option checked, you won't see the picture in its full glory.

The following solution tells you how to fix the problem.

How to fix it

1. Open the form or report in design view.

2. Click the icon.

3. On the Edit menu, point to the Object command for the type of object you're working with and then click Convert. For example, if you're working with a Microsoft Clipart object, point to Clip Object and then click Convert.

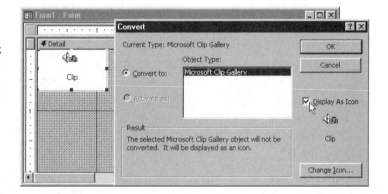

4. Clear the Display As Icon check box. ▶

5. Click OK and save the form.

If you just want a different icon...

If you do want to display an icon instead of the whole picture, but you don't like the default icon you've been offered, you can change it. Open the form or report in design view, and then click the icon. On the Edit menu, click the Object command and then click Convert. Click the Change Icon button, and then choose from the images provided or click Browse to locate a different icon file on your computer.

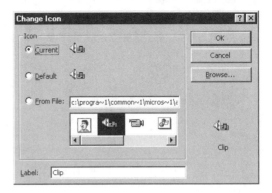

What kind of graphic file is best?

You can use several different types of graphic files with Access. For example, you can use bitmap files (.bmp or .dib), metafiles (.wmf or .emf), and other graphic files such as .gif and .jpg. Some file formats are better in certain situations than others.

Bitmap files are better if adjusting the size of the picture to fit the frame is not important and disk space is not limited. Bitmaps are also best to use if you want to be able to make small changes to the picture.

Metafiles are better if you need to be able to change the scale of the picture precisely to fit the frame without distortion. Metafiles are usually quite a bit smaller than bitmaps that display the same image, so metafiles take up less disk space.

Tip

You don't have to draw the image control frame the exact size of the picture you are going to add to a form or report. After you click the Image Control tool in the Toolbox, if you click in the design window, Access creates a one-inch square frame. When you insert the picture, the frame adjusts to fit the dimensions of the image.

I can't edit my OLE object

Source of the problem

Since life isn't perfect, at some point you're going to want to make some changes to the OLE object you placed in a handsome customized form. But when you go to make the changes, you find that you can't edit the object in form view, where you can actually see it as part of the full presentation. You double-click the object, and you see just the property sheet. The program you used to create the object doesn't open to help you edit the object in place.

There are several possible reasons why you can't change the object:

- You don't have the program that created the object installed on your computer. Without it, you're dead in the water.

- The object's properties are set to prevent editing in form view even though you can edit it in design view.

- The database is open read-only. When you double-click the object, the source program starts, but you get an error message when you try to save the changes.

- You converted the OLE object to a static image to save time when opening the form. Static images can't be edited in place, but you can resurrect the object from the original file.

The following solutions show you how to fix these problems.

How to fix it

To set the object's properties to allow editing, do the following:

1. Open the form in design view.

2. Select the object, and then click the Properties button on the toolbar.

3. Click the Data tab, and then set the Enabled property to Yes. ▶

4. Set the Locked property to No.

5. Save the form.

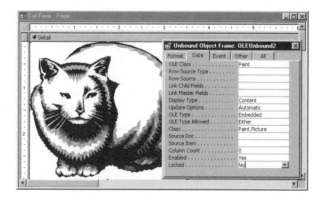

6. Switch to form view, and then double-click the object.

7. Make the changes you want, and then click outside the object in another part of the form.

8. Save the form.

If you see the error message shown in the figure after you make changes, you probably opened the database as read-only. To fix this, do the following: ▶

1. Click OK to clear the message.

2. Close the database.

3. Reopen the database normally.

4. Open the form in design view, and then double-click the object.

5. Make the changes you want, and then save the form.

If you have converted the object to a static image, remove the image and reinsert the object by following these steps:

1. Open the form in design view.

2. Click the image, and then press Delete.

3. On the Insert menu, click Object.

4. In the Insert Object dialog box, locate the object file you used before and then click OK.

5. Save the form.

> ### Is it bound or unbound? Linked or embedded?
>
> A few definitions may be in order at this point. A *bound* object is stored directly in an Access table as part of the stored data. For example, an employee's picture is a bound object.
>
> An *unbound* object is an element of a form or report design and has nothing to do directly with the table data.
>
> When you *link* an object to an Access form or report, the original object remains in the source application. Access reaches it by means of a pointer to the location where the object is stored. Linking saves disk space and ensures that the latest version of the object is retrieved.
>
> When you *embed* an object in an Access form or report, you are storing a static copy of it in the form or report. You can change the object in Access, but the original copy created in the source program does not reflect the changes.

The picture is distorted and doesn't fit the frame

Source of the problem

At the start of most videos you rent from a local shop, you often see a message stating that the film has been reformatted to fit your screen. The original footage has been nicely converted to a TV screen display. When you insert a picture in a form or report in Access, however, nobody sees to it that the picture looks right and fits the frame you drew. That's up to you.

An incorrect setting in the picture's Size Mode property has probably caused the distortion. The default setting is Clip. With this setting, the picture stays at its original size and, if it's bigger than the frame, only part of the picture shows. With the Stretch setting, however, Access resizes the picture to fit both the height and width of the frame. This setting can distort the picture if the original dimensions were much different from the frame you drew.

The Size Mode property not only leads to distortion, but it also can be the reason a picture doesn't fit the frame. The picture may appear cropped, or too much white space might appear in the frame. This problem can be especially bothersome when you're storing pictures in a field and the pictures are not all the same size.

If you're having trouble displaying a background picture in a form, the form's Picture Size Mode property might be set incorrectly. The problem could also be that the picture's alignment is not set so that it will resize when you change the size of the form window.

The following steps show you how to overcome these problems.

How to fix it

To cure a distorted picture, do the following:

I. Open the form or report in design view.

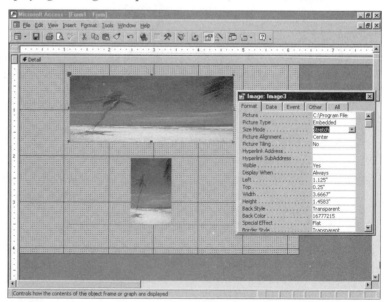

2. Click the picture, and then click the Properties button on the toolbar.

3. In the properties dialog box, click the Format tab and then change the Size Mode property to Zoom.

4. Drag the border of the picture frame to fit the picture.

5. Save the form or report.

If your bound pictures are all the same size, use the previous steps to adjust the frame to fit the pictures. If the pictures are not the same size, do the following:

1. Open the form in form view.

2. Click the picture, and then click the Properties button on the toolbar.

3. Click the Format tab, and then change the Border Style property to Transparent. ▶

4. Change the Back Color property to be the same color as the form background.

5. Save the form.

If you're having trouble with a background picture on your form, try these steps:

Tip

The Zoom setting is the best setting for pictures in the bitmap (.bmp) format because it preserves the picture's proportions. If you use the Stretch setting, the picture expands horizontally and vertically to fill the frame, which can cause distortion if the picture's dimensions differ significantly from the dimensions of the frame you drew.

1. Open the form in design view, and then click the Properties button on the toolbar.

2. In the properties dialog box, click the Format tab and set the Picture Size Mode property to Stretch.

3. If you want the picture to resize with the form window, set the Picture Alignment property to Center. If you don't want the picture to resize, set the Picture Alignment property to Form Center.

4. Switch to form view, and then save the form.

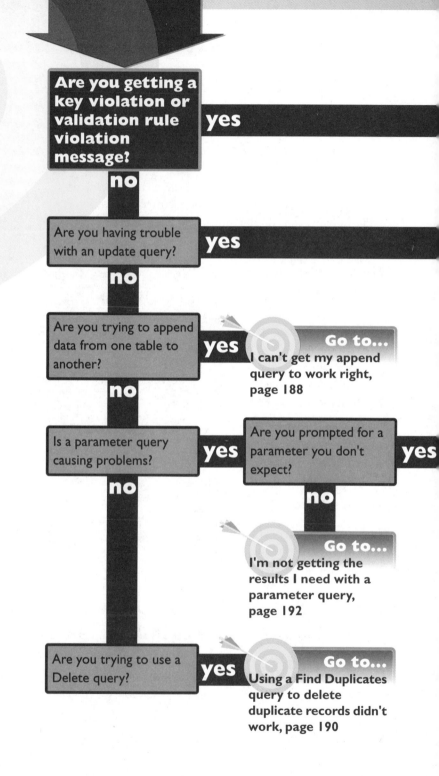

Are you getting a key violation or validation rule violation message?

yes

no

Are you having trouble with an update query?

yes

no

Are you trying to append data from one table to another?

yes

Go to...
I can't get my append query to work right, page 188

no

Is a parameter query causing problems?

yes

Are you prompted for a parameter you don't expect?

yes

no

Go to...
I'm not getting the results I need with a parameter query, page 192

Are you trying to use a Delete query?

yes

Go to...
Using a Find Duplicates query to delete duplicate records didn't work, page 190

Queries—Action

Go to...
My action queries cause
errors, page 186

Do you see a type
mismatch error message?

yes

no

Quick fix

You have put an expression in
the Update To cell that doesn't
match the field data type. For
example, you included the $
character in a currency field or
a character in a number field.

1. Open the update query
   in design view.

2. Click in the Update To
   cell of the field you need
   to change.

3. Type the correct
   expression for the new
   value in the Update To
   cell.

4. Save the query.

Quick fix

Referential integrity prevents
changing the primary key value
if there are child records.

1. Click the Relationships
   button on the toolbar.

2. In the Relationships
   window, right-click the
   line between the two
   tables and click Edit
   Relationships.

3. Select Cascade Update
   Related Records.

4. Click OK.

5. Run the update query
   again.

Quick fix

You might have misspelled or
renamed a field in the query
but not in the underlying table.

1. Open the query in design
   view.

2. Check for misspelled
   field names.

3. If you removed a para-
   meter from the query,
   click Parameters on the
   Query menu and delete
   it also from the Query
   Parameters dialog box.

If your solution isn't here
Check these related chapters:
Queries—Calculations, page 194
Queries—Selection criteria, page 214
Or see the general troubleshooting tips on page xiii.

My action queries cause errors

Source of the problem

Action queries are a quick way of getting things done. They're like cutting the whole corn field at once. But action queries don't always work right. You can run into problems because Access is very careful about what data you can add, delete, or update in a table. The following are three common problems that can come up with action queries:

- You tried to append or update records with primary key values that are already in the destination table. This causes a key violation error message.

- You tried to append or update records with field values that violate a validation rule set for the field. Or you might have violated the record validation rule set for the table. Either of these actions causes a validation rule violation error message.

- You enforced referential integrity (which demands that for every record on the "many" side of a relationship there is one and only one matching record on the "one" side) and tried to append, update, or delete records that result in a violation of referential integrity rules for the related tables. This causes a key violation error message.

The following solutions demonstrate the measures you can take to overcome these problems.

How to fix it

If you see the error message shown in the figure, you might have encountered key violation problems. Do the following: ▶

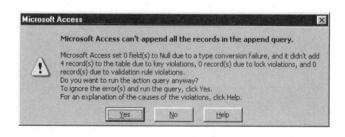

1. Click No in the message box to abandon the action query.

2. Open the table with the records you are appending (the source table) and make sure the records you are appending or updating don't include any AutoNumber field types. These can result in duplicate primary key values.

3. As necessary, edit the data in the source table that contains the primary key value so that it is no longer a duplicate of one in the destination table.

4. Close the source table.

5. Run the query again, and click Yes to confirm the append or update action.

If the error message includes a reference to one or more records violating validation rules, do the following:

1. Click No in the error message to abandon the query for now. ▶

2. Open the destination table in design view.

3. Select each field in turn and look at its Validation Rule property in the Field Properties area of the window. Make note of any rules and the fields they apply to.

4. Click the Properties button on the toolbar, and look for a record validation rule in the Table Properties dialog box. Make note of any rule.

5. Open the source table in datasheet view, and edit the fields as necessary to comply with the rules in the destination table.

6. Run the query again.

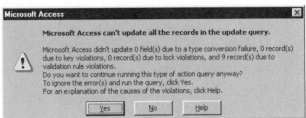

If you see a message about violating referential integrity rules that you have enforced between related tables, do the following:

1. On the Tools menu, click Relationships.

2. Right-click on the relationship line between the source and destination tables, and then click Edit Relationship on the shortcut menu.

3. Clear the Enforce Referential Integrity check box and click OK. ▶

4. Open the tables in datasheet view, and modify the tables one at a time so all the child records you're adding have a matching record in the parent table. Also, make sure you're not deleting a record or changing the primary key value of a record in the parent table if that record has matching records in the child table.

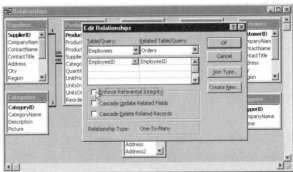

Warning

Before running a delete or other action query, run it as a select query and look at the records that will be affected by the query. If the records are the right ones, return to query design view and click Delete Query on the Query menu to change the type of query. Then, when you run the query, Access asks for confirmation that you want to delete all those records.

Tip

If you're planning to enforce the rules again after modifying the tables, be careful not to leave any field values that violate referential integrity.

I can't get my append query to work right

Source of the problem

Moving data from one table to another is only a little more complicated than dropping a bunch of folders in a file cabinet. All you need to do is tell Access what data you want to put in the table and in which fields you want the data to go. Sounds pretty simple, doesn't it? Then how come things go wrong and the data turns up in strange places or disappears altogether?

There are several problems that you might have encountered when creating and running an append query:

- When you created your append query, you placed the asterisk (*) from the field list for the source table in the Field row in the query grid to include all the fields from the table. Then you selected the asterisk for the destination table in the Append To cell as well. When you try to run the query, you get an error message. Using the asterisk shortcut method requires that the field names in the source table and the destination table match exactly. If one or more of the field names is not the same, the error message tells you the name of the source field that has no match in the destination table.

- You have a source field and a destination field that are defined with incompatible data types. For example, trying to append text data to a number field can cause an error message whether you have used the asterisk shortcut or added the fields to the query grid manually.

- You selected the wrong field in the Append To row in the query grid, so the appended data ended up in the wrong field. If the field names match, Access automatically fills in the Append To row, but if they don't, you need to enter the field names manually.

The following solutions show you how to overcome these problems.

How to fix it

If you see an error message about an unknown field name (as shown in the figure) and don't want to rename the table fields, do the following: ▶

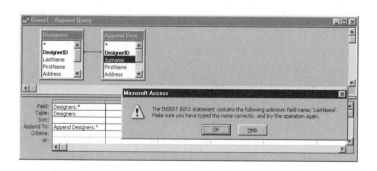

1. Click OK to clear the message, and then remove the asterisk column from the query grid.

2. From the list of fields for the source table, drag the first field to the query grid.

3. Click in the Append To row for that column, and then select the corresponding field from the destination table.

4. Repeat steps 2 and 3 until all the fields are added to the query grid.

5. Save and run the query.

If you see a message such as the one shown in the figure about failing to convert data types, do the following: ▶

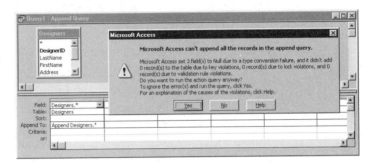

1. If you want to go ahead and run the append query and accept blank values in the incompatible field, click Yes.

2. Open the source table in datasheet view and fill in the missing values. You might also want to correct the mismatch in the types of data before trying to run the query again.

3. If you want to correct the data type mismatch before appending the records, open either the source or destination table in table design view and change the data type of the field to one compatible with the corresponding field in the other table.

4. Save the table and rerun the append query.

If the data turns up in the wrong fields after you run your append query, do the following:

1. Open the query in design view.

2. Click the Show Table button, and then select the destination table from the Show Table dialog box.

3. Click Add to add the table to the query, and then click Close.

4. Compare the field names in the source table field list with those in the destination field list. (Be careful, the matching fields might not be in the same order in both tables.)

5. Change the field in the Append To cell for the fields that were misplaced.

6. Save the query, and then run it again.

Tip

If the primary key field of the destination table is not an AutoNumber field, be sure to include the source field that corresponds to it in the append query.

Tip

If you're appending data to a table that's in another database, Access does not display a drop-down list of field names in the Append To row.

Using a Find Duplicates query to delete duplicate records didn't work

Source of the problem

After the tedious work of deleting duplicate records one at a time, turning the Find Duplicates query that the Query Wizard built for you into a Delete query sounds like a good idea. You run the query, but all of a sudden the table has no records at all. Using the Find Duplicates query as a Delete query can get you into trouble, as you can see. A Delete query deletes not only all the duplicate records, it also deletes any record that had a duplicate, including the original record. The only records it leaves in the table are those that had no duplicate values in the field in the first place.

The following solution provides a way to work around this problem, resulting in a table with only unique values in one or more fields.

How to fix it

Fixing this problem is a two-part process. First you create a new table. To do that, follow these steps:

1. In the database window, select the table with the duplicate values and then click the Copy button.

2. Click the Paste button on the toolbar.

3. In the Paste Table As dialog box, enter a name for the copy of the table and select Structure Only in the Paste Options area. Click OK. ▶

4. Select the new table, and click the Design button. In design view, select the field or fields in which you don't want duplicate values. Click the Primary Key

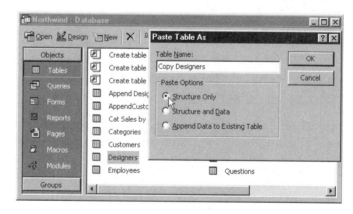

button. Be sure you don't include any AutoNumber field that you used in the original table as the primary key. ▶

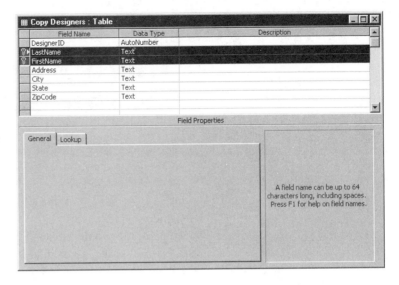

5. Save and close the table.

In the second phase of the process, append the records from the original table to the copy:

1. In the database window, click Queries and then click New.

2. Select Design View, and then click OK.

3. In the Show Table dialog box, click the Table tab and select the original table.

4. Click Add, and then click Close.

5. In the table field list, double-click the asterisk (*) to add all the fields to the query grid.

6. On the Query menu, click Append Query.

7. In the Append dialog box, select the table you created in the first phase and then click OK. ▶

8. Click the Run button, and then click Yes. Notice that the message mentions all the records that the original table contains.

9. Click Yes again in the message box about not being able to append all the records because of key violations. The records left out have duplicate values in the fields you chose as the primary key for the new table.

Warning
Always make a backup copy of a table you're using in an action query. This is especially important when working with Delete queries because you can't undo the deletion. With a backup copy, you can restore any data you inadvertently delete.

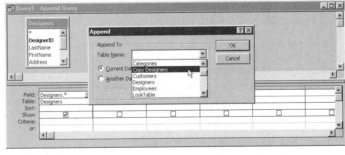

10. Open the new table and make sure there are no duplicates. Delete the original table and rename the copy.

I'm not getting the results I need with a parameter query

Source of the problem

You created a parameter query to give yourself some flexibility in choosing the records you want to see from the underlying table. But like a lot of other conveniences, this flexibility comes with a risk.

One of the problems you might have encountered is seeing the cryptic error message "Can't bind name *name*." You're probably using the query as the basis for a chart or a crosstab query. What Access is trying to tell you is that you didn't do a good job indicating the parameters you needed. You need to explicitly indicate the data types if you're using the parameter for a chart or a crosstab query. You might also see this message if you use a Yes/No field as a parameter in the query.

Using a lookup field in a parameter query can also produce unexpected results. You enter the value you've been looking at in the table in the parameter prompt, but nothing shows up in the query results. This is because (as always) what you see in a lookup field is not the same as what is stored in the field. So when you enter a value that is not stored in the field, Access won't find any matches.

The following solutions describe remedies for these problems.

How to fix it

If you see the message "Can't bind name," do the following:

1. Open the query in design view.

2. On the Query menu, click Parameters.

3. In the first Parameter row, type the first prompt you entered in the query design grid. Make sure you enter it exactly as it appears in the design grid.

4. In the Data Type row to the right, select the data type that matches the field. ▶

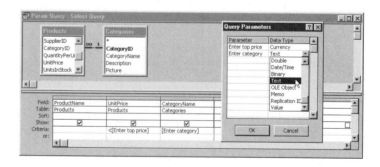

5. Repeat steps 3 and 4 for each parameter whose data type you need to specify.

6. Click OK.

7. Save the query.

If the field you want to use as the parameter is a lookup field, do the following:

1. Open the query in design view.

2. Click the Show Table button on the toolbar.

3. From the list of tables, select the table that contains the value you see in the lookup field. For example, if your query is based on a table that lists products and you want to enter the category of the product, add the categories table to the query. After you've made the selection, click Add and then click Close.

4. In the list of fields for the table with the lookup values, double-click the field that contains the displayed value to add it to the design grid.

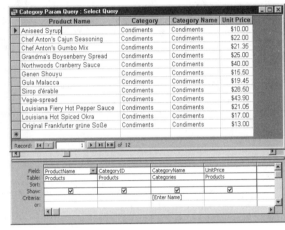

5. In the Criteria row for that field, type a prompt. For example, enter **[Enter Name]** in the Criteria row in the CategoryName column. ▶

6. On the View menu, click Datasheet View to run the query.

7. In the parameter prompt, enter the category name.

8. Save the query.

More parameter query tips

If you want the option to see all the records in the results of a parameter query, you can modify the query to allow that option. Instead of creating a separate query without the parameter prompt, you can add criteria to the parameter field column. After entering the prompt in the Criteria row, move down to the Or row and enter the same prompt followed by Is Null. When you click OK without entering a value in the parameter prompt, all the records are displayed because the parameter you don't enter is a Null value, one of the acceptable criteria.

You can also enter more advanced expressions in the Criteria row to see values between two values that you enter at the prompts. For example, the expression **Between [Enter start date] And [Enter end date]** will return all records whose value falls between the two dates you enter.

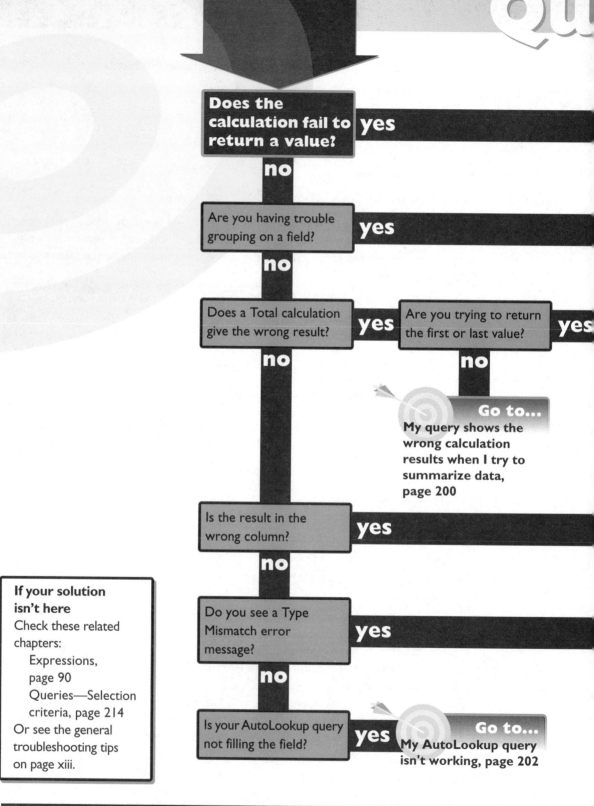

Does the calculation fail to return a value? yes

no

Are you having trouble grouping on a field? **yes**

no

Does a Total calculation give the wrong result? **yes** Are you trying to return the first or last value? **yes**

no no

Go to...
My query shows the wrong calculation results when I try to summarize data, page 200

Is the result in the wrong column? **yes**

no

If your solution isn't here
Check these related chapters:
Expressions, page 90
Queries—Selection criteria, page 214
Or see the general troubleshooting tips on page xiii.

Do you see a Type Mismatch error message? **yes**

no

Is your AutoLookup query not filling the field? **yes**

Go to...
My AutoLookup query isn't working, page 202

Go to...

I keep getting blanks instead of real values, page 196

Quick fix

You used the asterisk (*) to add fields to the query grid.

1. Remove the asterisk from the query grid.
2. Add the field you want to group by to the query grid.
3. Add the field you want to calculate with to the query grid.
4. In the Total row for the field you want to group by, select the function you need.
5. Click the View button to check the results.

Go to...

I get a strange result when I use the First function in a query, page 198

Quick fix

You placed the function in the wrong column.

1. Open the query in design view.
2. In the Total cell, replace the function with Group By.
3. Select the function in the Total cell of a different column.
4. Click View to check the results.

Quick fix

You're comparing text criteria with the result of using the Count function, which is numeric.

1. With the query open in design view, add a second instance of the text field to the design grid.
2. In the Total row of one column with the field, select Count.
3. Enter the text criteria in the Criteria row of the second column.
4. Click View, and check the results.

I keep getting blanks instead of real values

Source of the problem

You've seen the response a 12-year-old gives when he doesn't know the answer to your question. He just shrugs his shoulders in the universal gesture for "I don't know." That's sort of what Access does when you ask it to calculate a value in a query and Access doesn't know the answer. In Access, the shrug is called Null. Access believes it's better to leave the result blank than to guess at the answer.

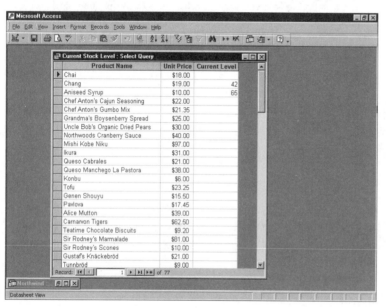

The reason Access comes up blank is that one of the fields you used in the expression for the calculated field includes blank records. In an arithmetic expression, if any of the values used in the expression is blank (Null), the entire expression is evaluated as Null, and Access shows blank values, as shown in the figure.

Another cause of the blank result in a query could be that you're combining text values in an expression by using the plus (+) operator instead of the normal concatenation symbol, the ampersand (&). The plus operator will usually work, but if one of the text values is blank, the entire expression is Null.

How to fix it

To fix the calculation problem resulting from blank records, use the Nz function to convert Null values to zero. Follow these steps:

1. Open the query you're working with in design view.

2. In the Field row for the field that includes blank records (Current Level in the figure), enter an expression such as **Nz([InStock],0)+Nz([OnOrder],0)-Nz([BackOrder],0)**. For InStock, OnOrder, and BackOrder, you would substitute the field names from your own database. ▶

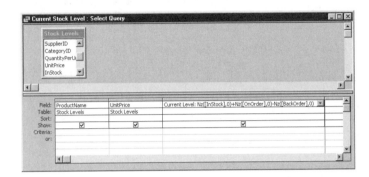

3. Save and run the query.

> **Tip**
> If you want to prevent problems with blank records from happening in the first place, open the table in design view and add a default value of 0 to each number field you expect to use in calculations.

If you see blank records instead of the text values you tried to combine with the plus sign (+), do the following:

1. Open the query in design view.

2. In the Field row for the field causing the problem, replace each plus sign (+) with an ampersand (&) and then save the query. ▶

3. Run the query.

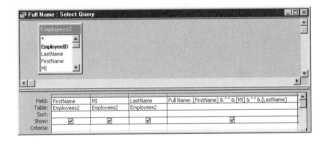

> **Tip**
> To place spaces between the text values, include a space between the field names enclosed in quotation marks.

I get a strange result when I use the First function in a query

Source of the problem

You tally up your recent rush of orders from all your faithful customers and want to look at the range of your success. So you create a query and sort the orders in descending order of total dollar amount. If you pick the first record in the query result, you'll see the order with the highest total amount, right?

Wrong! The First function, as well as the Last function, has a mind of its own. It totally ignores the sort order you set for a query. These functions also stubbornly ignore indexes and primary keys. What they do is return the first or last record on the basis of record number (the order in which the records were entered in the table), not by the first or last record in the current sort order.

This problem occurs when you use the wrong function in the query. The following solutions describe how to solve this problem.

How to fix it

To correct the problem, do the following:

1. Create a new query, basing it on the table with the values you want to sort.

2. In the Field row in the first column, enter an expression such as **Max Order: [UnitPrice]*[Quantity]**

3. Click the Totals button on the toolbar.

4. In the Total row, choose Max from the drop-down list.

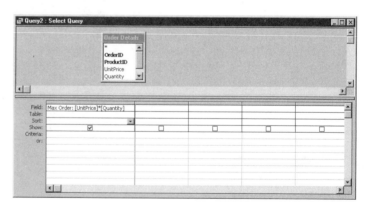

5. To see the smallest value among the records, copy the expression to the Field row in the second column in the query grid and change the name in the expression to Min Order.

6. From the drop-down list in the Total row, click Min.

7. Save and run the query. ▶

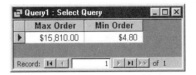

If you're looking for the first or last value in a single field, you can use the Top Values query property by following these steps:

1. Start a new query based on the table that contains the values you're interested in.

2. Drag the field name that contains those values to the first column in the design grid.

3. Choose Ascending in the Sort row if you want to see the lowest value in the field at the start of the query results, or choose Descending to see the highest value.

4. Right-click in the background of the upper pane of the query window, and then click Properties.

5. In the Top Values property, enter 1. ▶

6. Run the query.

Tip

When you close and reopen a query using one of the summarizing functions with an expression, you'll see that the function has been added to the expression in the Field row and the Total cell is changed from the function to Expression.

Tip

You can also simply enter 1 in the Top Values box on the Query Design toolbar. The number you enter there is added to the Top Values property in the query property sheet.

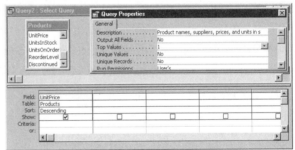

My query shows the wrong calculation results when I try to summarize data

Source of the problem

The whole point of grouping records in a query is to come up with summary information such as average time on a job or total orders by month. But when you run your query, you find that you worked an average of 36 hours per day or that your orders totaled $1,599,900,108 in March. (It was a busy month!) Access tries to make such summaries so easy you can do them blindfolded. But something has gone wrong somewhere. One of the following might have caused your problem:

- You grouped records on the wrong field.

- You placed the function you're using to summarize the data in the wrong column, or you chose the wrong function from the list.

- You're counting records with blanks in certain fields. If you're trying to count all the records, including the ones with blanks, you need to create a calculated field based on a special function.

The following solutions describe ways to fix these problems.

How to fix it

To correct a problem with grouping records on the wrong field, follow these steps:

1. Open the query in design view.

2. If the Total row isn't showing in the query grid, click the Totals button on the toolbar.

3. Verify that you have included the field you want to group by in the query grid.

4. In the Total row for that field, select Group By.

Tip

All the functions used to summarize data can be used with Number, Date/Time, Currency, and AutoNumber fields. Only the Min, Max, and Count functions can be used with Text fields. The only function you can use with Yes/No and OLE Object fields is Count.

5. Move to the Total row for the field whose values you want to summarize and select the function you need from the drop-down list. The list to the right will help you figure out which function to choose.

If you want to	Choose
Add all the values in the field	Sum
Find the average of the field values	Avg
Show the lowest value in the field	Min
Show the highest value in the field	Max
Count the number of non-Null field values	Count
Compute the standard deviation of the values	StDev
Compute the variance of the values	Var

If you want to include blank values when counting the number of records, do the following:

1. Create a new query, basing it on the table with the records you want to count, but don't add any fields to the grid.

2. Click the Totals button on the toolbar.

3. In the first Field row, enter an expression such as **TotalCities: Count(*)**.

4. In the Total row, choose Expression from the drop-down list.

5. Run the query. ▶

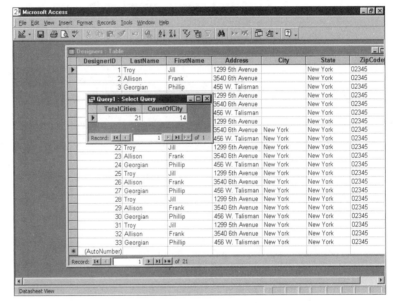

Tip

To see the difference between this method and counting field values that might include blanks, drag the City field name to the grid and choose Count in the Total cell.

My AutoLookup query isn't working

Source of the problem

Just when you think you've made data entry easier with AutoLookup, nothing happens. The insertion point sits blinking at you. Let's say you're entering new orders from your customers, and once you enter the customer's name you want the AutoLookup query to fill in the customer's address, phone number, and other boring information for you. If Access doesn't automatically fill in the data, you could have one of several problems:

Tip

A one-to-many relationship, the most common type, relates a single record in one table to any number of records in another table. A one-to-one relationship is used mainly as a lookup tool that relates a single record in one table to a single record in another table, possibly containing augmenting but seldom-used data. A many-to-many relationship exists in theory, but in Access it's implemented as two one-to-many relationships with a table in between. The "junction" table contains only those fields needed to link the two original tables with a one-to-many relationship.

- The fields in the query might not be from one or more tables that are part of a one-to-many relationship.

- The linking field you used in the query design might be wrong. The linking field must be the field from the table on the "many" side. For example, when working with orders and customers, the customers table is on the "one" side (the parent table); the orders table is on the "many" side (the child table). (This makes sense—one customer can place many orders, but an order is sent to a single customer.)

- AutoLookup will also not work if the field joining the tables from the "one" side includes duplicate values. All the records in this field must be unique. On the other hand, a customer name field cannot be the primary key or a unique index in an orders table (the "many" side of the relationship).

- The record you want to look up might not exist in the table on the "one" side. If Access is going to look up information in a table that it will use to fill in fields in another form, that information had better exist.

The following solutions give you ways to correct these problems.

How to fix it

The first thing to do is check the relationship between the tables and fields that are in the query design grid:

1. With your database open, click the Relationships button on the toolbar.

2. Right-click the relationship line linking the tables you're working with (Orders and Customers in this example), and then click Edit Relationship on the shortcut menu.

3. Check the related fields and make sure the relationship type is One-To-Many. ▶

4. Click OK, and then open the query in design view.

5. If the linking field in the query grid is from the table on the "one" side, delete the column containing the field from the query grid.

6. Drag the linking field from the table on the "many" side to the query design grid.

7. Save the query.

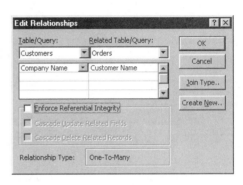

If the field you're using in your AutoLookup query includes duplicate values, try the following:

1. Open the table on the "one" side in design view, and then click the field that links this table with the table on the "many" side.

2. In the Field Properties area, change the field's Indexed property to Yes (No Duplicates).

3. Save the changes to the table.

4. Open the table on the "many" side in design view.

5. Click the field that links this table with the table on the "one" side.

6. Change the Indexed property to No. ▶

7. Save the changes.

8. Run your query again.

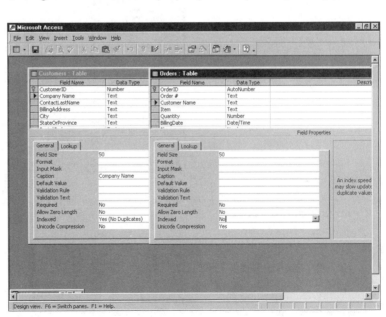

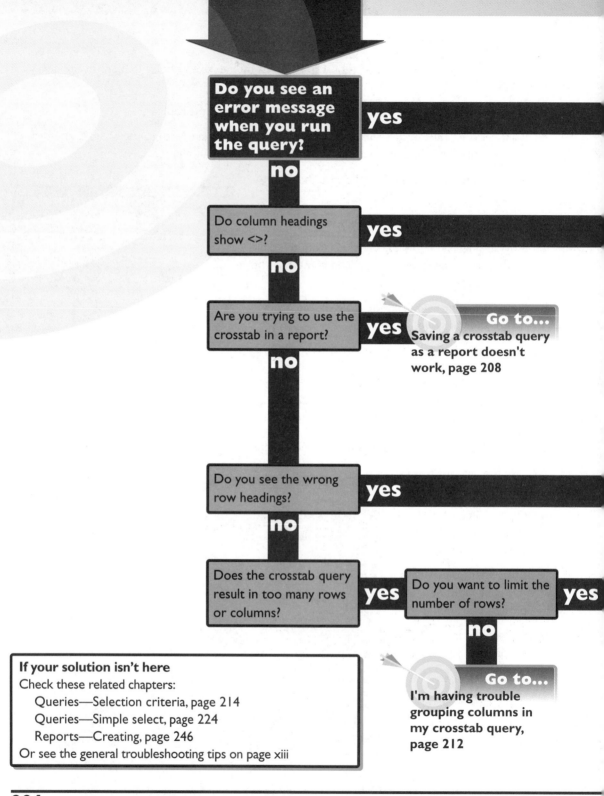

Do you see an error message when you run the query?

yes

no

Do column headings show <>?

yes

no

Are you trying to use the crosstab in a report?

yes

Go to...
Saving a crosstab query as a report doesn't work, page 208

no

Do you see the wrong row headings?

yes

no

Does the crosstab query result in too many rows or columns?

yes

Do you want to limit the number of rows?

yes

no

Go to...
I'm having trouble grouping columns in my crosstab query, page 212

If your solution isn't here

Check these related chapters:

Queries—Selection criteria, page 214
Queries—Simple select, page 224
Reports—Creating, page 246
Or see the general troubleshooting tips on page xiii

Does the error message refer to too many columns?

yes →

Go to...
Too many columns in my crosstab query caused an error message, page 206

no

Quick fix

You have not defined the parameters for the query.

1. Open the query in design view.

2. Click Parameters on the Query menu.

3. In the first Parameter cell, type the first prompt you entered in the design grid.

4. In the Data Type cell to the right, click the data type that matches the field.

5. Repeat for each parameter.

Quick fix

A field with Column Heading in its Crosstab cell contains a Null value.

1. Return to the query design view and enter **Is Not Null** in the Criteria row of the field.

2. Run the query again.

Quick fix

You have selected the wrong fields in the query grid.

1. Open the query in design view.

2. Click in the Field row of the row heading you want to change, and select a different field name from the list.

3. Repeat for each field you want to change.

4. Run the query.

Go to...
I'm having trouble grouping rows in my crosstab query, page 210

Too many columns in my crosstab query caused an error message

Source of the problem

You're trying to create a crosstab query that figures out how many orders your customers have placed for your delicious products over the past few quarters. You build the query in the query design grid, but when you try to run it, you get an error message about too many column headings. The problem is that you have far too many distinct values in the field you designated as the column heading in the crosstab query. If you use a field such as an order date, each different date results in a separate column heading.

The solution lies in grouping the records. The following solution shows how to correct this error.

How to fix it

If you see this message, do the following: ▶

1. Click OK to clear the message.

2. In the query design grid, remove the field that's resulting in too many column headings. In the Field row for that column, add an expression that groups the values in the field. For example, you could group date values by quarter by entering an expression such as **Expr1: Format([*DateField*], "q")**. This expression extracts the numeric value of the quarter in which the date falls. ▶

3. Run the query again.

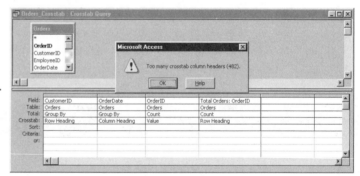

As easy as 1, 2, 3, 4

When you use the Format function to extract the number of the quarter, the column heads will read 1, 2, 3, 4. Although these headings are more helpful than the 482 dates that caused the error in the example, they aren't as informative as they could be. With the crosstab query in design view, add "**Qtr** " & to the start of the expression you entered in the Field row for the column heading field. Be sure to add a space after Qtr—if you don't, the text will run together with the numeric quarter value. Now when you run the query, the column headings provide more information and are more suitable for creating a chart based on the query.

Customer	Total Orders	Qtr 1	Qtr 2	Qtr 3	Qtr 4
Alfreds Futterski	7	2	2	1	2
Ana Trujillo Emparedados y hela	4	1		2	1
Antonio Moreno Taqueria	7	1	3	2	1
Around the Horn	13	4	2		7
Berglunds snabbköp	18	7	2	5	4
Blauer See Delikatessen	7	2	4	1	
Blondel père et fils	11	3	3	4	1
Bólido Comidas preparadas	3	1			2
Bon app'	17	6	3	1	7
Bottom-Dollar Markets	14	8	4		2
B's Beverages	10	4	4	2	
Cactus Comidas para llevar	6	3	2		1
Centro comercial Moctezuma	1			1	
Chop-suey Chinese	8	1	3	1	3
Comércio Mineiro	5	2	2	1	
Consolidated Holdings	3	3			
Drachenblut Delikatessen	6	1	2		3
Du monde entier	4	1		3	
Eastern Connection	8	2	4		2

Record: 1 of 89

Crosstab Queries 101

No matter what you think, crosstab queries are not really aliens from a different planet. They're useful tools for illustrating trends over time and relative proportions of totals. You can think of crosstab queries as a spreadsheet-like version of a chart or graph. A crosstab query summarizes the data you use rather than showing each and every record. The data is correlated with two types of information. In the example in this solution, orders are counted and grouped both by customer and by the quarter in which the order was placed.

> **Tip**
>
> If you use the Crosstab Query Wizard to create your query, it will group values such as dates for you. You have a choice of year, quarter, month, date (including the month, date, and year), or date and time.

Fields in your database are used as the three building blocks in a crosstab query: a row heading, a column heading, and a value. The values for the row heading field appear in a column at the left side of the crosstab, and the values for the column heading field are displayed (surprise!) at the top of each column. The field you select as the value is summarized as the number of records, the total of the values, or the average of the values. These values are then displayed in the body of the crosstab.

Whether you use a field as a row or column depends on what you want to emphasize. You can easily switch back and forth to get the result you want. But if you want to use subgroupings of one of the fields (individual cities within each state, for example), you must specify that field as a row heading. You can use only one field as the column heading.

You can select up to three fields as row headings that act as subgroupings for the data values. Each additional row heading multiplies the number of records in the query result. Two row headings doubles the number and three row headings triples it. If you use more than one row heading, be sure to arrange your row headings in the query grid in the order you want the results grouped.

Saving a crosstab query as a report doesn't work

Source of the problem

The Crosstab Query Wizard did just what you ordered it to and produced a very useful summary of your company's performance. Now all you need to do is put it in a report that you can distribute to all your admiring stockholders.

First you try to make a table from the crosstab query that you can use as the basis for the report. You use a Make-Table query to create the table from the crosstab query. Unfortunately, the table you create undoes all the summarization that the crosstab query so carefully calculated, expanding to include all the detail records in a plain vanilla report. If you were summarizing orders by customer and quarter, the table would show a record for each customer and each quarter in which an order was placed. Each customer would have up to four records, one for each quarter.

Next you try the clever Save As command to save your crosstab query as a report. What you get is a default tabular report with all the data, but it's not in the form of a crosstab—it doesn't show the columns, values, and rows with the summarized and coordinated values you want. Using the AutoReport tool results in the same flat report.

The following solution shows how to correct the problem and make a report out of a crosstab query.

How to fix it

1. In the database window, click Reports and then click New.

2. In the New Report dialog box, select the crosstab query you want to save as a report and then click OK.

3. On the View menu, click Sorting And Grouping.

4. In the Field/Expression column, select the field you want to use to group records so that you can summarize associated data. This is the field you used as a row heading in the crosstab query. ▶

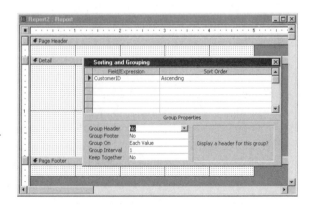

5. In the Group Properties area of the dialog box, select Yes in the Group Header box and then close the Sorting And Grouping dialog box.

6. In the report design window, click the Field List button on the toolbar if the field list is not already showing.

7. From the field list, drag the query's row heading fields to the group header section in the report design window.

8. Drag the column heading fields to the detail section of the report design window.

9. In the detail section, remove the attached labels from the column heading fields.

10. In toolbox, click the Label icon and add labels to the group header section to identify the fields that represent the column headings. (If the toolbox isn't displayed, first click the Toolbox button on the toolbar.)

11. Click the Label icon again, and add a title for the report in the Page Header section. ▶

12. Preview the report. ▶

You can save some space in your report by placing the column heading field labels in the Page Header section. Then the labels are not repeated in each group.

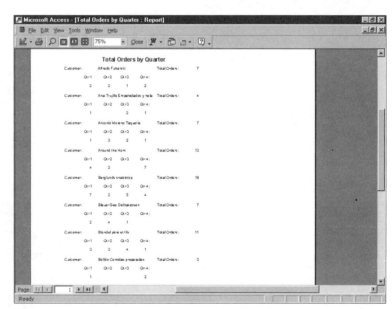

You can't update the data in a crosstab query. The crosstab query creates a static snapshot. To update the data in the crosstab with the latest table data, close and reopen the crosstab query.

I'm having trouble grouping rows in my crosstab query

Source of the problem

Creating summaries of your sales activities doesn't help much if what you end up with is a table with a record for each individual order and a column for each employee who made the sale. That information won't fit on a slide or in a report. You have to find a way to group some of these numbers to get a better overall picture of what you're trying to illustrate.

Unfortunately, the Crosstab Query Wizard can work on only one table or query at a time, but in a relational database, it's likely that the data you need to summarize is contained in related tables. If you're using the Crosstab Query Wizard, another problem might be that you aren't able to group values into rows the way you need them. The wizard can group records only with specific data types, such as dates. It can't, for example, group numbers such as sales totals by numeric ranges.

The following solution shows how to solve this problem using a helpful function named Partition. This is a two-phase solution involving a select query used as the basis for the crosstab query.

How to fix it

First, create a query that summarizes the numeric values you want to group in the crosstab query:

1. In the database window, click Queries and then click New.

2. In the New Query dialog box, click Design View and then click OK.

3. In the Show Table dialog box, click the Both tab. Select the tables or queries that contain the data you want in the crosstab query. Click the Add button, and then click Close.

4. In the query window, make sure the tables or queries are linked by a matching field. If they are not, select the field in one table or query and drag it to the matching field in the other.

5. From the field list for the primary table, drag the matching field to the query grid.

6. Drag the field containing the values you want to summarize to the query grid.

7. Rename the value column you just added by entering **Amount:** in the Field row in front of the field name to create an expression.

8. In the next empty column, enter an expression such as **Year:Year([*DateField*])**. The Year function extracts the year value from the date field.

9. Click Totals on the View menu.

10. Change the Total cell in the Amount column to Sum.

11. Save and name the query, and then run the query. ▶

Now create the crosstab query based on this select query:

1. Start a new query as you did in steps 1–4 above, basing it on the query you just created.

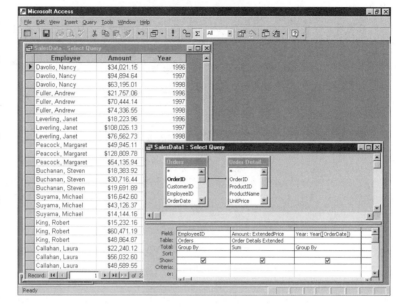

2. On the Query menu, click Crosstab Query.

3. In the first column, enter an expression such as **SalesRange: Partition([Amount], 0,100000,10000)**. This expression uses the Partition function to group the values in the Amount field beginning with 0 and ending with 100,000, in intervals of 10,000.

4. In the Crosstab row for this column, select Row Heading, and select Ascending in the Sort row.

5. Drag the field you want to see as column headings to the query grid. In the Crosstab row, select Column Heading.

6. Drag the field you want to use as a value to the query grid.

7. In the Crosstab row for this column, select Value. In the Total row, select Count.

8. Save and run the query. ▶

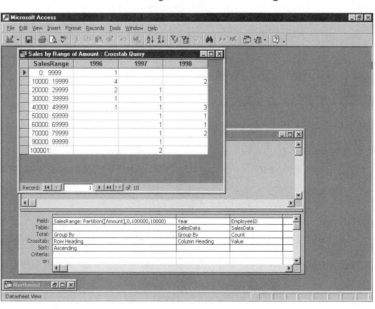

I'm having trouble grouping columns in my crosstab query

Source of the problem

It's easy to group column headings in a crosstab query by year or by quarter in a date field, but it's not so easy to group by other data types. For example, if you create a crosstab query that links customers with the amount of each order they've placed, you get thousands of columns—and an error message, by the way. To solve this problem, you need to find a different way to group the column heading field.

You can do this with the Switch function. The Switch function looks at a list of expressions you enter and returns a value related to the first expression that turns out to be true. You can use this handy function in a crosstab query to group the columns by numeric ranges. However, when you see the results, the columns are not in the right order. They're arranged alphabetically instead of in order of dollar value ranges. The following solutions show you how to fix your column groups with the Switch function and how to solve problems you might encounter in the process.

How to fix it

1. In the database window, click Queries and then click New.

2. In the New Query dialog box, click Design View and then click OK.

3. In the Show Table box, click the Both tab and then double-click the table or queries that contain the records you want in the crosstab query. Click Close.

4. On the Query menu, click Crosstab Query.

5. From the field list for the table that contains the field you want as a row heading, drag the field to the design grid.

6. In the Crosstab row, select Row Heading and then select Ascending in the Sort row.

7. From the field list for the table that contains the field whose values you want in the crosstab query, drag the field to the design grid.

8. In the Total row for that field, select Count. In the Crosstab row, select Value.

9. In the Field row in the next column, enter an expression such as **Expr1: Switch([ExtendedPrice]<250, "<$250",[ExtendedPrice] Between 250 And 1000, "$250-$1,000", [ExtendedPrice]>1000, ">$1,000")**. This expression uses the Switch

function to compare the value in the ExtendedPrice field with numeric ranges. If the first comparison is True, the column heading is set to the value enclosed in the next set of quotation marks. For example, if the ExtendedPrice value is less than 250, the column heading is set to <$250 and the record is included in the count value for that column. ▶

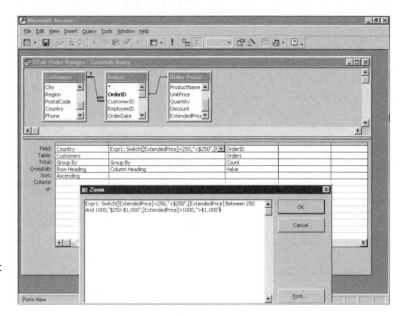

10. In the Crosstab row for that column, select Column Heading.

11. Run the query.

If your column headings are numeric values, the columns might not appear in the right order. To fix this problem, do the following:

1. Return to the query design.

2. Right-click in the background of the upper pane, away from any of the field lists, and click Properties on the shortcut menu.

3. In the Column Headings property box, enter the column headings in the order in which you want them to appear in the query results. Separate the column headings with commas and enclose the headings in quotation marks. ▶

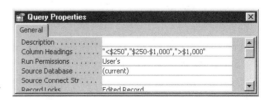

Queries

Is your query retrieving the wrong records?

yes →

no ↓

Are you prompted for a parameter when you run the query?

yes → **Quick fix**

If you're prompted for a parameter when you run a select query, do this:

1. Open the query in design view.

2. Compare the field names you used in the query to those in the table field lists.

3. Correct any misspellings and save the query.

4. If you want to keep the name you used in the query, open the table in design view, change the field name there, and then save the table.

no ↓

Does the query retrieve more records than you expect?

yes → **Do you want just the top few values?** **yes** →

no ↓

Go to...

I see too many records in the query results, page 220

no ↓

Does the query retrieve fewer records than you expect?

yes →

Selection criteria

Are you trying to find wildcard characters or operators in a field value?

yes

Quick fix

You need to treat wildcards and operators differently in a criterion.

1. If you're looking for one of the wildcard characters or an operator in a field by itself, use the = operator instead of Like. Access adds quotation marks around the character.

2. If you're looking for a wildcard character or operator that's part of a string, enclose the wildcard or operator in brackets: Like "[*]*" returns all values that begin with an asterisk.

no

Are you using wildcard characters to search for records?

yes

Go to...
What's up with my wildcard characters?, page 218

no

Go to...
I get the wrong records when I combine criteria, page 216

Quick fix

You need to select which records you want to see:

1. If you want the highest values, click Descending in the Sort row of the field you're using as the criteria.

2. If you want the lowest values, click Ascending in the Sort row.

3. On the Query toolbar, click the Top Values list and select the number or percentage of records you want to see.

Go to...
My query doesn't return as many records as I expected, page 222

If your solution isn't here
Check these related chapters:
- Filtering, page 100
- Queries—Calculations, page 194
- Queries—Simple select, page 224

Or see the general troubleshooting tips on page xiii.

I get the wrong records when I combine criteria

Source of the problem

You want to see a list of all books about dogs and cats, except for any books about the moot subject of training cats. Everyone knows those books would be empty covers. To find just the combination of information you want to see, you need to combine search criteria. The query design grid provides the Criteria and the Or rows where you place criteria in various arrangements.

If you're getting the wrong results with your query, you might have entered the correct criteria but just in the wrong place. You might, for example, have tried to combine two values with the And operator in the Criteria row for a single field. Doing this rarely works for text fields because one field can't have two values at the same time. The only reason you would combine criteria in this way would be to find a memo field with both text values somewhere in the field. What you might have wanted to see are records with either of the two values in a text field. In this case, you need to use the Or operator in the Criteria row to combine the values or place the second value in the Or row itself.

Another problem you might have stems from combining criteria in two rows and two columns. If you place criterion A in the Criteria row and criterion B in the Or row of one column and then enter criterion C in the Criteria row of another column (without any criteria in the Or row), you'll see records that meet criteria A and C, plus all the records that meet only criterion B.

The following solutions look at how to solve these problems.

How to fix it

If you want to find records with two values in a memo field, do the following:

1. In the database window, select the query and then click the Design button.

2. In the query grid, click in the Criteria row for the memo field and enter an expression such as **"*dog*" And "*cat*"**. When you move to another cell, Access adds the Like operator to both values. ▶

3. Run the query. You'll see all records that have the words *dog* and *cat* in the same memo field.

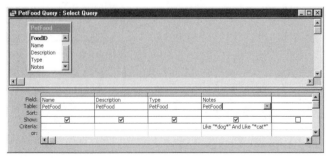

If you're trying to find records with either of two values in a single field, do the following:

1. Open the query in design view.

2. In the Criteria row of the field you're searching, enter the first criterion—for example, **"*cat*"**. Again Access adds the Like operator.

3. Click in the Or row of the same column, and then enter the second value you want—for example, **"*dog*"**.

4. Click the Run button to display the results of the query.

Tip
The asterisk wildcard character represents any number of characters. The words *dog* and *cat* can be embedded anywhere in the memo text, and the expression will locate them.

If you're combining criteria in more than one column, you might not have arranged them correctly. Try the following:

1. Enter a criterion in the Criteria row of the first column and in the Or row of the same column.

2. Add a criterion in the Criteria row in another column. This criterion is combined with the criterion in the Criteria row of the first column with the And operator.

3. To apply the criterion in the Criteria row of the second column to both groups of records from the first column, copy the criterion to the Or row of the second column. ▶

4. Run the query, and you'll see records that meet both pairs of criteria.

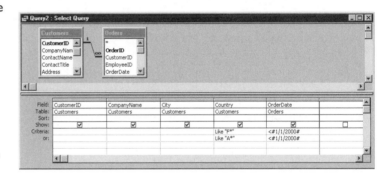

Tip
You can use the Cut, Copy, and Paste commands to move or copy criteria from one cell to another.

The logic may not seem so logical

Combining selection criteria with And and Or can get rather confusing. Whether the record is included in the query results depends on the outcome of the full expression. And the outcome of the expression depends on the outcome of each of its components and on how they're combined. An expression using an And combination is true only when both criteria are true. If only one of them is true, the whole expression is false and the record is not selected. On the other hand, when criteria are combined with the Or operator, if either of the criteria is true, the whole expression is true and the record is selected.

What's up with my wildcard characters?

Source of the problem

When you send out invitations to your gala open house, you'd better get all the details right or the wrong guests will show up on the wrong day wearing the wrong outfits. The last thing you want is to have your boss and her good-looking spouse show up at midnight in their bathing suits for a slide show of your latest ski trip. If you leave any gaps in the information and expect Access to come up with the right answers, you'd better give it a clue about what fits in the gaps. Wildcards can do just that if you choose them wisely.

Query criteria are invitations for certain records to show up in certain circumstances when you run the query. If you see the wrong records or the wrong values in the query results, the criteria in the invitation might be goofed up. One of the following is probably your problem:

- You used the wrong operator with a wildcard character. For example, using the equals sign (=) with a wildcard character causes Access to look for the wildcard character itself rather than use it to represent other characters.

- You got an error message indicating an invalid value because you used the wrong wildcard for the type of data you're searching through. For example, entering the question mark (?) wildcard to search for a number in a date field will cause an error. The question mark wildcard character is intended to replace any single character in a text field.

The following solutions show you ways to cure these problems.

How to fix it

If you're having trouble using a wildcard character to search for records, follow these steps:

1. In the database window, select the query and then click the Design button.

2. Click in the Criteria row for the fields where you've entered wildcard characters.

3. Replace the equals sign (=) with **Like** or the not equal to sign (<>) with **Not Like**. ▶

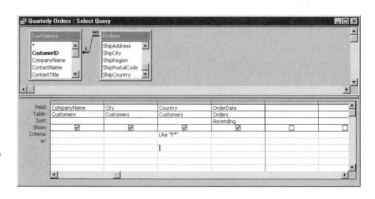

If you see a message about an invalid value, such as the one shown in this figure, do the following: ▶

1. Click OK to close the error message.

2. In the Criteria row for the field where you've used a wildcard, replace the invalid wildcard character with * or a date value such as 01.

3. Run the query again.

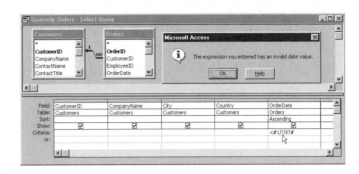

Tip

To find dates before a certain date, use the < operator combined with the actual date. To find a date in a specific month and year, use the * wildcard in place of the day value. Similarly, you can use the * wildcard in place of the month or year as well.

Tip

If you're looking for the wildcard character itself in the field value, you can use other wildcard characters to find its occurrence in any part of the value. The expression [*] finds all records that contain an asterisk (*) anywhere in the field.

Wildcards aren't so wild after all

Wildcard	Purpose
*	Used as the first or last character in the criteria. The * matches any number of characters in the field value. For example, "c*" finds any word that begins with the letter c.
?	Matches any single alphabetic character in a text field. For example, "c??e" finds care, cave, core, and so on.
#	Matches any single numeric character. For example, 25# finds 251, 252, 253, and so on.
[ ]	Used to enclose specific characters, and matches any one of them. For example, "c[aou]ll" finds call, coll, and cull but not cell or cill.
!	Used within the square brackets. The exclamation point matches any character not in the brackets. For example, "c[!ao]ll" finds cell and cull but not call or coll.
-	Used within the square brackets. The hyphen defines an ascending or descending range of characters to match. For example, "c[a-d]d" finds cad, cbd, ccd, and cdd.

I see too many records in the query results

Source of the problem

You open the door just a crack, and half the world shows up. Too many records crash the party when you've tried to invite just a few selected ones. That's what criteria are for in a query; they're like a formal invitation to a party. So why do you see so many unwanted guests in your query results?

One reason you could be flooded with records is that the query you're running is based on more than one table, but the tables aren't related in the query's design. In this case, you're swamped with what mathematicians call a *Cartesian product*—for each record in one table you get the whole set of records from the other table, not just a matching record. In other words, if one table has 100 records and the other has 250, the result will show 25,000 records.

Other causes of seeing too many records aren't so dramatic:

- The tables are not joined in the right way.

- Criteria in the query are not selective enough to narrow down the result. The criteria might be combined with the Or operator, which increases the number of records that meet the criteria.

The following solutions give you some pointers on how to solve these problems.

How to fix it

If the tables you've included in the query aren't related at all, do the following:

1. In the database window, select the query and then click the Design button.

2. In the query window, select the field from one table and drag it to the matching field in the other table. ▶

3. Save the query.

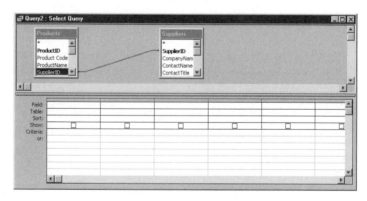

To change the way two tables are joined, follow these steps:

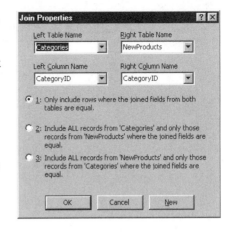

1. In the database window, select the query and then click the Design button.

2. In the query window, right-click the relationship line between the two tables and then click Join Properties on the shortcut menu.

3. In the Join Properties dialog box, select the first option (labeled with the number 1) to create what Access calls an *inner join*. ▶

4. Repeat for other relationships between tables in the query.

5. Click OK, and save the query.

If you want to enter criteria that will limit the records further, try one or more of the following steps:

1. In the database window, select the query and then click the Design button.

2. In the query grid, click in the Criteria row for a field without selection criteria entered and add criteria. This criteria will be combined with criteria entered for other fields to reduce the number of records.

3. Move criteria for a field from the Or row to the Criteria row. This will further restrict the number of records that appear in the query results.

4. Add selection criteria to existing criteria using the And operator.

5. When you have the results you want, save the query.

My query doesn't return as many records as I expected

Source of the problem

It's hard to know which is worse, having the whole town crash your party or having no one show up at all. You keep wondering what you might have said that keeps everyone away. If your query displays very few or no records at all, it might indeed be something you said. In the form of the selection criterion, that is.

If you see fewer records than you expected, one of these situations is probably the source of your problem:

- You accidentally entered criteria that no record could meet. For example, you might have combined two values with an And operator in a text field. The field can't have two values in the same record, so no records will meet these criteria.

- You placed criteria in the Criteria row of too many columns. Access interprets this combination of criteria using an implied And operator. That means few records will meet all the criteria.

- The criteria values you used are too limiting. Using wildcard characters can add some leeway.

- You want to include records that have no value in the field you're setting criteria for, but you didn't enter criteria that will select blank records.

The following solutions give you some ways to correct these problems.

How to fix it

First select the query in the database window and click the Design button. Then do the following:

1. In the query design grid, check criteria you entered for misspellings, spaces in the wrong place (for example, in field names not enclosed in brackets in an expression), and extra characters that might be in the way.

2. Remove any mutually exclusive values from criteria combined with the And operator, or change the And operator to an Or operator to allow both values. For example, change the criteria **"cat" And "dog"** to **"cat" Or "dog"**.

3. If criteria are entered for more than one field, remove criteria from the Criteria row for one or more fields, or move those criteria to the Or row for that column.

Tip

After each change, switch to datasheet view to see whether that change cured the problem.

To make the criteria more flexible (which should result in the display of more records), use wildcard characters as follows:

1. Replace one or more characters with a wildcard character. The question mark (?) can be used to represent a single character; the asterisk (*) represents any number of characters.

2. If you're already using wildcards, check to make sure you're using the right wildcard for that data type. (See the table in the solution "What's up with my wildcard characters?" on page 219 for examples of other wildcard characters you can use in selection criteria.) ▶

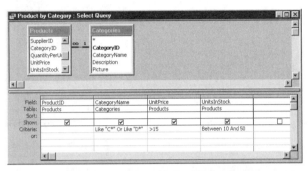

3. Switch to datasheet view to see the results. ▶

Tip

If you use = or <> with wildcards, Access looks for the wildcard character itself, not what it represents.

To include records with blank (or Null) values in a field, do the following:

1. Open the query in design view.

2. In the Or row for a field that already contains criteria in the Criteria row, enter **Is Null**.

3. Save and run the query.

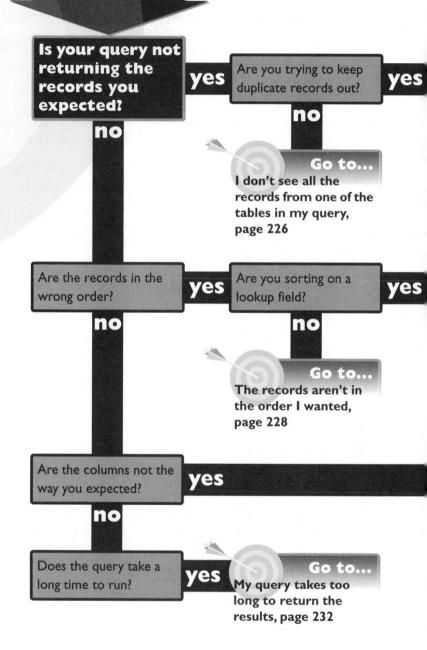

Is your query not returning the records you expected?

yes → **Are you trying to keep duplicate records out?**

yes →

no ↓

Go to...
I don't see all the records from one of the tables in my query, page 226

no ↓

Are the records in the wrong order?

yes → **Are you sorting on a lookup field?**

yes →

no ↓

Go to...
The records aren't in the order I wanted, page 228

no ↓

Are the columns not the way you expected?

yes →

no ↓

Does the query take a long time to run?

yes → **Go to...**
My query takes too long to return the results, page 232

Quick fix

You need to change the query properties.

1. In query design view, click the Properties button on the toolbar.

2. If the query includes only one field, change the Unique Values property to Yes.

3. If you want unique records based on all the fields in the data source (whether they are in the query or not), change the Unique Records property to Yes.

Go to...

I can't sort on a lookup field in my query, page 234

Do the columns show the wrong names?

yes

Quick fix

The query usually shows the field names from the underlying table.

1. To change the name in the query result, select the column in the design grid.

2. Click Properties.

3. Change the field's Caption property to the name you want to see.

no

Go to...

The query doesn't display the number of columns I expected, page 230

If your solution isn't here

Check these related chapters:

Queries—Calculations, page 194

Queries—Selection criteria, page 214

Relationships, page 236

Sorting, page 266

Or see the general troubleshooting tips on page xiii.

I don't see all the records from one of the tables in my query

Source of the problem

You know that your favorite customer, Paris Specialties, is in your database, but when you run your query, you don't see their name. Did they forget to pay their last bill or what? So you open the Customers table and, sure enough, they're still there. That's a relief, but why didn't they show up in the query?

When you don't see a record you expect to see in a query, it's probably because of the type of join that's used in the query to relate the tables the query is based on. If the tables have a one-to-many relationship and are using the most common type of join—the inner join—the query displays only those records where the fields joining the tables are equal. In other words, in a query matching customers with orders, if a customer doesn't have a matching order, the customer isn't included in the query results. Likewise, if an order isn't related to a customer, the order record isn't included.

By changing the type of join, you can return records without a match in the related table. The following solution shows you how you can create a query to show all the records on the "one" side of a table relationship (all the customers, in this example) even if there are no related records on the "many" side (the orders).

How to fix it

To change the type of join used in the query, do the following:

1. In the database window, select the query and click the Design button.

2. Right-click the relationship line between the two tables you're concerned with, and then click Join Properties on the shortcut menu.

3. In the Join Properties dialog box, select option 2, which will return all the records from the table on the "one" side of the relationship (Customers, in this example). ▶

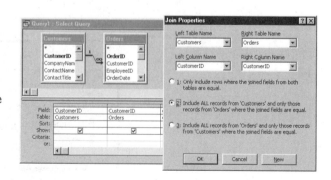

4. Click OK.

5. You can repeat these steps to change the type of join for other relationships in the query.

6. Click the View button on the toolbar to show the results of the query in datasheet view.

Warning

If you change the type of join in the Relationships window, all instances of the related tables are affected. Changing the type of join in the query design window affects the relationship only for that query.

Tip

If you have enforced referential integrity, you won't see any order records without matching customers in the database when you run your query. The symbols (1 and ∞) at the ends of the relationship line in the query design indicate that you have enforced referential integrity. If you haven't, there will be no symbols.

Joining a table to itself can be useful

Suppose your table includes a field that refers to another field in the table. How are you going to retrieve the value from another record in the same table? Pulling yourself up by your bootstraps might work, but a better idea is to use a self-join. A great example of a self-join is a query that returns employees' names and the names of their managers, who are also employees and have records in the same table. You can see this example using the Employees table in the Northwind sample database that comes with Access. The Employees table includes data about all the employees, including the managers, but the Reports To field contains the EmployeeID value, not the name of the manager. To see the manager's name in a query result instead of the employee ID, you need to put two copies of the same table in the query design. Then draw a relationship between the tables to link the fields in a self-join. In order to avoid having two column headings that are the same in the query result, right-click a column and then click Properties. Enter a name, such as Reports

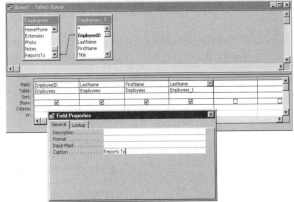

To, in the field's Caption property. When you run the query, you'll see records only for those employees who have a value in the EmployeeID field. The EmployeeID value in the query result is replaced by the last name of that employee because of the self-join.

The records aren't in the order I wanted

Source of the problem

Ducks are often easier to line up than the results of an Access query, in spite of all the help you can get with the query design. In the tables, the records are all neatly lined up, but when you combine them in a query, the order of things seems to get turned around. You might have selected the wrong sort order or set it for the wrong field in the query design grid. If you're sorting on more than one field, you might not have arranged the fields in the right order in the query. Here are a couple more reasons why the records might not be in the order you want:

- You hid the field you're sorting on in the query results.

- You're trying to sort on a field added to the query by dragging the all-fields asterisk (*) to the query grid.

The following solutions offer ways to overcome these difficulties.

How to fix it

To select the field to sort on and set up the sort order, do the following:

1. In the database window, select the query and then click Design.

2. In the query design grid, examine the sort order selected in the Sort row of the fields.

3. For any field you don't want to sort by, remove the sort settings by choosing Not Sorted from the Sort row's drop-down list. ▶

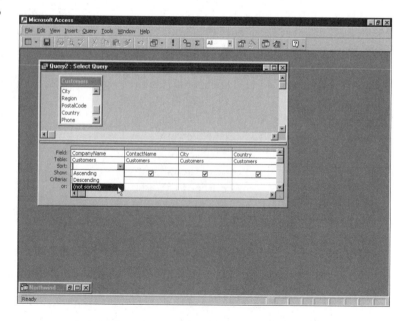

4. In the Sort row for the field you do want to sort by, select the sort setting you want.

5. If you have chosen a setting in the Sort row for more than one field, make sure the field you want to sort by first is at the left, with the other sorting fields arranged in sort precedence from left to right.

6. If the sorted field doesn't appear in the query result, make sure the Show box is checked for that field.

If you added all the fields to the grid by dragging the asterisk from the field list and want to sort by one of the fields, do the following:

1. Open the query in design view.

2. From the list of fields, drag the field you want to sort by to the query design grid.

3. In the Sort row, set the sort order for the field.

4. Clear the Show box, and then run the query. ▶

5. Repeat these steps with other fields if you want to sort on more than one field. Be sure to arrange them from left to right in the order you want the sort carried out.

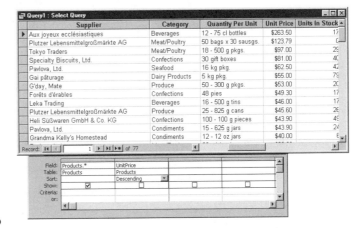

Seeing is believing

You might want to see the fields in the result of a query in a different order than the order in which they're set up in the query design grid. If you sorted on multiple fields in the design grid and you want the fields to appear in a different order in the result, you can add a copy of the field to the query grid in the position you want it to appear in the query result. (In the figure, you'll see that a copy of the City field has been added.) Clear the Show box in the columns used for multiple-field sorting so you won't see two copies of the field values in the query results.

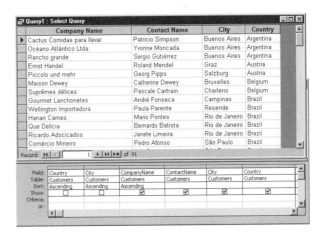

The query doesn't display the number of columns I expected

Source of the problem

What you expect and what you get can be very different, whether you're opening your mail or dropping a quarter in a slot machine in Las Vegas. Sometimes you expect a lot more than you see, and sometimes you expect a lot less. Access queries can surprise you just as much.

If you see too many columns in the query result, you might have unintentionally included more fields than you really need in the query design. You might have used the asterisk (*) shortcut to place all the fields from a table in the design grid. You might also have set one of the default options that includes all the fields from the underlying tables and queries in a query, whether you add them to the query design grid or not.

If your query shows too few columns, you might not have included the fields or tables you need. Another cause of this problem could be that you've hidden the fields by clearing the Show box in the design grid. If you do this, the columns won't show up in the results. Hidden columns can further complicate things when they don't appear where you left them in the design grid. When you save and close a query, Access, in a frenzy of removing clutter, moves hidden columns to which you've added selection criteria or sort settings to the far right of the design grid, possibly off the screen and out of view. If a field has no criteria or sort settings, it's removed altogether from the design grid, and when you reopen the query in design view, the field is no longer there.

How to fix it

If you see too few columns in your query, do the following:

1. In the database window, select the query and then click the Design button.

2. In the list of fields for the table, double-click the name of the field you want to add to the query. If you want a field in a specific place in the query design grid rather than in the first empty column, click the field name in the list of fields and drag it to that position in the grid.

3. To add another table or query to the query you're working with so that you'll have access to those fields as well, click the Show Table button on the toolbar.

4. In the Show Table dialog box, click the Both tab and select the table or query you want to add. Then click Add.

5. Click Close in the Show Table dialog box, and then add the fields you want to the query, following step 2 above.

6. To restore any fields that Access doesn't display in the query result, scroll right in the grid and check the Show box. ▶

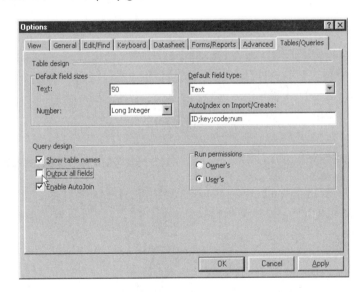

If you see too many columns, try this:

1. Open the query in design view.

2. If you added the fields to the query design grid using the asterisk shortcut, delete the column with the asterisk from the design grid and add the fields you need in the query, one at a time, by dragging the field name from the field list to the query grid.

3. If you need some of the fields for selection criteria, sorting, or calculations but don't want to see these fields in the query results, hide them by clearing the Show box for those fields.

4. If you still see all the fields from the underlying tables even though they're not included in the design grid, click Options on the Tools menu.

5. Click the Tables/Queries tab, and clear the Output All Fields check box. ▶

6. Click OK.

Tip

Changing the Output All Fields setting affects all new queries, not existing ones. So if you're starting a new query and you change this option, delete the query and start over so the change will take effect.

My query takes too long to return the results

Source of the problem

If you have time to refill your coffee cup while your query is running, the query is too slow. If the coffee cools off before the results of the query appear, it's *really* too slow. A lot of factors can affect a query's performance. You can correct or minimize many of these. Some of the most common causes of poor query performance are the following:

- A field linking the tables isn't indexed, or fields used for sorting or selection criteria in the query aren't indexed.

- Some of the fields in the query are defined with an unnecessarily large data size. This wastes disk space and slows down the query.

- You included more fields than you need in the query. Queries with lots of fields take more time to display their results.

The following solutions describe how to correct or avoid these problems.

How to fix it

To create indexes for the fields in the tables the query is based on, do the following:

1. In the database window, select a table included in the query and then click Design.

2. Select the field that is used to link the tables in the query.

3. In the Field Properties area, click in the Indexed property box and select Yes (Duplicates OK). ▶

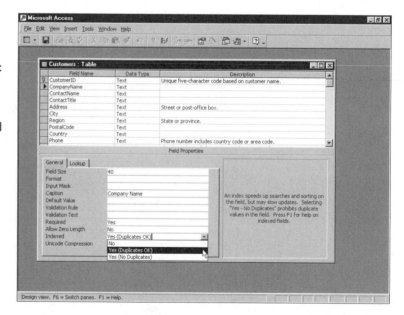

4. Repeat step 3 for each field you plan to sort on or set criteria for in the query.

5. Look at the fields with Text as their data type and reduce the Field Size property to the smallest size that will hold your data. The default field size for a text field is 50 characters, but your field might require fewer.

6. Look at the fields with Number as their data type and reduce their field size, if possible. The Field Size property setting determines the amount of disk space used by the number field. For example, the Byte field size setting can be used to store positive integers from 1 through 255 and only uses 1 byte of disk space. An Integer field size setting can be used to store larger positive or negative integers and uses only 2 bytes.

7. Save and close the table.

To reduce the number of fields in a query, do the following:

1. Open the query in design view.

2. In the query design grid, remove any fields you don't need in the query results.

3. If you need a field for sorting or for criteria but don't need to see the field in the query result, clear the Show box for that field.

More help speeding up queries

Access has a couple of other tools you can use to help speed up your queries. The Performance Analyzer looks at your query design and comes up with suggestions, recommendations, and ideas that might help the query's performance. To run the Performance Analyzer, point to Analyze on the Tools menu and click Performance. Click the Queries tab (in Access 97, the name of the tab is simply Query), and select all the queries you want examined, or click Select All to give them all the once-over. Click OK. After a few moments, the Analyzer displays its advice. You can review and accept the recommendations individually or all at once.

As you work with your database, it becomes scattered around on the disk. Queries take longer to find records for display or update. Access provides a tool you can use to consolidate your database for easier data retrieval. Point to Database Utilities on the Tools menu, and then click Compact And Repair Database. ▶

If you're using Access 97, the compact and repair utilities are two separate operations. To get the best results, repair the database first and then compact the results.

I can't sort on a lookup field in my query

Source of the problem

Lookup fields were invented to make entering data faster and more accurate. All you need to do is select a value from the list and you're home free. Unfortunately, that's not quite true—in spite of the old saying "What you see is what you get." What you see in a lookup field is a far cry from what Access stores in the record. And when you try to sort on a lookup field in a query, you're sorting on the stored value, not the value you're looking at.

If your query results aren't in the order you expected, you might be sorting on a lookup field. It's easy to find and fix the problem, as the following solution demonstrates.

How to fix it

If you think the field you're trying to sort on is a lookup field, do the following:

1. Open the table the query is based on in design view.

2. Select the field you're trying to sort on, and then click the Lookup tab. If you see a SELECT statement in the Row Source property, the field is getting its value from another table or query. ▶

3. Close the table design window, and open the query in design view.

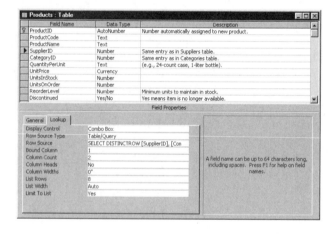

Tip

You might encounter a similar problem if you try to filter records in your query based on the value in a lookup field. When you filter on a lookup field, you must enter the stored value in the Criteria row in the query grid.

4. Run the query. You'll see that the records are not sorted correctly (by Supplier name in this example). ▶

5. Click in the column that contains the lookup field, and then click Sort Ascending or Sort Descending on the toolbar.

6. Click the View button to return to the query design, and then click Save.

7. Click the View button again, and you'll see that the records are now sorted in the correct order because the sort order you set in the datasheet view is saved with the query. ▶

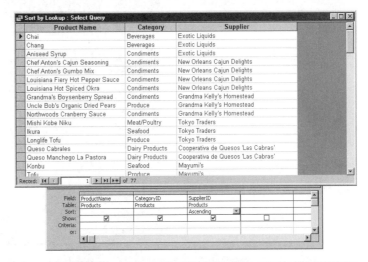

Where do lookup fields look?

The most popular sort of lookup field gets its values from another table or query. This is called a "lookup list." The biggest advantage of

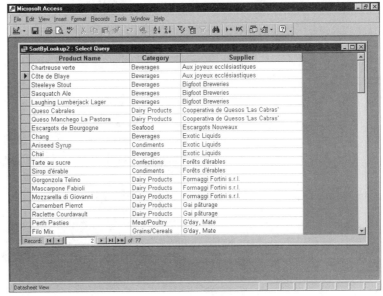

this type of lookup field is that the tables with the lookup field and the table with the values are related. When the values in the list change, the list is still available to the lookup field.

Another type of lookup field gets values from a list called a "value list." These values are entered in the Row Source property of the lookup field itself. This property is found on the Lookup tab in the Field Properties pane of the table design window. Other properties of a lookup field determine which value is bound to the field and which is displayed on the screen.

If you try to filter records in a query based on a lookup field, you'll experience the same problem as with sorting. You must enter the stored value in the Criteria row in the query grid. However, you can apply the filter to the query results and retrieve the set of records you want. But, unlike the sort order, the filter is not saved with the query design.

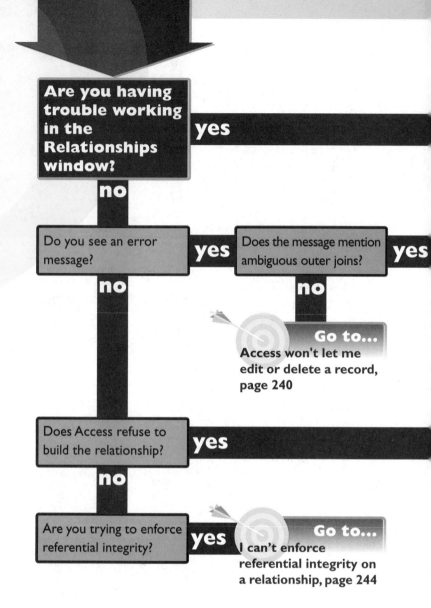

Are you having trouble working in the Relationships window?

yes

no

Do you see an error message?

yes

Does the message mention ambiguous outer joins?

yes

no

no

Go to...

Access won't let me edit or delete a record, page 240

Does Access refuse to build the relationship?

yes

no

Are you trying to enforce referential integrity?

yes

Go to...

I can't enforce referential integrity on a relationship, page 244

Relationships

Are you trying to edit or delete a relationship?

yes → **Quick fix**

One or more of the tables might be open.

1. Click the Window menu, and select the table from the list of open tables.
2. Close the table.
3. Repeat to close other related tables.
4. Return to the Relationships window and make the necessary changes.

no

Go to...

I get an error message about ambiguous outer joins, page 238

Go to...

I can't build the relationship I want in a query, page 242

Are you having trouble telling which tables another table is related to in the Relationships window?

yes → **Quick fix**

Too many tables are in the layout or they aren't in a clear arrangement.

1. Select a table that you don't need in the layout, and click Hide Table on the Relationships menu.
2. Select the table whose relationships you want to see, and click the Show Direct Relationhips button on the toolbar.

If your solution isn't here
Check these related chapters:
   Queries—Simple select, page 224
   Table design, page 276
Or see the general troubleshooting tips on page xiii.

Relationships **237**

I get an error message about ambiguous outer joins

Source of the problem

Access is usually pretty good at understanding what you want it to do. But even Access can get confused once in a while, especially when it can interpret your instructions in a couple of different ways. That's the case sometimes when you've created a query with multiple tables and at least one of the joins is an outer join. Access informs you of its confusion by showing an error message complaining of "ambiguous outer joins." This means that you've related the tables in such a way that you would get different results depending on the sequence in which you applied the table relationships.

The best way to fix this problem is to create two queries—the first to process one of the joins and the second to use the results of the first query with the third table. This process is illustrated in the following solution.

How to fix it

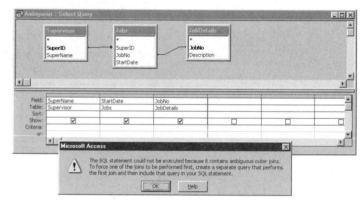

1. Click OK to clear the message, and then close the query design window. ▶

2. In the database window, click Queries, and then click New. In the New Query dialog box, click Design View and then click OK.

3. On the Tables tab in the Show Table dialog box, select the tables you want to use with an outer join, click Add to place them in the query, and then click Close.

4. In the field list, select the primary key field from one table and drag it to the matching field in the other table.

5. Right-click the relationship line between the tables, and then click Join Properties on the short-cut menu.

---

6. In the Join Properties dialog box, select the outer join (option 2 or 3) that results in the records you want and click OK. ▶

7. From the field lists, drag the fields you want to display in the query results to the design grid.

8. Save and name the query.

9. Start a new query as you did in steps 1 and 2. In the Show Table dialog box, click the Queries tab, select the query you created at the beginning of this solution, and then click Add. Then click the Tables tab and add the third table you want to use in your query. Click Close.

10. Drag the linking field from the query to the table. Access creates an inner join by default.

11. From the field lists, drag the fields you want to display in the query to the design grid.

12. Save and name the query.

13. Click the Run button. You see only the records with matching values in both linking fields. ▶

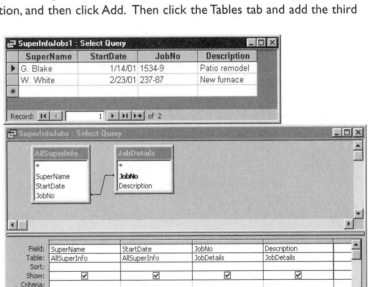

The thing about joins

Time out here for a few definitions to be sure we're on the same page. The type of join tells Access to include specific records from specific tables in the query results. The most common type of join, the inner join, retrieves only those records with matching values in the linking fields of both tables. An outer join, on the other hand, is one in which all records from one table are included, but only matching records from the other table are included. An outer join can be either left or right. A left outer join includes all the records from the parent table (the table on the "one" side of a one-to-many relationship) but only the matching records from the child table. A right outer join includes all the records from the child table and only the matching records from the parent table.

Access won't let me edit or delete a record

Source of the problem

All you're trying to do is clean up some of the tables in your database. Sounds simple enough—just change some field values and delete records you don't need anymore. But Access has a different slant on the edits and deletions you want to make and shows you a message that says, "The record cannot be deleted or changed because table '*tablename*' includes related records." The message shows the name of a table that's related to the one you're working with—a table that would be left with loose ends if your changes were carried out. This message appears because the tables are bound by *referential integrity*. Referential integrity helps preserve the relationships between the data in your database, but it also causes the error message when you try to change the value of the primary key field in a record in the parent table that has one or more related records in the child table or when you try to delete a record from the parent table that still has related records in the child table.

Access realizes that keeping your data up-to-date and free of errors can be a time-consuming problem, so it provides two options for you to use when referential integrity is in force. Here is an explanation of these options.

How to fix it

To fix the problem with editing a table's primary key field, do the following:

1. With your database open, click Relationships on the Tools menu.

2. Right-click in the middle of the relationship line that links the two tables you want to work with, and then click Edit Relationship on the shortcut menu.

3. In the Edit Relationship dialog box, select the Cascade Update Related Fields check box. ▶

4. Click OK.

5. Repeat steps 2 through 4 to add the Cascade Update Related Fields option to any other relationships involving the table you want to edit.

6. Close the Relationships window.

7. In the database window, select the parent table and click Open. Make the necessary changes in the primary key values. Access doesn't ask for confirmation for the updates.

If you're trying to delete a record from the parent table, do the following:

Tip
You can set one cascade option or the other—you don't need to set them both.

1. Open the Edit Relationship dialog box, following steps 1 and 2 in the previous solution.

2. Select the Cascade Delete Related Records check box.

3. Click OK.

4. Follow steps 1, 2, and 3 to edit each relationship line that involves the table you want to delete records from.

5. Close the Relationships window.

6. In the database window, select the parent table and click Open. Delete records as necessary.

7. Click Yes to confirm the deletion of the records in the child table as well as the parent record. ▶

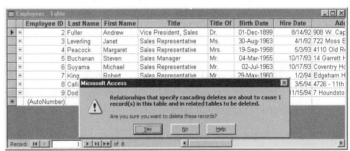

What exactly is referential integrity?

Referential integrity is a set of rules that tries to keep a database intact and free of loose ends. In a one-to-many table relationship, referential integrity ensures that no related records on the "many" side can exist without a matching parent record on the "one" side. This means you can't accidentally delete a parent record that still has child records, and you can't change the primary key field in a record in the parent table if that record still has related records in the child table. The rules also apply to tables in a one-to-one relationship.

In order to set referential integrity, the matching field from the parent table must be a primary key or have a unique index. Both tables in the relationship must be in the same database, and the related fields must have the same data type, with this exception: an AutoNumber field can be related to a Number field with a field size set to Long Integer.

You can tell whether referential integrity has been enforced on a relationship by looking at the symbols that appear at the ends of the relationship line in the Relationships window. In a one-to-many relationship, the line will show a 1 at the "one" end and an infinity sign (∞) at the "many" end. A one-to-one relationship shows a 1 at both ends of the line.

I can't build the relationship I want in a query

Source of the problem

When you first started working with the magic of relational databases, it seemed that the sky was the limit. At last you had a tool that would help you store all the data you needed and turn it into worthwhile information with the click of a button. You could relate tables just the way you wanted to and draw out all the information you needed. But now, when you try to get the most from your Access database, there seem to be relationship rules that tie your hands. The source of your problem might be your choice of where to create these relationships. You can create some relationships in the Relationships window that you can't create when building a query. Here are a couple of problems you might run into trying to relate two tables in a query design:

- You're trying to relate the tables using fields with different data types. For example, you're trying to relate an AutoNumber field to a text field. If you're doing this, you'll likely see an error message about a type mismatch.

- You're trying to use a memo, OLE Object, or hyperlink field in the relationship.

The following solution describes ways to correct these problems.

How to fix it

If you see an error message in the query design view about a type mismatch, do the following:

1. Click OK to clear the message. ▶

2. Right-click the relationship line between the tables, and click Delete from the shortcut menu.

3. If the primary key field in the parent table is an AutoNumber field, select that field and drag it to the matching Number field in the child table. This creates the relationship line between the tables.

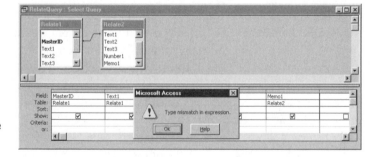

4. If the child table has no matching field with the Number data type, close the query design window. Then, in the database window, select the child table and click Design.

5. Add a field to the table, selecting Number from the Data Type list. On the General tab in the Field Properties area, set the Field Size property to Long Integer.

6. Save the table design.

7. If no data has been entered in either table in the query or data has been entered only in the parent table, return to the query design and set the relationship. If you have already entered data in the child table, open that table in datasheet view and edit the records to include values in the new number field to match values in the parent table. Then return to the query design.

If you have tried to relate the tables with a memo field and you get an error message, try the following:

1. Click OK to clear the message, and then close the query design. ▶

2. In the database window, select the table with the memo field and then click Design.

3. If the memo field doesn't contain more than 255 characters in any record, select the memo field and choose Text from the Data Type list.

4. If you get an error message because a record contains too many characters, click Yes to truncate the excessive text or switch to datasheet view and edit the memo field data to less than 256 characters. ▶

5. Save the table and return to the query design.

6. Draw the relationship line between the tables, and continue with the query design.

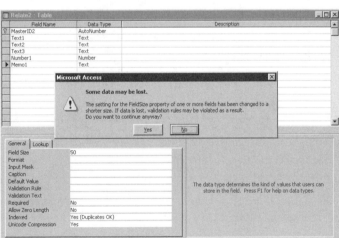

I can't enforce referential integrity on a relationship

Source of the problem

It's one thing to create happily related tables, and it's another thing to insist they all toe the line and obey the house rules. When you first build relationships between your tables in the Relationships window, you're responsible for making sure the fields creating the relationships have the same data type and content. After all, if one field contains dates and the other contains text, no values are going to match.

To help you crack the whip and get your tables to play by the rules, Access provides a tool. This tool could have been named something simpler than "referential integrity," but that's what we've got. Referential integrity keeps records in a database tightly integrated. Choosing to enforce referential integrity is easiest before you've entered any data in the tables, but you can try to do it later. If you tried to apply referential integrity to a table relationship in the Relationships window and encountered a problem, one of the following might be the cause:

- Existing data in the tables already violates referential integrity. There might be a record in the child table with no matching record in the parent table.

- The field in the parent table you're using to form the relationship might not be a primary key field or unique index.

The following solutions help you correct these problems.

How to fix it

If you see a message that existing data violates referential integrity, follow these steps:

1. Click OK to clear the message. ▶

2. In the database window, click Queries and then click New. In the New Query dialog box, select Design View and then click OK.

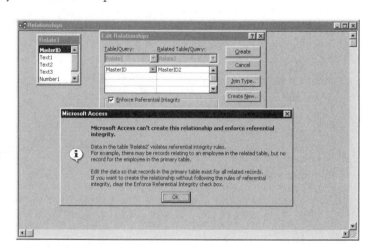

3. On the Tables tab in the Show Tables dialog box, select the two tables and click Add to place them in the query. Click Close.

4. Drag the primary key field in one table to the matching field in the other table to create the relationship line.

5. From the field list, drag the matching fields from both tables to the design grid.

6. Right-click the join line, and then click Join Properties from the shortcut menu.

7. In the Join Properties dialog box, select the join type that includes all the fields on the many (child) side and only those on the one (parent) side that match. This way you can see which child records have no parent.

8. Click OK, and then click the Run button.

9. In the query datasheet, edit the records so that each field in the child table matches one in the parent table. You might need to open the parent table in datasheet view to find the correct related record because not all the parent records are included in the query.

10. After editing the child records, close the datasheet.

11. On the Tools menu, click Relationships. In the Relationships window, right-click the relationship line between the tables and choose Edit Relationship. In the Edit Relationship dialog box, select Enforce Referential Integrity.

If you see a message about the primary table not having a unique index, try these steps:

1. Click OK to clear the message.

2. Right-click in the parent table title bar, and click Table Design on the shortcut menu.

3. Select the field you want to use in the relationship, and set the Indexed property to Yes (No Duplicates). ▶

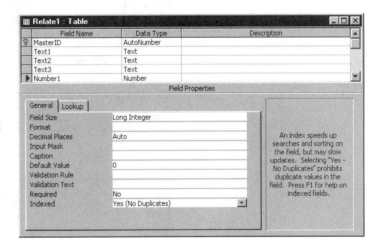

4. Save and close the table design window.

5. In the Edit Relationships dialog box, select the Enforce Referential Integrity check box and then click OK.

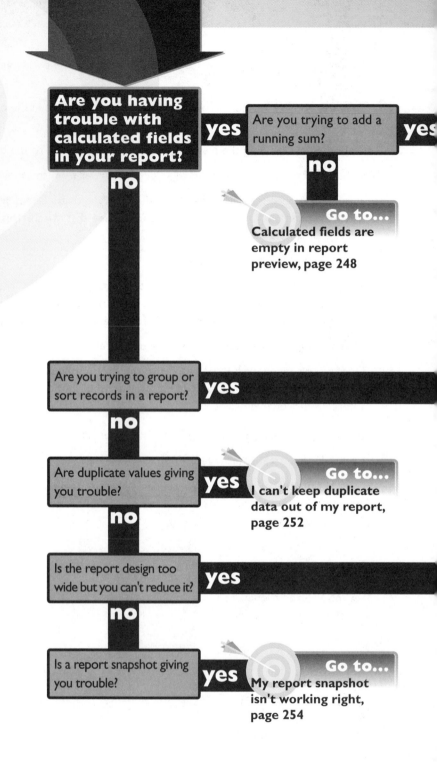

Are you having trouble with calculated fields in your report?

yes → Are you trying to add a running sum? **yes**

no

Go to...
Calculated fields are empty in report preview, page 248

Are you trying to group or sort records in a report? **yes**

no

Are duplicate values giving you trouble? **yes**

Go to...
I can't keep duplicate data out of my report, page 252

no

Is the report design too wide but you can't reduce it? **yes**

no

Is a report snapshot giving you trouble? **yes**

Go to...
My report snapshot isn't working right, page 254

Quick fix

You need to place the control for the running sum in the detail section of the report, not the group footer section.

1. Add a text box control to the detail section of your report.
2. Right-click the control, and then click Properties.
3. On the Data tab, enter the name of the field you want to tally in the Control Source property box.
4. In the Running Sum property, select Over All to keep the sum going through the report or Over Group to reset the sum to zero at each new group.

Do you want to sort on a field not in the report?

yes

no

Go to...

I can't group records in a report the way I want, page 250

Quick fix

You don't have to show the field in the report to sort records with it.

1. Make sure the field you want to sort with is in the table or query used by the report.
2. Click Sorting And Grouping on the View menu.
3. Enter the field name in the Field/Expression box and choose the Sort Order.

Quick fix

There is probably a line drawn across the report design.

1. Drag the report section boundaries down one at a time to locate lines drawn to the right margin.
2. Resize the lines to fit the width you want.
3. Restore the section heights to their original settings.

If your solution isn't here

Check these related chapters:

Controls—Managing data, page 12
Controls—Placing & formatting, page 24
Reports—Previewing & printing, page 256
Or see the general troubleshooting tips on page xiii.

Calculated fields are empty in report preview

Source of the problem

We've all been taught that arithmetic never fails to give us the right answer if we ask the right question. Two plus two always equals four, right? Then how come some of the calculated fields in your report have the right answer and some of them are blank? The answer to that question lies in the Access philosophy that no answer at all is better than the wrong answer.

When you put a calculated text box control in a report, you enter an expression that calculates the value the control displays. If the expression uses any of the math operators and one of the fields in the expression includes Null (or blank) values, the entire expression is calculated as Null and the field is blank in the report. If some of the calculated values are blank and others show the values you expected, chances are one of the fields you used in the expression includes a Null value in some records.

The following solution shows a way to solve this problem.

How to fix it

When you preview your report, you see blanks where there should be results of a calculation in both the detail and the group header sections. Follow these steps:

1. In the database window, select the report and then click Design.

2. Click the control that sometimes displays blank fields.

3. On the toolbar, click the Properties button.

4. In the Control Source property box, enter an expression using the Nz function—for

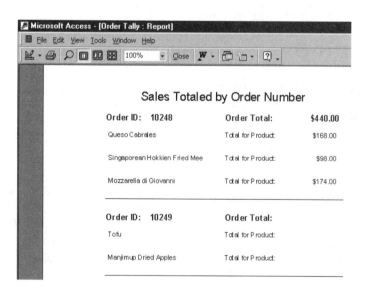

example, **Nz([UnitPrice])*Nz([Quantity])*Nz((1-[Discount]))**. UnitPrice, Quantity, and Discount are the fields whose values are being used in the calculation. The Nz function changes all Null values to zero to prevent the expression from returning blank values. ▶

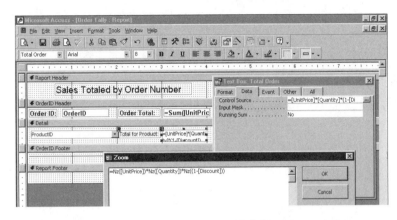

5. Click the Preview button to view the report.

6. If you included the calculated field in the group header, you'll see that it's still blank. Click the View button to switch to design view.

7. In the group header section, right-click the control that displays blanks and click Properties on the shortcut menu.

8. In the Control Source property box, add an expression using the Nz function as in step 4 above.

9. Preview the report again.

Heading blanks off at the pass

If you have access to the tables used in the report and can modify their design, you can make sure the field you use in the calculation doesn't contain Null values. In the database window, select the table used in the report and open it in design view. Select a field you want to use in a calculation. In the Field Properties pane, set the Required property for that field to Yes. Set the Required property to Yes for any other fields that you want to use in calculations.

Click the Save button, and then click Yes when you see the message about testing existing data for compliance with the change in the Required property setting. You'll probably see another message indicating that existing data violates the new setting. Click Yes to keep the setting and continue. (If you click No, you'll return the Required property to No; if you click Cancel, you'll stop the testing altogether.) Save the table, and then click the View button to switch to datasheet view. Click in the field (or fields) with the new setting, locate the records with blank fields, and enter the required data. You can then return to the report design and enter the calculations you need free from concern.

Tip

If you see *#Error* instead of a blank or a value in a control in the group header section of your report, you might have entered an expression in this control that uses the name of a calculated control you put in the detail section of your report. When entering an expression in the group header control (which uses the Sum function), you have to include the entire expression from the calculated control in the detail section. You can't simply refer to the name of the control.

I can't group records in a report the way I want

Source of the problem

They say there's safety in numbers. If that old adage is true, a report that groups a bunch of records to come up with conclusions can be a big help at the next corporate get-together. Access makes it so easy to group records to display summaries of your data that it's hard to imagine anything going wrong. But Murphy is alive and well—even in Access. Some of the problems you might have faced include the following:

- Your records aren't really grouped. You might have failed to include a group header or footer in the report design. You must set one of these properties to Yes in the Sorting And Grouping dialog box or the records will be just sorted and not grouped.

- You're grouping by two different fields, and you grouped the fields in the wrong sequence. For example, if you're trying to group by year and then by quarter within each year, you might have set the quarter group above the year group in the Sorting And Grouping dialog box. This would group by quarter first and then by year within each quarter.

The following solutions provide ways to overcome these problems.

How to fix it

To make sure your records are grouped, follow these steps:

1. In the database window, select the report and then click Design.

2. On the View menu, click Sorting And Grouping.

3. In the Field/Expression column, click in the row for the field you entered earlier for grouping the records.

4. In the Group Properties pane, set either the Group Header or Group Footer property to Yes. You can set both to Yes if you like. ▶

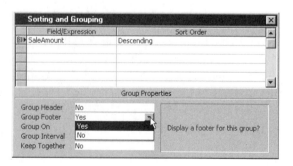

5. Close the Sorting And Grouping dialog box, click the Save button, and then preview the report.

To change the order of record grouping in the report, do the following:

1. Open the report in design view, and then click Sorting And Grouping on the View menu.

2. In the Sorting And Grouping dialog box, click the row selector (the small gray box at the left end of the row) for the field you want to move. ▶

3. Drag the row selector up or down to position the field where you want it.

4. Close the Sorting And Grouping dialog box, and then click the Preview button to view the report.

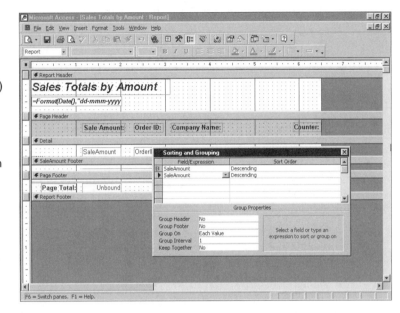

Heads up on headers

When you have large groups of records that span more than one page in your report, it's handy to have the group header information printed on the spillover pages. By doing this, you can keep track of the column headings and other information without having to look back at the page that contains the group header. To do this, click the section boundary for the group header section and then click the Properties button on the toolbar. Set the Repeat Section property to Yes. Unfortunately, if a new group happens to start at the top of a page, you might see two lines of the group header information.

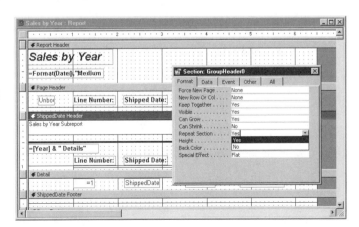

I can't keep duplicate data out of my report

Source of the problem

Long lists of duplicate values not only clutter up a report, they can also cause someone studying your report (like your boss) to doze off as her eye follows the tedious repetition. A report can be cleaner and more effective if you can find a way to print the value only once. But the other values in the records are important, so you can't simply leave the records out. You might have had trouble in a couple of situations:

- You created a report with records that are sorted on one or more fields and have found many records with the same values in those fields clustered together. While all the information is important, you still don't need all those copies.

- You grouped the records by one or more fields and the duplicate values all appear in the detail section because they occur in each record. ▶

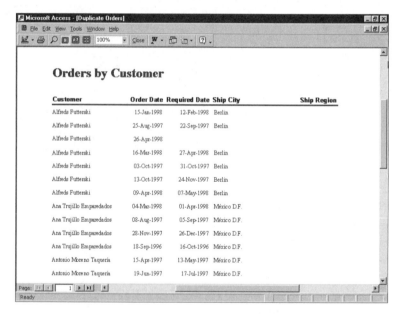

The following solutions describe ways to solve problems with duplicate data in reports.

How to fix it

If your report is based on sorted records, follow these steps:

1. In the database window, select the report and then click Design.

2. Click the control that displays duplicate values, and then click the Properties button on the toolbar.

3. In the property dialog box, set the control's Hide Duplicates property to Yes. ▶

4. Repeat steps 2 and 3 for other controls that you have sorted on and found duplicate values.

5. Click the Save button, and then preview the report. ▶

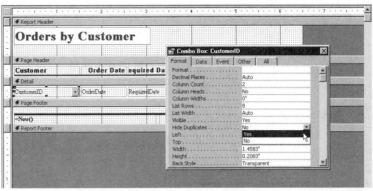

If you grouped records in the report and don't want to see the duplicates in the detail section, you can use one of the two following ways to solve the problem, depending on whether you want the detail value printed on the same line or in the group header. If you want to print the duplicate value on the same line as the first record in the detail section, leave the field in the detail section of the report and then follow these steps:

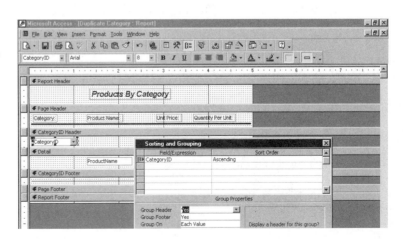

1. Right-click the field control, and then click Properties on the shortcut menu.

2. Set the Hide Duplicates property to Yes.

If you don't need the duplicate value printed on the same line as the first detail record, follow these steps:

1. Click the field in the detail section and drag it to the group header section. ▶

2. Click the Preview button to view the report.

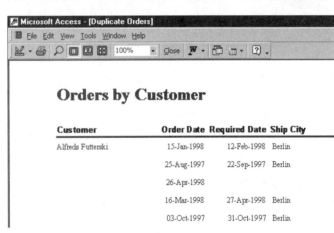

My report snapshot isn't working right

Source of the problem

Whoever invented the report snapshot is a genius and an honest supporter of preserving our forests. Report snapshots, which are new to Access 2000, provide a way to distribute a high-fidelity version of the report that preserves all the layout, graphics, and other embedded objects without having to print a gazillion copies. It's a separate file that can be e-mailed to anybody. Then they can print as much of the report as they need.

Just because it's a great invention doesn't mean a report snapshot can't cause trouble. For example, you might have had trouble creating or opening a snapshot. If you have permission to open the file and it is in fact a snapshot file (with an .snp file extension), it might be too big for the disk space available on your computer. Or you might not have the Snapshot Viewer program installed. Access usually installs the viewer when you create a report snapshot, but you might not yet have created and saved one.

Another problem you might have encountered is that you created and saved the report snapshot and now you can't find it. The snapshot is saved as a separate file outside the Access database. You decide where to store the file when you export the report.

The following solutions describe how to combat these problems.

How to fix it

If you see a message that the snapshot file is too big for remaining disk space, do the following:

1. On the Windows desktop, click the Start button and point to Programs.

2. Click Windows Explorer. (Depending on your version of Windows, you might need to click Accessories first.)

3. Select a folder that you use often, such as My Documents, and on the View menu, click Details.

4. On the View menu, point to Arrange Icons and click By Size.

5. Scroll down to the bottom of the list, select large files that you no longer need, and then click Delete on the File menu.

6. Continue deleting files until you have enough disk space to save the report snapshot.

> **Warning**
> Be careful which files you delete. Don't delete files with an .exe file extension or those with the extension .dll, for example. These are program and system files needed to run the programs on your computer.

If the Snapshot Viewer isn't installed, you have not created any report snapshots yet. Run the Microsoft Office Setup program again to add it.

1. To start the setup, click Start on the Windows taskbar, point to Settings, and then click Control Panel.

2. Double-click Add/Remove Programs, and then scroll down to select Microsoft Office.

3. Depending on your version of Windows, click Add/Remove or Change. Follow the instructions in the series of dialog boxes to install the Snapshot Viewer.

If you exported a report to a report snapshot and can't find the snapshot, the first place to look is where the file would be stored by default:

1. In the database window, select a report.

2. On the File menu, click Export.

3. In the Export Report dialog box, select Snapshot Format in the Save As Type box. ▶

4. If you see the file you want, note the folder that's open, click Cancel, and return to the database window.

5. On the Windows desktop, click Start, point to Programs, and then click Windows Explorer. (Depending on your version of Windows, you might need to click Accessories first.)

6. In the Folders pane, open the folder that you viewed in step 4. ▶

7. In the right pane, double-click the snapshot file you want to view. The Snapshot Viewer starts automatically.

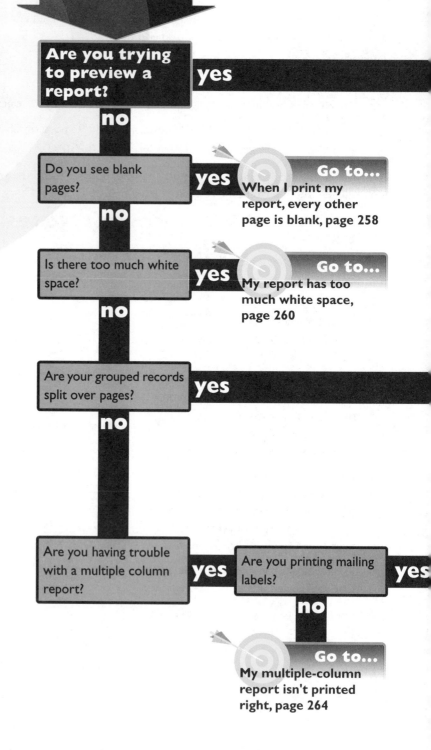

Reports—Pre

Are you trying to preview a report? — **yes**

no

Do you see blank pages? — **yes** — Go to... **When I print my report, every other page is blank, page 258**

no

Is there too much white space? — **yes** — Go to... **My report has too much white space, page 260**

no

Are your grouped records split over pages? — **yes**

no

Are you having trouble with a multiple column report? — **yes** — **Are you printing mailing labels?** — **yes**

no

Go to... **My multiple-column report isn't printed right, page 264**

Is data missing from the report preview? **yes**

Quick fix

You might be looking at the report in layout preview, which shows just enough data for you to see how each section will look.

1. To preview the full report, close layout preview by clicking Design View on the View menu.
2. On the View menu, click Print Preview.

no

Are you prompted for a report title you don't expect? **yes**

Quick fix

You set the title control so you can print the report with a different title each time. Do the following:

1. Open the report in design view.
2. Look for a text box control in the report or page header containing a prompt expression—for example, =[Enter report title:].
3. Delete the control.
4. Save the report design.

Quick fix

The Keep Together properties are not set correctly.

1. Open the report in design view, and then click Sorting And Grouping on the View menu.
2. Set the Keep Together group property to With First Detail.
3. Close the Sorting And Grouping dialog box.
4. Right-click the group section bar, and then click Properties.
5. Set the Keep Together property to Yes.

Go to...

Some of my mailing labels are blank, page 262

If your solution isn't here
Check these related chapters:
    Reports—Creating, page 246
Or see the general troubleshooting tips on page xiii.

When I print my report, every other page is blank

Source of the problem

It's bad enough to print on only one side of the page, but to find that your report was printed on only every other page is really too much. A quick look at the pages with words and numbers on them convinces you that you aren't missing any data from your report. Was your printer just taking a quick breath after pumping out each page?

Actually, the reason this problem occurs—and it occurs often—is very simple. Something is causing your report design to be wider or longer than the page you're trying to print on. There are several reasons for this:

- The total width of the report plus the right and left margins exceeds the specified page width.

- Some controls have been placed outside the page dimensions, so some of the data appears on a spillover page or the page might be blank. This could occur if you used the Report Wizard.

- The settings in the Page Setup dialog box are overriding the settings in the report itself.

The following solutions give you ways to solve these problems.

How to fix it

If every other page is printed blank, follow these steps:

1. In the database window, select the report and then click Design.

2. Look at the controls near the right edge of the report. Move or resize these controls so they're not as close to the edge.

3. Click the right edge of the report page (not the report design window) and drag it to the left to reduce the report width.

4. Click the Preview button and look at several pages.

5. If these steps didn't work, click Page Setup on the File menu and then click the Margins tab. ▶

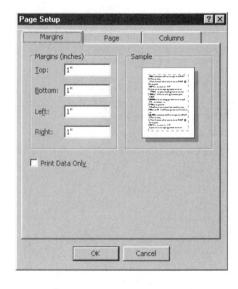

6. Reduce the width of the right or left margin, or both. Click OK.

7. Click the Preview button to view the report.

If you used the Report Wizard to create the report, you probably didn't select the Adjust The Field Width So All Fields Fit On A Page check box. Since you can't go back and change settings in the Report Wizard, you'll have to correct this by hand.

1. With the report open in design view, move the controls in all the sections to fit within the page width you need. For example, if you're printing on standard 8.5-by-11-inch paper, narrow the report design to 6.5 inches. Custom paper might require a narrower print width.

2. Click the right border of the report page and drag it to the width you want.

3. Click the Preview button to see whether you still have empty pages. If you do, return to design view.

4. On the File menu, click Page Setup and then click the Columns tab.

5. In the Column Size area, select the Same As Detail check box. ▶

6. Click OK, and then click the Preview button to view the report.

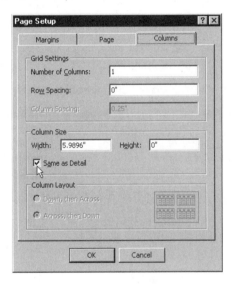

Practice good report management

It's always a good idea to preview several pages of a report before printing it to avoid problems such as the ones mentioned in this solution. It's even more important to catch errors before they show up in print if you're printing on expensive paper stock or mailing labels.

My report has too much white space

Source of the problem

Busy people, like our bosses, don't want to spend their time flipping pages in a report that's too long. "Keep it simple" is the motto. Reports should present information in a concise and easily interpretable style. One way your report can take up too many pages is by leaving too much empty space. Here are some possible causes of this problem:

- You left too much space between the controls in the report design, either vertically or horizontally.

- You left too much space between the report sections when you designed the report.

- Some of the controls you added to the report design are larger than they need to be to contain the data they display.

- Some of the text box controls are bound to varied-length text fields and are empty or only partially filled for some records, leaving too much white space. You can set these controls so that they shrink to fit the contents.

Here are ways to modify the report design to fix these problems.

How to fix it

1. In the database window, select the report and then click Design.

2. Hold down the Shift key and click controls spaced vertically. On the Format menu, click Vertical Spacing and then click Decrease. ▶

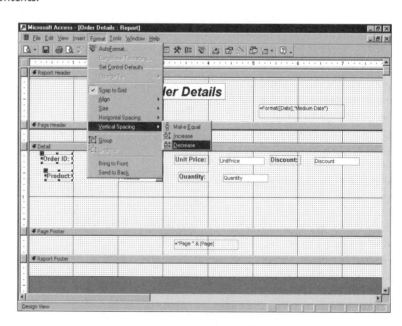

3. Click unnecessary labels, and then press Delete to delete the labels and close up the horizontal spacing. After removing the labels, you can probably move more controls to the same line.

4. Right-click any text box controls, and then click Properties on the shortcut menu. In the Height property box, reduce the setting as much as possible.

5. Drag controls to reposition them at the top of the sections they occupy. Drag the section boundaries up to reduce the space between the information printed in the sections. If there are no controls in the header or footer sections, reduce these areas to 0.

6. Click the Preview button to view the report. ▶

Tip

After each change to the report design, switch to print preview to see the effect on reducing white space. When you're satisfied with the result, save the report.

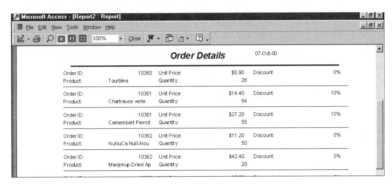

To set up text box controls so that they display only the amount of information necessary, do this:

1. With the report open in design view, right-click a control that's the cause of empty space and then click Properties on the shortcut menu.

2. Click the Format tab, and set the Can Shrink property to Yes. Repeat for other controls.

3. Right-click the detail section border, and click Properties on the shortcut menu.

4. Set the Can Shrink property to Yes. ▶

5. Click the Preview button to view the report.

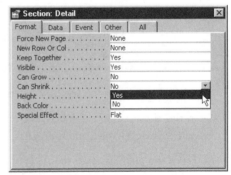

Some caveats on Can Shrink

You should know a few things about using the Can Shrink property to reduce white space. Can Shrink reduces only the height of the section or control and doesn't affect the space between controls. You can apply the Can Shrink property to the report header and footer sections as well as the detail section, but the page header and footer sections have no Can Shrink property. The height of a large control can prevent other controls in the same section from shrinking because the section shrinks line by line—there's no point in shrinking one control if another gets in the way.

Some of my mailing labels are blank

Source of the problem

One of the prized talents of Access is its ability to take a table full of names and addresses and turn it into pages of printed mailing labels. Access can do this with the help of Microsoft Word's Mail Merge feature or all on its own. Mailing label stock is expensive, and when you see a page of printed labels missing a few addresses, it's not a trivial problem. You can't really put the page back through the printer to fill up the blanks. Here are two reasons you might have encountered blank mailing labels:

● If the blanks occur in groups, the underlying table might have no values in the fields you're sorting the records on. (This could also be true if the blank labels are scattered, but they're not so obvious.)

● If you see a blank row at the bottom of the label page, you might be using a printer that skips the last row. You don't lose any of the data, but the last row of labels on the sheet are wasted.

The following solutions describe how to solve these problems.

How to fix it

If you see groups of blank labels, do the following:

1. In the database window, click Queries and then click New.

2. In the New Query dialog box, select Design View and then click OK.

3. In the Show Table dialog box, click the Table tab, select the table that contains the names and addresses, click Add, and then click Close.

4. From the field list, drag the fields you want to use in the labels to the query grid.

5. In the Criteria row of each field, enter **Is Not Null**. ▶

6. Click the Run button on the toolbar.

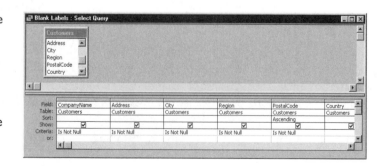

7. If you're happy with the results, save the query. If you're not, return to the query design view and make more changes to the selection criteria.

8. When you're satisfied with the query results, re-create the mailing labels based on the new query instead of the original table.

Some printers set a large top margin by default, which causes the last row of labels to be printed on the next page. If the last row of your labels is blank, try the following:

Tip

If you don't specify a sort order when you create labels with the Label Wizard, the labels are arranged in ascending order based on the first field in the table. If you base the labels on a query, they're sorted by the values in the left-most column in the query grid.

1. In either design view or print preview, click Page Setup on the File menu.

2. Click the Margins tab, and change the Top setting in the Margins section to 0.25. ▶

3. Click OK.

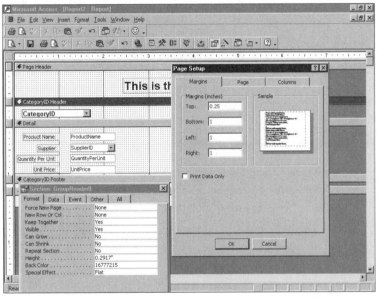

You don't have to depend on the Label Wizard

You can always create your own label design by starting a new multiple-column report with only a detail section. There are several neat tools you can use to create just the right disk label or personalized bookplates for the books in your library. The three functions that eliminate spaces when you put variable-length text values together are very useful for creating labels. The RTrim function removes spaces after the last character, while LTrim removes the spaces before the first character. Plain old Trim removes both the leading and trailing spaces. When you use these functions, be sure to add a space between the text controls or they will run together. For example, the expression =Trim([FirstName]&" "&[LastName]) displays the first and last names separated by a space but without any leading or trailing spaces.

The Can Shrink and Can Grow field properties are also very useful. Setting Can Shrink to Yes will prevent blank lines in mailing labels. Setting Can Grow to Yes adjusts the field vertically to accommodate extra lines in the printed label. See the solution "My report has too much white space" for information about applying the Can Shrink property.

My multiple-column report isn't printed right

Source of the problem

When you have a long list of items to print in a report, it helps save space if you build the report to show the data in multiple columns. The Access Report Wizard is no help in this project, so you're on your own.

Multiple-column reports can present you with some unique problems that you don't have to worry about when designing regular reports. They require special consideration when it comes to arranging the data on the page and making sure that the report is readable—that the header information actually points to the corresponding data, for example. You might have encountered one of the following problems while building a multiple-column report:

● You told Access you wanted to see the data arranged in three columns in the report, but when you preview the report you see only one.

● You decided to add another column to the report, but Access warns you that there isn't enough room for the new column. In another case, the additional column is printed on the next page instead of with the other columns the way you wanted.

The following solutions show you how to combat these and other problems with multiple-column reports.

How to fix it

If you see only one column instead of the number you specified in the Page Setup dialog box, do the following:

1. In the database window, select the report and then click Design.

2. On the File menu, click Page Setup.

3. On the Columns tab, in the Column Size section, clear the Same As Detail check box.

4. In the Width box, enter a smaller number. For example, if you're building a three-column report, enter 2" as the column width. Click OK. ▶

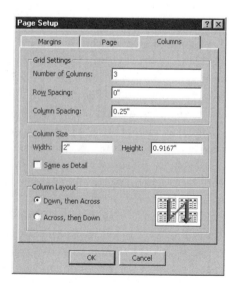

5. In the report design window, right-click the group header bar and then click Properties on the shortcut menu.

6. On the Format tab, set the New Row Or Col property to Before Section. Set the Repeat Section and Keep Together properties both to Yes.

7. Click the Preview button to view the report.

If you chose to arrange the columns across and then down in the Page Setup dialog box, you might see the warning message shown in the figure. ▶

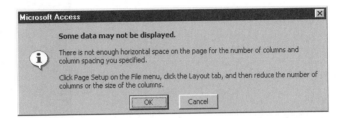

Microsoft Access

Some data may not be displayed.

There is not enough horizontal space on the page for the number of columns and column spacing you specified.

Click Page Setup on the File menu, click the Layout tab, and then reduce the number of columns or the size of the columns.

OK   Cancel

1. Click Cancel in the message box to return to the report design view.

2. On the File menu, click Page Setup.

3. On the Columns tab, reduce the number of columns and reduce the column width. Click the Margins tab, and reduce the width of the left and right margins. Click OK.

4. In the report design window, move or rearrange the controls in the report design to fit in the narrower column width.

5. Click the Preview button to view the report.

Designer tips for multiple-column reports

In a multiple-column report, the record data can all run together and be very confusing if you don't add a few cosmetic touches. If you arranged the columns so that the data reads down and then across the page ("snaking columns"), put a dividing line in the group footer section and set the group header section's New Row Or Col property to Before Section.

If you arranged the columns across and then down, put a dividing line in the detail section beneath the detail controls and set the group header section's New Row Or Col property to Before & After.

Tip

You won't see this warning message if you have the columns arranged down and then across. The column that doesn't fit on the page just moves to the next page in the report.

Tip

The formula for calculating the maximum width of your multiple-column report is *Column width*Number of columns + Column spacing*(Number of columns –1) + right margin + left margin*, which must add up to less than or equal to the page width.

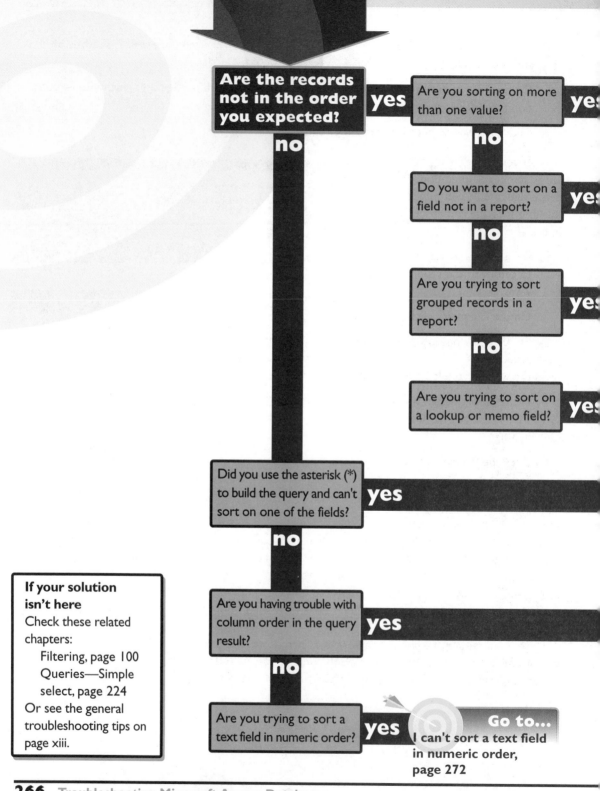

Are the records not in the order you expected? — yes → **Are you sorting on more than one value?** — yes

no

Do you want to sort on a field not in a report? — yes

no

Are you trying to sort grouped records in a report? — yes

no

Are you trying to sort on a lookup or memo field? — yes

no

Did you use the asterisk (*) to build the query and can't sort on one of the fields? — yes

no

Are you having trouble with column order in the query result? — yes

no

Are you trying to sort a text field in numeric order? — yes → **Go to...** I can't sort a text field in numeric order, page 272

If your solution isn't here
Check these related chapters:
   Filtering, page 100
   Queries—Simple select, page 224
Or see the general troubleshooting tips on page xiii.

Sorting

Go to...
My records aren't in the order I want, page 268

Quick fix

If the field is part of the underlying table or query, do the following:

1. Open the report in design view.
2. Click the Sorting And Grouping button.
3. In the Field/Expression column, select the field to sort by and then set the sort order.

Go to...
I can't sort grouped records in a report the way I want, page 274

Go to...
I'm having trouble sorting on lookup and memo fields, page 270

Quick fix

The sort field must appear individually in the query grid.

1. Open the query in design view.
2. Drag the field to the grid next to the column with the *.
3. Set the desired sort order.
4. Clear the Show box for the added field.

Quick fix

You need to add the field you want to sort by to the query again.

1. Open the query in design view.
2. Drag a second instance of the sort field to the grid where you want it to appear in the query result.
3. Check the Show box for this field.
4. Clear the Show box for the first instance of the field.

My records aren't in the order I want

Source of the problem

Sorting records in Access can be easier than sorting your laundry on wash day. It's a very mechanical process that you shouldn't have to think about too deeply. But to make it simple and achieve the correct results, you have to get all the pieces together in the right places at the start. Access, like all computer programs, does only what you say, not what you meant to say. If you sort on the wrong field or in the wrong order, you're likely to get the wrong results.

When you're sorting on more than one field and you get the wrong results, the problem is usually that you sorted your data in the wrong sequence. Access first sorts by one field and then, within each group of equal values in that field, sorts by the next field, and so on. You tell Access which field to start with by where you place fields in a datasheet or the query grid. Fields are arranged in order of sorting precedence, from left to right. In a report, you can sort on more than one field by using the Sorting And Grouping feature.

The following solutions show you ways to solve this assortment of problems.

How to fix it

If you're sorting records by more than one field in a datasheet, follow these steps:

1. In the datasheet, drag the column containing the field you want to sort by first to the left of the other columns you want to sort by. This column doesn't need to be at the far left of the datasheet. ▶

2. Drag the other columns you want to sort by to positions to the right of and adjacent to the first column, in order of sorting precedence.

Address	Country	City	Region	Postal Code	Phone	
Obere Str. 57	Germany	Berlin		12209	030-0074321	030
Avda. de la Constitución 2222	Mexico	México D.F.		05021	(5) 555-4729	(5)
Mataderos 2312	Mexico	México D.F.		05023	(5) 555-3932	
120 Hanover Sq.	UK	London		WA1 1DP	(171) 555-7788	(17
Berguvsvägen 8	Sweden	Luleå		S-958 22	0921-12 34 65	092
Forsterstr. 57	Germany	Mannheim		68306	0621-08460	062
24, place Kléber	France	Strasbourg		67000	88.60.15.31	88.
C/ Araquil, 67	Spain	Madrid		28023	(91) 555 22 82	(91
12, rue des Bouchers	France	Marseille		13008	91.24.45.40	91.
23 Tsawassen Blvd.	Canada	Tsawassen	BC	T2F 8M4	(604) 555-4729	(60
Fauntleroy Circus	UK	London		EC2 5NT	(171) 555-1212	
Cerrito 333	Argentina	Buenos Aires		1010	(1) 135-5555	(1)
Sierras de Granada 9993	Mexico	México D.F.		05022	(5) 555-3392	(5)
Hauptstr. 29	Switzerland	Bern		3012	0452-076545	
Av. dos Lusíadas, 23	Brazil	São Paulo	SP	05432-043	(11) 555-7647	
Berkeley Gardens	UK	London		WX1 6LT	(171) 555-2282	(17
Walserweg 21	Germany	Aachen		52066	0241-039123	024
67, rue des Cinquante Otages	France	Nantes		44000	40.67.88.88	40.
35 King George	UK	London		WX3 6FW	(171) 555-0297	(17
Kirchgasse 6	Austria	Graz		8010	7675-3425	767
Rua Orós, 92	Brazil	São Paulo	SP	05442-030	(11) 555-9857	
C/ Moralzarzal, 86	Spain	Madrid		28034	(91) 555 94 44	(91
184, chaussée de Tournai	France	Lille		59000	20.16.10.16	20.
Åkergatan 24	Sweden	Bräcke		S-844 67	0695-34 67 21	
Berliner Platz 43	Germany	München		80805	089-0877310	089
54, rue Royale	France	Nantes		44000	40.32.21.21	40.

3. Select the columns for the fields you want to sort by.

4. On the toolbar, click the Sort Ascending or Sort Descending button. The records will be sorted following the order in which you arranged the fields.

If you need to sort by more than one field in a query, follow these steps:

1. In the database window, select the query and then click Design.

2. In the query grid, position the fields from left to right in order of sort precedence. The fields don't need to be in contiguous columns.

3. In the Sort row, set the sort order for each field.

To sort records in a report by more than one field, do the following:

1. In the Database window, select the report and then click Design.

2. On the View menu, click Sorting And Grouping.

3. In the Field/Expression list, select the name of the field by which you want to sort first. ▶

4. In the Sort Order column, select the sort order you want.

5. Select the second field you want to sort by, and then set the sort order for that field.

6. Click the Preview button on the toolbar to see the results of the sort process.

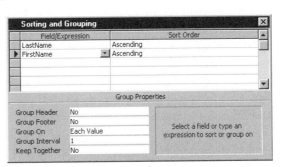

What about sorting in a form?

If you're sorting records in a form, you can sort on only one field, so you have to use other methods to fine-tune the sort order if you need to sort by more than one field—creating a query on which to base the form.

Create the query, basing it on the tables containing the data you'll work with in the form. In the query design window, add the fields that will appear in the form to the query design grid. Set the sort order for the query by positioning the fields in the query grid in left-to-right sequence, according to sort precedence. Then save and name the query.

Now that you have the query, create the new form and base it on the query. The form inherits the sort order you set up in the query. You can, of course, place the fields anywhere you want on the form design and the records will still be sorted correctly.

I'm having trouble sorting on lookup and memo fields

Source of the problem

Lookup fields can be deceiving. For one thing, they display a different value from the value stored in the table that the lookup field refers to. This means that sorting on a lookup field can have unsettling results. When you design a query to retrieve records and set the sort order for a lookup field in the query design grid, you sort on the stored value, not on the value that's displayed. If that isn't confusing enough, when you sort the records by the lookup field in the query results datasheet, you're sorting by the displayed value, not the stored value.

Sorting on memo fields can also present problems. Why anyone would want to sort records on the basis of what is usually miscellaneous text is a mystery, and Microsoft probably didn't think anyone would want to, so they didn't provide sorting for memo fields in most situations. If you set the Order By property for a form to the name of a memo field, it is ignored. In datasheets and form views, the sort buttons aren't available when you click in a column or control for a memo field. In addition, a memo field name isn't included in the Sorting And Grouping dialog box in report design. Although the online help in Access says you can't sort on memo fields, there are exceptions to this statement.

The following solutions show you how to solve these problems.

> **Tip**
> The same sorting problem happens when you try to filter records in a query based on the value in a lookup field. To achieve the correct results, you must use the stored value in the filter expression instead of the displayed value in the Criteria cell of the query grid or in the Advanced Filter/Sort window.

How to fix it

If you're trying to sort on a lookup field, follow these steps:

1. In the database window, select the query with the lookup field you want to sort by and click Open. Review the order of the returned records.

> **Tip**
> If you use a query that's sorted by a lookup field as the basis for a form, you'll encounter the same sorting problem. Click in the lookup field's control in form view, and then click the Sort Ascending or Sort Descending button.

2. Click in the lookup field's column in the query result datasheet. ▶

3. On the toolbar, click one of the Sort buttons to sort by displayed values.

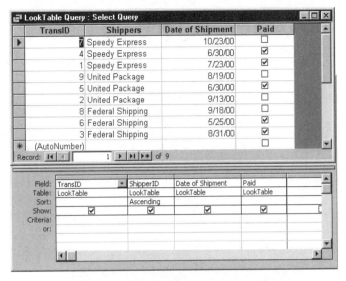

To sort on a memo field in a report, follow these steps:

1. In the database window, select the report and then click Design.

2. On the View menu, click Sorting And Grouping.

3. In the Field/Expression box, type the name of the memo field. ▶

4. In the Sort Order box, select the sort order you want.

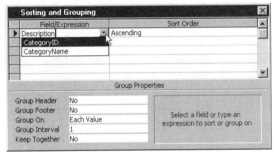

Tip

If you're trying to sort on a memo field in a form, create a query that includes the memo field and set the sort order for the memo field in the Sort row of the query design grid. Then you can use the query as the basis for a form.

Other tricky sorts

You can never sort on an OLE Object field, no matter where it sits or how hard you try. Whether you can sort on a memo or hyperlink field depends on where it occurs—in a table, query, form, or report. Here are some general guidelines:

● You can't sort on memo or hyperlink fields in tables or forms.

● You can always set the sort order for a memo or hyperlink field in a query.

● You can sort on memo and hyperlink fields in a report if you type the field name in the Field/Expression box in the Sorting And Grouping dialog box. The memo and hyperlink names are not included in the drop-down list in the box.

I can't sort a text field in numeric order

Source of the problem

Everyone has to mix apples and oranges once in a while. Similarly, sorting numeric data in a text field might sound unusual, but at times it's important to do so. For example, let's say you've created a database to manage projects and the individual tasks within each project. To identify tasks, you use a field named ProjectItem, which is composed of a series of numbers followed by no more than one letter. In this field you have entries such as 101A, 25A, 25B, 59A, 632B, 250C, 1001C, and 5000.

When you sort a text field, the values are sorted from left to right in alphabetic order. When you sort a field with the Number data type, the values are sorted in numeric order. With a field such as ProjectItem, which includes both numbers and letters, you need to split the value into the numeric portion and the alphabetic portion to sort the field numerically. You need to maintain a certain field value structure, however, to sort in this way. Notice that the sample values above limit the number of trailing alphabetic characters to one. The normal sorting order for this field yields the results shown in the figure.

The following solution shows you how to solve the problem of sorting text fields in numeric order.

How to fix it

1. In the database window, click Queries and then click New. In the New Query dialog box, click OK.

2. In the Show Table dialog box, select the table that includes the field with both numbers and letters. Click Add, and then click Close.

3. Drag the fields you want to the query grid, including the field with text and numbers. You probably want at least the primary key field in the query results.

4. In the Field row of a blank column in the query grid, enter an expression such as **NBR: Val([ProjectItem])** to retrieve the number portion of the field value. NBR is the name of the expression. Val is a function that returns the numeric value of a field. (See "About the functions used in this solution" on the next page for a more detailed explanation.)

5. In the Sort row for this column, set the sort order to Ascending.

6. Clear the Show box for that column.

7. In another new column, add an expression such as **LTR: IIf(Val(Right$([ProjectItem],1))=0, Right$([ProjectItem],1),"")** . The LTR expression isolates the alphabetic portion of the field

value. It uses the IIf function to test the right-most
character in the field with
numbers and letters. If the
value of that character is 0,
the character is alphabetic
and is included in the sort
process. Otherwise, it is
ignored. ▶

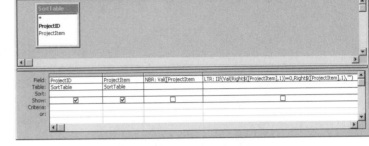

8. In the Sort row for this
column, select Ascending.

9. Clear the Show box in that column.

10. Run the query. ▶

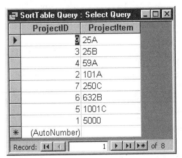

Tip

When you close a table after
sorting the records in it,
you're asked if you want to
save the changes you made,
including the sort order. Click
Yes to save the sort order. The
next time you open the table,
the records will appear in the
same order. If you click No,
the records revert to their
original primary key order.

Tip

Another way to sort numbers
numerically in a text field is to
fill the field with leading zeros.
The numbers will all be the
same length and will sort in
correct numeric order. If you
know there will never be alphabetic characters in the
field, simply change the data
type of the field to Number.

About the functions used in this solution

The Val() function returns the numeric value of the field
and ignores any alphabetic characters. It actually stops
reading the numbers as soon as it encounters the first
non-numeric character. The IIf() function returns one
value if the condition specified in the function is true and
another value if it is false. In our example, this function
tests the right-most character to see if it is alphabetic
(value = 0). If the character is alphabetic, Access adds the
character to the value of the expression. If it is not, the
function ignores that character completely. The Right$()
function returns a string of characters containing a specified number of characters (1 in this case) from the right
end of a string.

I can't sort grouped records in a report the way I want

Source of the problem

You've created an innovative report that clearly demon-strates an upward trend in your business. The report groups records by the values in one of the fields, but when you pre-view the report the records in the detail section don't appear in the order you want. They're no longer in the order that you estab-lished in the table or query you used as the basis for the report.

This problem happens because when you group records in a report, the sort order the report inherits from the table or query the report's based on is over-ridden by the settings you make in the Sorting And Grouping dialog box.

In this example, records were sorted by product within product category, but after the records are grouped in the report, the sort order is disrupted. ▶

The following solu-tions give you ways to overcome this problem.

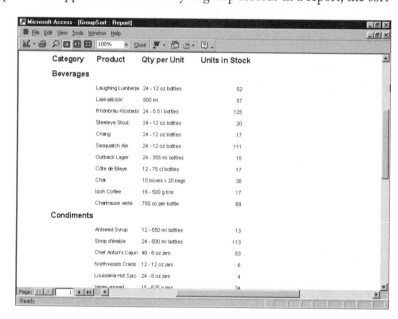

Tip

A report inherits several properties from the table or query it's based on. If you look at the report's Order By On property before you group the records, you'll see that it is set to Yes. After grouping, it's set to No.

How to fix it

If the records in the detail section of your report are not in the right sort order, do the following:

1. In the database window, select the report and then click Design.

2. On the View menu, click Sorting And Grouping.

3. In the first empty row below the row that sets the grouping, select the field you want to group the records by from the drop-down list. ▶

4. Leave Group Header and Group Footer properties for this field set to No.

5. Click the View button on the toolbar to preview the report. ▶

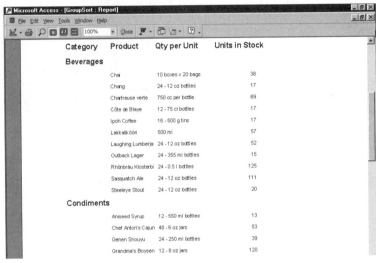

Rejecting inherited sort orders

If you haven't grouped records in a report but you still want to change the sort order the report inherits from its underlying table or query, open the report in design view, click the Properties button on the toolbar, and then set the Order By property to No. This reverts to the sort order in which the records were entered. You can also change the sort order for the report. To do this, leave the Order By On property set to Yes and enter the field name you want to sort by in the Order By property box, enclosed in brackets. If you want descending order instead of the default ascending order, type **DESC** after the field name. You can sort on more than one field by entering the field names separated by commas. You can also mix and match ascending and descending sort orders this way. For example, to sort the records by CategoryName in ascending order first and then by ProductName in descending order within each category, enter **[CategoryName],[ProductName] DESC** in the Order By property box.

Chasing those blanks away

If you don't want to include blank records in the groups in your report, create a new query and add the fields you want to see in the report to the query design grid. Click in the Criteria row of a field that you suspect contains blank values (either Null or zero-length strings) and enter the expression **Is Not Null.** Enter this expression for other fields that might contain blank values.

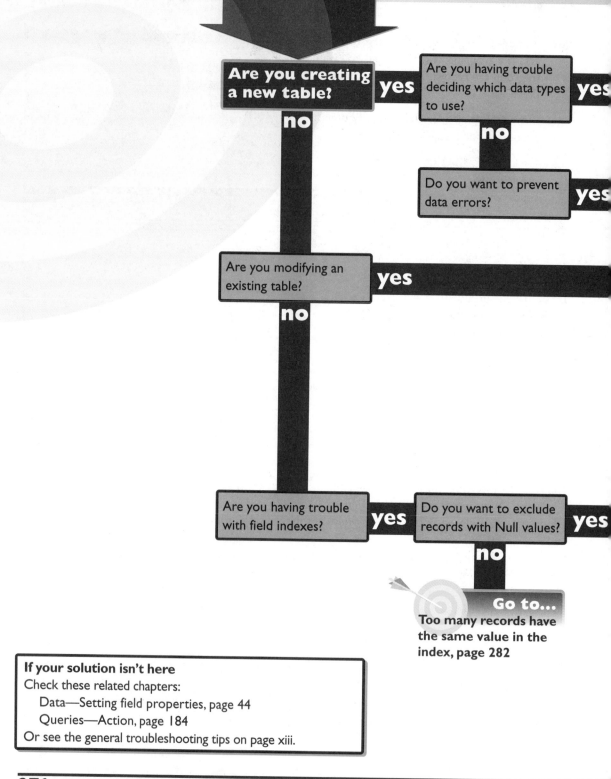

Are you creating a new table?

yes → Are you having trouble deciding which data types to use? → yes

no ↓

Are you having trouble deciding which data types to use?

no ↓

Do you want to prevent data errors? → yes

Are you modifying an existing table?

yes →

no ↓

Are you having trouble with field indexes?

yes → Do you want to exclude records with Null values? → yes

no ↓

Go to...
Too many records have the same value in the index, page 282

If your solution isn't here
Check these related chapters:
Data—Setting field properties, page 44
Queries—Action, page 184
Or see the general troubleshooting tips on page xiii.

Table design

Go to...

I don't know which data types and properties to choose in a new table, page 284

Go to...

I need to control errors in my data, page 280

Are you having trouble trying to delete a primary key field?

yes

no

Are you trying to set a primary key field?

yes

Go to...

I get an error message after designating a primary key, page 278

Quick fix

First delete the relationship between the field and other tables.

1. On the Tools menu, click Relationships.

2. Right-click the relationship line from the primary key field to the table it's related to.

3. Click Delete on the shortcut menu.

4. Return to the table design, and delete the primary key field.

Quick fix

1. Open the table in design view.

2. Click the Indexes button on the toolbar.

3. Select the name of the index from which you want to exclude Null values.

4. If the index doesn't have a name, re-create and name the index.

5. Set the Ignore Nulls property to Yes.

I get an error message after designating a primary key

Source of the problem

Primary keys are the essential key (no pun intended) to relational databases. They ensure that you don't enter duplicate records, and they provide a means to relate information in different tables. Because the rules governing primary keys are strict, it's easy to encounter problems.

If you don't designate a primary key field before you save a new table design, Access reminds you of this and asks whether you want to add one. You can click No to save the table without a primary key, but by clicking Yes, you have Access add an AutoNumber field named ID to the table and set it as the primary key.

If you enter records into the table before you designate a primary key field and save the table, you might see a message indicating some trouble. For example, you might have entered duplicate values in the field you want to designate as the primary key—but values in the primary key field need to be unique. Or the primary key field in one or more records might be blank. You can't leave a blank (or Null) value in a primary key field. The following solutions show how to get around these problems.

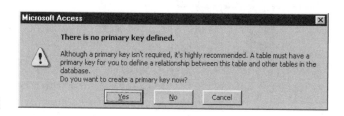

How to fix it

If you're trying to set a primary key and you get a message about duplicate values, follow these steps:

1. On the toolbar, click the Primary Key button to remove the primary key designation from the field.

2. Save changes to the table design, and then click the View button to switch to datasheet view.

3. Click in the column for the field you want to use as the primary key, and then click the Sort Ascending button to sort the records in that field.

4. Locate the duplicate values and edit them so they're no longer the same.

> **Tip**
> You can also create a primary key using two fields instead of just one. Then there may be no duplicates in the combination. Simply select both fields in the table design and click the Primary Key button.

5. Click the View button to switch to design view.

6. Select the field you want to use as the primary key, and then click the Primary Key button. ▶

7. Click the Save button.

If the message indicates that a record contains a Null value in the primary key field, follow these steps:

1. Click the Primary Key button to remove the primary key designation.

2. Click the Save button to save changes to the table design, and then click the View button to switch to datasheet view.

3. Click in the column for the field you want to use for the primary key, and then click the Sort Ascending button on the toolbar to display the blank records at the top of the column.

4. Enter data in the records where the field is blank.

5. Click the View button to switch to design view.

6. Select the field you want to use as the primary key, and then click the Primary Key button.

7. Click the Save button.

Do I really need a primary key?

No, you don't have to choose a primary key for every new table. But Access tries to help by reminding you when you haven't chosen one, and it even offers to create one for you. While primary keys are not required, they are recommended. If you plan to use the table in a relationship with other tables, you'll need to specify a primary key field, or at least a unique index.

Letting Access create a primary key field by adding a field to the table with the AutoNumber data type assures that no two records will be the same, an important feature in a relational database. If you specify as the primary key one of the fields you added to the table to contain data, it's up to you to make sure you don't enter duplicate values in it.

Tip
An additional advantage to having a primary key field in the table is that the records in the datasheet appear sorted by the primary key value by default. Of course, you can still sort the records any way you want.

I need to control errors in my data

Source of the problem

Humans, being what they are, make mistakes when entering data. Working with Access, you can try to prevent errors from being stored along with valid data in your database. Once incorrect or invalid data is in place, it's hard to find and correct. It's a lot more productive to keep it out of your database in the first place.

What can you do ahead of time to help ensure data accuracy? If a field's values must lie within a range of values or must be one of a few specific items in a list of values, you can apply a validation rule that limits the values entered in the field. The rule is enforced when you enter or edit data in that field, whether in datasheet view, in a form, or with an append or update query. You can also display a message to indicate that invalid data has been entered. Each table also has a validation rule property that you can use to compare field values and set restrictions. A record validation rule is enforced when you move to another record. A table can have only one record validation rule, so if you need more than one criterion, combine them in a single expression with *And* and *Or* operators.

How to fix it

To set up a field validation rule, follow these steps:

1. In the Database window, select the table and then click Design.

2. In the table design window, select the field you want to apply the rule to, and then click in the Validation Rule property box.

3. Enter an expression that controls the values the field can contain. For example, if the value in a date field must be less than one year from today, enter the expression **<Date()+365**. If the value in a number field must be greater than 0, enter **>0**. The rule can also limit the field to a short list of values—for example, **"Small" OR "Medium" OR "Large"**. Be sure to enclose any text in double quotation marks in the Validation Rule property box. ▶

4. Click in the Validation Text property box.

5. Enter a message that explains what's wrong with a value when an incorrect value is entered. ▶

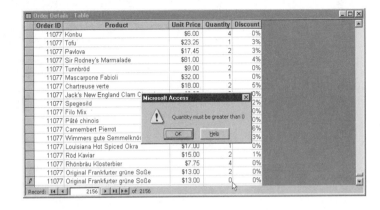

To set up a record validation rule for a table, do the following:

1. In the Database window, select the table and then click Design.

2. Click the Properties button on the toolbar.

3. In the Validation Rule property box, enter the record validation rule expression. For example, you could enter an expression that compares two amounts, such as **[SalesPrice]>[UnitPrice]**.

4. In the Validation Text property box, enter explanatory text about the rule. ▶

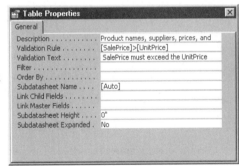

A few more tips about validation

If you add a field validation rule after data has been entered, Access offers to test the existing data against the rule. If you click No in response to the offer, you can still test the data later by switching to table design view and clicking Test Validation Rules on the Edit menu.

If users are entering data in a form, you can spare them the anxiety of reading an error message by placing a label control next to the text box control that explains the requirements of the field data. This can save time as well as create a user-friendly atmosphere for those who enter data.

Too many records have the same value in the index

Source of the problem

You create indexes for tables in a database for the same reason authors create indexes for their books—so you can find things in a hurry. If an index entry in a book refers you to 100 different pages, it's not much help. The same goes for table indexes. One reason to create an index for a table is to speed up queries, sorting, and searches by building a list of values that is shorter than the number of records in the table. The index points to the records with the specified values. If the field you set as an index for the table contains a lot of records with the same value, the index doesn't speed up your queries, sorting, and searches very much.

If this is the case, you probably need to modify the index to add another field. Multiple-field indexes help distinguish between the many records that have the same value in the first field. You can use up to 10 fields in a single index. The second field groups records that have the same value in the first field, which results in smaller groups of records with the same combined-field index values. If you don't want more than one record with the same value in the index, you can set either a field property or an index property to prevent duplicates.

The following solution shows how to solve your indexing problems.

How to fix it

To add another field to an existing index, do the following:

1. Open the table in design view.

2. On the toolbar, click the Indexes button.

3. In the Field Name drop-down list, select the name of the field you want to index first (ShipVia, in this example).

4. In the Index Name column, change the name of the new index from the field name to a more descriptive name (Route, in this example).

5. Click in the next empty row in the Field Name column, and then select the second index field from the list (ShipRegion, in this example).

Indexes: Orders		
Index Name	Field Name	Sort Order
OrderDate	OrderDate	Ascending
PrimaryKey	OrderID	Ascending
ShippedDate	ShippedDate	Ascending
ShipPostalCode	ShipPostalCode	Ascending
Route	ShipVia	Ascending
	ShipRegion	Ascending

Index Properties

Primary	No
Unique	No
Ignore Nulls	No

The name for this index. Each index can use up to 10 fields.

6. Leave the Index Name row blank for the second field.

7. In the Index Properties area, set the Unique property to Yes if you want to prevent duplicate combined values.

8. Set the Ignore Nulls property to Yes if you want to keep records with Null values in the index.

Tip

In the example, the index named Route will find order records shipped by each shipper and, within shipper, by ShipRegion. Notice that the ShipVia Indexed property was changed to No when the second field was added to the index.

Timesaving hint

You can save time by creating fields that Access will automatically index for you. All you have to do is give the field a name that ends with the characters *ID, key, code,* or *num*—and presto!, the Indexed property for the field is automatically set to Yes (Duplicates OK).

For example, you could add a field named CompanyCode, and it would be automatically indexed. If you want to add other trailing characters to the list of auto-indexes, click Options on the Tools menu and then click the Tables/Queries tab. In the Table Design area, look at the list in the AutoIndex On Import/Create box. To further personalize your database design, you can add other character combinations to the list, separated by a semicolon. ▶

Memo, OLE Object, and hyperlink fields don't have Indexed properties, so you can't index one of

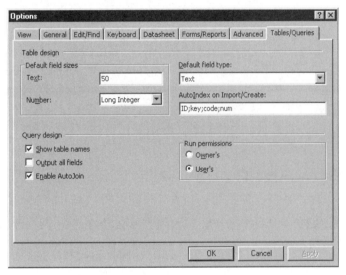

them individually in the table design. However, you can create an index on a memo field by selecting the name from the drop-down list in the Indexes dialog box. Typically, you wouldn't want to index a memo field because most records would contain different data in the memo. OLE Object and hyperlink field names don't appear in the list in the Indexes dialog box.

I don't know which data types and properties to choose in a new table

Source of the problem

You've carefully split your data into several tables for your new database, but the problem of choosing field data types and setting field and table properties still faces you. There are several issues you need to consider if you want to end up with an efficient, easy-to-use database. Proper selection of field data types and appropriate table and field properties is essential to smooth data management.

For example, should you index a field? When you index a table by a field, Access creates a list of values from the field along with pointers to their locations in the table. Indexes speed up searching and sorting significantly if there aren't too many different values. A table's primary key field is automatically indexed, but you can create additional indexes on one or more fields.

The following solution describes ways to understand what data types to select for the fields in your tables and which fields to use in an index.

How to fix it

To decide what data type to choose for a field, consider the following:

Choose this data type	For this type of data
Text	Values containing both letters and numbers. Even if you plan to store only numbers but don't expect to do any calculating, using the Text data type is often the best.
Memo	Variable-length text values. You can use the spell checker tool on memo fields just as you would on text fields.
Number	Numeric values you plan to sort on or use in calculations.
Currency	Fields that will contain monetary values. In calculations, the Currency data type rounds off the results to two decimal places, which can help prevent errors due to the way Number fields truncate values.
AutoNumber	To create a primary key field that contains none of your actual data but will guarantee a unique value in every record. It's a good idea to place an AutoNumber field at the top of the field list in the table design.
Date/Time	Date and time values you plan to sort on or use to perform date arithmetic, such as computing the time between two dates.
Yes/No	If you simply want the equivalent of a check mark in the field.

Table properties and how to set them

To set table properties, click the Properties button on the toolbar with the table open in design view. The text you enter in the Description property is displayed in the database window when you select the Details view. The Filter property sets the selection criteria that's saved with the table when you choose to save changes you've made in the datasheet. The Order By property specifies the sort order that's saved with the table.

Tip

Data-related field properties are discussed in "Data—Setting field properties" on page 44. The Indexed property is discussed in more detail earlier this chapter, on page 282.

Which fields to use for indexing

Consider these factors when choosing which fields to index:

- Fields you expect to search in for specific values.

- Fields you expect to sort by.

- Fields you expect to use in a relationship with another table. This can speed up processing if the field is indexed.

If you don't want duplicate values in the field, choose Yes (No Duplicates) in the Indexed property box in the table design window; otherwise, choose Yes (Duplicates OK). When you set a field's Indexed property to Yes, it's automatically added to the list in the Indexes dialog box. Remember, if you expect the field to contain the same value in a lot of records, indexing won't help much.

Making your own rules

All objects in Access databases have default property settings. Access tries to use settings that will please most everyone, but you don't have to leave it at that. The default data type is Text, as you can see when you move to the Data Type column after entering a new field name in the table design. The default Text field size is 50 characters, and for Number fields, it's Long Integer. Sure, you can change the field size on a field-by-field basis, but it would be easier to change the default if a larger or smaller size is more appropriate for your work.

To change these default settings for all the tables in your database, click Options on the Tools menu and click the Tables/Queries tab. Enter a number for the Text field size, and select from the list of Number field sizes. Change the default data type if you want, and then click OK.

Are you having trouble seeing all the buttons on a toolbar?

yes → **Did you change the toolbar?** → **yes**

no ↓

Is a button missing? → **yes**

no ↓

Do you need to reset the built-in toolbar buttons? → **yes**

Are you trying to hide a toolbar? → **yes**

no ↓

Are you having trouble customizing a toolbar? → **yes**

no ↓

Are you having trouble docking a toolbar? → **yes**

Quick fix

1. Right-click the toolbar, and then click Customize.
2. On the Toolbars tab, click the Properties button.
3. From the Docking list, select Allow Any.
4. Select the Allow Moving check box.
5. Click Close twice.

Toolbars

Go to...
I can't restore my built-in toolbars, page 288

Go to...
Some of the built-in buttons aren't displayed, page 292

Go to...
I can't reset my built-in toolbar buttons, page 290

Quick fix

1. Right-click the toolbar, and then click Customize.
2. On the Toolbars tab, select the toolbar you want to hide.
3. Click the Properties button.
4. Select the Allow Showing/Hiding check box.
5. Click Close.
6. Clear the check box in the Toolbars list.
7. Click Close again.

Are you trying to change a button image?

yes

Go to...
When I try to paste an image on a button, it doesn't look right, page 296

no

Go to...
I can't customize the toolbar I need, page 294

If your solution isn't here
Check these related chapters:
   Menus, page 160
Or see the general troubleshooting tips on page xiii.

I can't restore my built-in toolbars

Source of the problem

Toolbars look so sturdy, it hardly seems possible that they can be drastically changed. But buttons can be removed or rearranged, and the icon on a button can be different from the one you remember and have grown accustomed to. You might even see only one toolbar where you used to see two, or a button might trigger an action you don't expect.

If you or someone else changed a toolbar, you have two paths of reclamation to consider:

- Resetting the entire original toolbar, including all of its buttons. When you reset the entire toolbar, all the buttons revert to their original behavior so that they perform the same action when you click them as they did when Access was first installed. The buttons appear in their original positions on the toolbar and display the same icons.

- Restoring the default toolbar settings that were in effect when you first installed Access, including settings such as allowing docking, moving, resizing, and showing/hiding. Restoration is not available for custom toolbars because they have no original properties, only the ones you created.

The following solutions show you some ways to fix these problems.

How to fix it

To reset a toolbar to its original structure, follow these steps:

1. On the View menu, point to Toolbars and then click Customize.

2. Click the Toolbars tab, and select the name of the toolbar you want to restore.

3. Click Reset, and then click OK to confirm the change. ▶

4. Click Close, or keep the Customize box open to reset more toolbars.

If you want to restore the default options of a toolbar, do the following:

1. On the View menu, point to Toolbars and then click Customize.

2. In the Customize dialog box, click the Properties button.

3. From the Selected Toolbar list, select the name of the toolbar whose properties you want to restore. ▶

4. Click the Restore Defaults button, and then click Yes to confirm the action.

5. If you want to restore other toolbars, select each one and click Restore Defaults again.

6. When you've finished, click Close in the Toolbar Properties dialog box and then click Close in the Customize dialog box.

Tip

After you open the Toolbar Properties dialog box, you can make changes to several toolbars without returning to the Customize dialog box. Simply select the next toolbar from the Selected Toolbar list and make the changes.

Do's and don'ts of restoring and resetting built-in toolbars

You might have noticed in the Toolbar Properties dialog box that some of the properties are dimmed—this indicates that they can't be changed. The Toolbar Name, Type, and Show On Toolbars Menu options can't be changed in a built-in toolbar. In addition, the Restore Defaults button and the Reset button (in the Customize dialog box) become available only after you have made a change in the original built-in toolbar.

Tip

Buttons on the built-in toolbars sport helpful screen tips that clue you in to what the button will do—just in case the picture doesn't communicate the idea well enough. If the tips have been removed or changed, you can restore them, too. On the Toolbars tab of the Customize dialog box, select the toolbar from the list. Click the Options tab, select the Show ScreenTips On Toolbars check box, and then click Close.

Tip

If you're a keyboard fan, you can also have the shortcut key shown in the screen tip. On the Options tab of the Customize dialog box, select the Show Shortcut Keys In ScreenTips check box.

I can't reset my built-in toolbar buttons

Source of the problem

When you created your own personal toolbars, you probably took a shortcut and borrowed some of the built-in buttons such as Print or Copy. Of course, the buttons weren't exactly what you wanted, so you added a few touches of your own. Maybe you used a new icon, or perhaps you replaced an image with text. Now you want all of those buttons back the way they were. It's easy to restore the default settings and style for an individual button on a toolbar, whether it's located on a built-in toolbar or on a custom toolbar you created yourself. The following solution shows how to reset built-in toolbar buttons.

How to fix it

To reset the buttons on a built-in toolbar, do the following:

1. If the toolbar that contains the built-in button you want to reset isn't already displayed, point to Toolbars on the View menu and select the toolbar from the list. If the toolbar is attached to a form or report, open the form or report to display the toolbar.

2. Right-click the toolbar, and choose Customize from the shortcut menu.

3. Right-click the button on the toolbar, and then click Reset on the shortcut menu. If you just want to restore the button image, right-click the button and then click Reset Button Image on the shortcut menu. ▶

> **Tip**
> If the toolbar you want doesn't appear in the list, you can display it by selecting it on the Toolbars tab of the Customize dialog box.

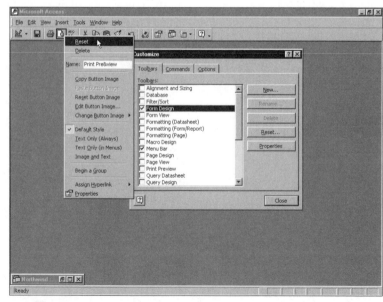

4. Click Close in the Customize dialog box, or keep it open for more adjustments.

Resetting buttons in a list

Things are a little different with toolbar buttons that display a list when you click them. Think of these lists as if they were shortcut menus. For example, in form design view, clicking the View button displays a list of available form views you can choose from. You can't reset the View button, but you can reset each of the items in the list that's displayed. On the View menu, point to Toolbars and then click Customize. Click the Toolbars tab, and then select the toolbar from the Toolbars list. Click the

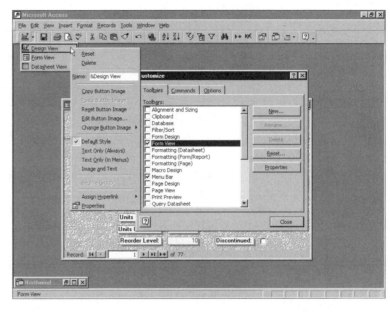

down arrow next to the button that displays the button you want to reset, and then right-click the button you want to reset. Click Reset to restore all the button's default properties or click Reset Button Image to restore only the original image on the button. In the Customize dialog box, click Close.

What is a button style?

On the shortcut menu that's displayed when you right-click a button, you have four styles to choose from to apply to individual toolbar buttons. Default Style shows only an image on buttons. However, when you apply Default Style to a menu, only text is displayed. Text Only (Always) shows only the name of the button or menu, with no image, on buttons and menus. You can change the name by entering a different name in the drop-down property list or by changing the Caption in the Properties dialog box. Text Only (In Menus) is used for menus and shows only the name of the menu or the caption. Image And Text shows both the name of the button or menu and an image, if one has been selected.

When you display text on a button, you can also specify a shortcut key, just as with menus and menu commands. Edit the name of the button, and include an ampersand (&) just before the key you want as the shortcut key. If you don't want text on the button, you can still show a shortcut keyboard combination, if one can be used for that button. Click the Options tab of the Customize dialog box and select both Show ScreenTips On Toolbars and Show Shortcut Keys In ScreenTips.

Some of the built-in buttons aren't displayed

Source of the problem

One of your friendly old toolbars suddenly looks shorter than it used to. Some of its buttons are missing. It might be that you or someone else changed the startup settings to keep the toolbars from appearing. Or it could be that this was one of those times when Access 2000 tried to help you by saving display space. It does this by placing two toolbars together in the same row at the top of the window. There might not be room for all the buttons on the combined toolbars to be shown on your screen. You'll see the More Buttons button (>> with a down arrow) at the right end of the toolbar if this is the case. You will also see the More Buttons button if there's not enough room to display all the buttons on a single toolbar. Perhaps you added buttons to the toolbar or resized the Access window to a narrower width. A button might also be missing because it's been moved to another toolbar. You can easily move it back or add a copy of the button to the original toolbar.

The following solutions show how to deal with each of these problems.

How to fix it

To change your startup settings so that toolbars appear, follow these steps:

1. On the Tools menu, click Startup.

2. Select the Allow Built-in Toolbars check box to restore a complete set of built-in toolbars. Click OK. ▶

3. Close and reopen the database to activate the changes.

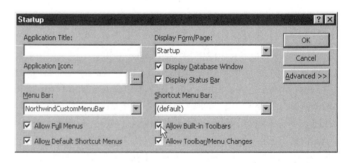

If some of your buttons are missing, choose the appropriate action from this list:

1. If you see the More Buttons button, click it to display the missing buttons.

2. If you have two toolbars in the same row, click the vertical bar at the left end of the second toolbar (the bar will

> **Tip**
>
> If you're reluctant to change the startup options but still want to see all the built-in toolbars, simply hold down the Shift key when you open the database.

appear between the toolbars sharing the row) and drag the toolbar down to its own row.

3. If the Access window is too narrow, widen it or use the More Buttons button to see the other buttons.

4. If the toolbar is floating, you can drag one of the edges to resize it so that all the buttons are visible.

If you want to add a missing button back to a built-in toolbar, follow these steps:

1. Right-click the toolbar, and then click Customize on the shortcut menu.

2. Click the Commands tab, and then select the category the button belongs to.

3. In the Commands list, locate the missing button and drag it to the toolbar.

4. Drop the item when you see the dark I-beam. ▶

5. Click Close in the Customize dialog box.

Tip

If you can't move or resize a toolbar, one of the Allow check boxes in the Toolbar Properties dialog box might be cleared. Click the Properties button on the Toolbars tab of the Customize dialog box.

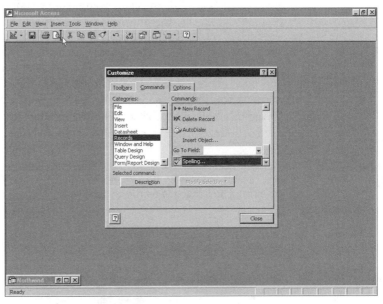

Tip

Not all buttons are found in the most logical category. For example, the Spelling button falls under Records rather than Edit. Often a button is related to the menu where a corresponding menu command can be found—but not with Spelling, which is found on the Tools menu.

Keeping buttons the way you want

Once you've struggled to get your built-in toolbars customized just the way you want them, you might not want anyone else adding more buttons or even restoring the toolbar to its original plain vanilla style. To prevent changes to a toolbar after you've restored or customized it to your requirements, click Toolbars on the View menu and then click Customize. In the Customize dialog box, select the built-in toolbar on the Toolbars tab and then click the Properties button. Clear the Allow Customizing check box, and then click Close in the dialog boxes.

I can't customize the toolbar I need

Source of the problem

You've got some really great ideas about creating a friendly and useful customized workplace for your database. You especially want some customized toolbars containing just the buttons you need, looking just the way they should. But something gets in the way, and you can't get the toolbar the way you want. You can run into problems trying to customize a toolbar for a couple of reasons:

- In the Startup dialog box, the Allow Toolbar/Menu Changes check box isn't selected. That means you aren't allowed to change any toolbar, menu bar, or shortcut menu, whether it's a built-in one or a custom one you created. In fact, if this check box is cleared, the Customize dialog box isn't even available to you.

- The Allow Customizing check box for the specific toolbar you want to work on is cleared. This means you can't make any changes to the toolbar even if you created it in the first place.

How to fix it

To set the startup options so that you can customize toolbars in a database, follow these steps:

1. Open the database you're working with.

2. On the Tools menu, click Startup.

3. Select the Allow Toolbar/Menu Changes check box, and then click OK. ▶

4. Close and reopen the database to apply the change.

To make sure you can customize an individual toolbar, follow these steps:

1. With the toolbar displayed, right-click the toolbar and then click Customize on the shortcut menu.

2. On the Toolbars tab, click Properties.

3. From the Selected Toolbars list, select the name of the toolbar you want to customize.

4. Select the Allow Customizing check box. ▶

5. Click Close in the Toolbar Properties dialog box and again in the Customize dialog box.

Tip

Even if the Allow Toolbar/ Menu Changes check box is cleared, you can still move, size, and dock the toolbar, unless you have forbidden these actions with the individual toolbar's Allow Moving, Allow Resizing, and Docking property settings.

Tip

After you make changes to the toolbar, you might want to clear the Allow Customizing check box again to keep others from making more changes.

Why doesn't the toolbar go away?

When you display a toolbar that doesn't usually appear during your current activity, it remains on the screen until you manually remove it. This goes for built-in toolbars as well as your own custom toolbars. If you haven't attached the toolbar to a form, report, or other database object and you open it by selecting it from the Toolbars shortcut menu, you must get rid of it yourself. Right-click the toolbar, and then clear the check box next to the toolbar name in the shortcut menu.

It works the other way, too. If you close a toolbar in a window where it normally appears, it won't show up when you start the associated activity. To see the toolbar, you have to select it from the list of toolbars that you want to display.

Forming a toolbar

If you created a custom toolbar that contains just the activities you need for working in a specific form, you can set a form property that replaces the default toolbar with yours. To display a custom toolbar when a form opens, open the form in design view, click the Properties button on the toolbar, and then click the Other tab. Click the down arrow next to the Toolbar property box, and then select the custom toolbar name from the list. The selected toolbar will replace the default built-in toolbar that normally appears when you open a form in form view.

When I try to paste an image on a button, it doesn't look right

Source of the problem

The image you place on a custom toolbar button is supposed to give you a clue about what will happen when you click the button. Unfortunately, when you're working with a special picture file that you want to show on the button, you can often run into problems getting the button to look the way you want. If you imported an image from another source, such as clip art or a scanned drawing, the graphic image might be a different size than the built-in images that fit perfectly on the standard buttons. You should be sure to adjust the scale of the bitmap image before importing it to the toolbar button. Enlarging or reducing an imported image after placing it on the button can produce blurred results.

The images that come with Access are all sized properly at 16 by 16 pixels. If you start with one of them and use the Button Editor to create a custom image, the image should work just fine. Here are some solutions for making custom toolbar buttons appear the way you want.

How to fix it

To replace a button image with one of the other images that comes with Access, do the following:

1. Right-click the toolbar, and then click Customize on the shortcut menu.

2. Right-click the button you want to change, and then point to Change Button Image on the shortcut menu. ▶

3. Click the new image you want to use, and then click Close in the Customize dialog box.

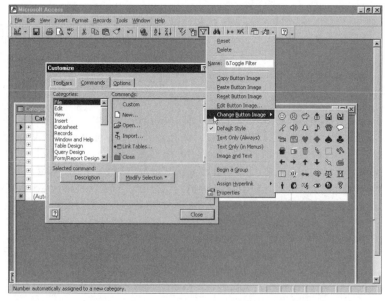

To edit one of the toolbar button images that comes with Access, use the Button Editor:

1. Right-click the toolbar that contains the button you want to edit, and then click Customize.

2. Right-click the button with the image you want to change, and then click Edit Button Image.

3. In the Button Editor, click the color you want in the color palette.

4. Use the pointer to click and drag over the pixels you want to change the color of. The Preview pane shows what the button will look like on the toolbar. ▶

5. To erase pixels, click the Erase box and then click and drag the mouse pointer over each of the pixels you want to get rid of. Click a color to turn erasing off.

6. Click Clear to start over, or click OK to keep the changes and return to the Customize dialog box. Click Cancel to restore the button's original image.

Warning

If you used a built-in command such as Print as the basis for the custom button, when you paste the new image on this copy of the button, the image will appear on the button in all the toolbars that include that button. All your Print buttons will show the new image.

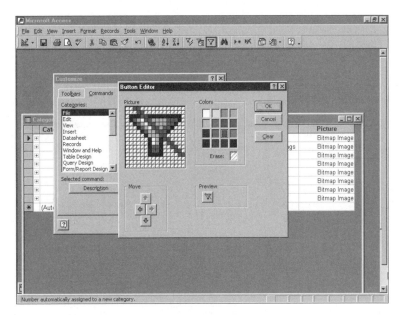

If you want to use your own bitmap image, do the following:

1. Use a graphics program such as Microsoft Paint to adjust the size of the button before importing it.

2. After editing the image, save the file in the graphics program and then copy the image to the Clipboard.

3. Return to Access, right-click the toolbar, and click Customize on the shortcut menu.

4. Right-click the button on the toolbar that you want to add the image to, and then click Paste Button Image.

Tip

Don't forget that the button's style property must be set to allow the image to be displayed. Right-click the button and select either Default Style or Image And Text to show an image on the button.

Index

Symbols and Numbers

A and *a* used to create input masks, 51
Access Picture Builder, 31
action queries. *See* queries, action
ActiveX calendar control, 176–77
ActiveX controls, 36, 37
ActiveX Controls dialog box, 37
Add Colon property, changing settings for, 22
adding. *See* adding *under specific topics*
Adjust The Field Width So All Fields Fit On A Page, 259
Advanced Filter/Sort, 102, 104–5, 106, 109, 270
After Update event property, 157
Align buttons, 121
aligning
    background pictures in forms, 124–25, 182, 183
    items in option groups, 27
    labels with text boxes, 120–23
    numbers after exporting to text files, 80–81
    text boxes, 115
    values to the left using ! symbol, 49
Allow Built-in Toolbars option, 292
Allow Customizing option, 293, 294, 295
Allow Default Shortcut Menus option, 166
Allow Docking option, 295
Allow Full Menus option, 166
Allow Moving option, 295
Allow Resizing option, 295
Allow Toolbar/Menu Changes option, 294, 295
ampersand (&). *See* & (ampersand)
Analyze It With MS Excel (Office Link) command, 89
And operator
    described, 217
    in Filter By Form, 102–3, 108
    multiple validation rules combined using, 47, 280
    Or operator compared to, 108
    selection criteria combined using, 216, 221, 222
"An error occurred trying to import file..." error message, 148
appending. *See* adding; appending *under specific topics;* copying; importing
Append To row in query grid, 188, 189
"A problem occurred while Microsoft Access was communicating with the OLE server or ActiveX Control" error message, 181
arithmetic operators, 91. *See also* calculations; *specific operators*
arranging. *See* arranging *under specific topics*
arrow keys, using to move controls, 121
arrows on menus, 166, 292
AS clauses in SQL statements, changing SumOf*<fieldname>* in legend labels, 7
asterisk (*). *See* * (asterisk)
AutoIndex On Import/Create, 283

AutoKeys macro group, 158, 159
Auto Label property, changing settings for, 22
AutoLookup queries not working, 202–3
AutoNumber fields
    in append queries, 189
    converting fields to, 52
    cutting from or pasting into, 61
    described, 284
    editing, 56
    including in appended records, 186
    as primary keys, 278, 279
    referential integrity and, 241
    relating to text fields, 242–43
    summarizing functions used with, 200
Auto Order button, 127
Auto Resize property of forms, 115, 116
Auto Tab property, 127
Avg() function in expressions, 92
axis, tick marks on, 9

Back Color property, 27, 183
background pictures, 124–25, 182, 183
Back Style property, 27
backward compatibility. *See* converting
backward slash (\) indicating integer division, 91
beeping when entering data into fields, 62
Best Fit option, 55
bitmap files, 179, 297
blank column headings after importing, 146
blank fields. *See also* Null values
    converting databases created in earlier versions of Access, 37
    counting records with, 200, 201
    displaying None as field value instead, 49
    expressions used for skipping over, 96–97
    in report previews, 248–49
    searching for, 69
    sorting records on, 262–63
blank forms instead of showing data, 134–35
blank lines in mailing labels, 96–97
blank mailing labels, 262–63
blank pages when printing reports, 258–59
blank properties, 25
blank records, not including in groups in reports, 275
blank results from calculation queries, 196–97
blank values. *See* Null values
.bmp (bitmap) files, 179, 297
Boolean operators. *See specific operators*
borders, options placed near, 26–27
Border Style property, 183
Border Width property, 27
Borland Database Engine, 140, 142

converting, to Access 2000, *continued*
    Microsoft Access 2.0 databases, 36–37
    out-of-memory error messages, 42–43
    overwriting old databases, 39
  to Access 97 from Access 2000, 41
  charts to static images, 11
  fields to other data types, 52–53
Convert option, 178
copying. *See also* pasting
  Ctrl+C stops working, 158
  Excel worksheets into databases, 147
Count function, 92, 195, 200
Country setting, 49
creating. *See* creating *under specific topics*
Criteria row of query design grid, 216, 217, 270, 275
crosstab queries. *See* queries, crosstab
Crosstab Query Wizard, 207, 210
Ctrl+C stops working for copying, 158
Ctrl key represented by ^ in macro names, 158
Currency data type, 284
Currency fields, 200
currency values, symbols for, 49. *See also* numbers
custom controls, 36, 37
Customize dialog box
  customizing toolbars, 294–95
  pasting images on command buttons, 296–97
  restoring and resetting command buttons, 292–93
  restoring and resetting menu bars, 162–63
  restoring and resetting menus, 164–65, 170–71
  restoring and resetting toolbars, 288, 289, 290–91
customizing, 294–95. *See* customizing *under specific topics*
custom menus, 168–69

DAO 3.6. *See* Microsoft DAO 3.6
data
  accuracy, ensuring, 46–47, 280–81
  appending, 55, 149, 188–89
  beeping heard when entering, 62
  blank forms displayed instead of, 134–35
  changing display of, 70–71
  color of, 49
  controls larger than necessary for, 260, 261
  Date function as source of, 91
  displayed in controls coming from expressions, 16, 17
  entering and editing
    pasting records into datasheets, 58–61
    unable to enter dates into input masks, 62–63
    unable to find records with partial field values, 64–65
  importing into tables, 144, 145
  incorrect, 46–47, 280
  labels explaining requirements of, 281
  missing from report previews, 257

data, *continued*
  precedence of settings, 5
  sample shown in a chart, 2–3
  size defining fields, 232, 233
  "Some data may not be displayed" warning message, 265
  subforms displaying incorrectly, 136–37
  templates for entry (input masks), 50–51
  unable to add in tables, 56–57
  unable to fit in columns, 55, 57
  validation rules and, 46–47, 59, 280–81
databases
  Access 97 opened as read-only in Access 2000, xiv
  appending data from one to another, 189
  blank fields in, 37
  Borland Database Engine, 140, 142
  consolidating using compact and repair utilities, 233
  converting Access 2.0 to Access 2000, 36–37
  copying Excel worksheets into, 147
  holding Shift key while opening, 166, 292
  opening as read-only, 56, 180, 181
  overwriting, 39
  secured, converting to Access 97 from Access 2000, 41
Database Utilities, 233
Data Entry property, 132, 134, 135
data entry templates (input masks), 50–51
data series in charts, 9
datasheets
  changing display of, 70–75
  changing size and behavior of, 76–77
  default formats for, 71
  entering and editing data
    pasting records into, 58–61
    unable to enter dates into input masks, 62–63
    unable to enter or edit data in tables, 56–57
    unable to find records with partial field values, 64–65
  order of columns changing when tab order is changed, 126
  sorting records in datasheets by multiple fields, 268–69
  subdatasheets
    adding to new queries, 67
    default view of, 73, 76
    displaying, 70, 71
    filters built for, 101
    missing from display, 71
    viewing data in/displaying, 72–75, 76–77
  viewing data, 68–69, 70–75, 76–77
datasheet view of subforms, 136, 137
Data Type column, 285
data types. *See also specific data types*
  appending spreadsheets or text files to tables, 148, 149
  append queries and, 188, 189
  assigned to fields when importing, 146, 147
  choosing in new tables, 284
  converting fields to different types, 52–53
  described, 284
  incompatible, defined for source field during append queries, 188, 189

duplicate values, *continued*
  of primary keys
    appended records containing, 186
    appended spreadsheets or text files containing, 148, 149
  setting properties to prevent, 282
dynamic link libraries (library files), 39, 40–41

Edit Button Image command, 297
editing. *See* editing *under specific topics*
Edit Relationships dialog box, 185, 203, 240, 241, 245
e-mail, sending reports in, 78
embedded objects, 181
.emf files (metafiles), 179
empty fields. *See* blank fields
Enabled property, unable to edit OLE objects, 180
Enforce Referential Integrity, 187, 245
entering. *See* entering *and* adding *under specific topics*
equals sign (=). *See* = (equals sign)
#Error
  evaluated expressions causing, 92–93
  in fields instead of field values, 16–17
  in group headers, 249
  in linked Excel spreadsheets, 138
error messages. *See also specific error messages*
  about ambiguous outer joins, 238–39
  about being out of memory, 42–43, 174, 175
  about dividing by zero, 98–99
  about invalid values, 56–57, 219
  about key violations, 186
  about missing macros, 154–55, 168, 169
  about missing object libraries, 40–41
  about not finding linked files, 139
  about syntax errors when applying filters, 101
  about too many indexes, 42, 43
  about type mismatches, 185, 194–95, 242–43
  about unknown field names during append queries, 188
  about validation rules, 45
  about validation rule violations, 186
  crosstab queries causing, 204–5, 206
  Help button in boxes, xiii
  when appending data, 55
  when clicking hyperlinks, 32–33
  when pasting records into datasheets, 58–61
errors
  compilation, 38–39
  controlling by ensuring accuracy of data, 46–47, 280–81
  syntax, 39
  when exporting to Excel, 86–87
event property boxes, Access looking for macros when blank or containing spaces, 154–55
events, macros attached to, 156–57. *See also specific events*
Event tab, macro names in, 156–57
Excel. *See* Microsoft Excel

exclamation mark (!). *See* ! (exclamation mark)
expanded view of subdatasheets, 72, 73, 76–77
Export Errors tables, 86–87
exporting
  to dBASE or Paradox, 84–85
  to Excel, 86–89
  to formats not in list of available types, 85
  reports to snapshot files, 255
  selected records, 79
  sending reports in e-mail, 78
  to text files, 79, 80–81
  to Word, subforms not showing up, 82–83
Export Report dialog box, 255
Expression Builder, 93, 95, 281
expressions. *See also* calculations; *specific function and operator names*
  blank records in fields used in, 196, 197
  closing and reopening queries with summarizing functions, 199
  combining text values in, 196, 197
  control names in, 16, 17
  in Control Source property box, 16, 17
  data displayed in controls coming from, 16, 17
  Date(), source of data, 91
  dates in, 98–99
  for emphasizing values with special formatting, 45
  equals sign preceding, 16, 17
  #Error displayed when evaluating, 92–93
  field names in, 16, 17, 95
  in Message argument box, 153
  Now(), source of data, 91
  Null values and, 20–21
  quotation marks enclosing, 17
  for skipping blank fields, 96–97
  spaces in field or control names, 16, 17
  square brackets enclosing spaces in field or control names, 16, 17
  text combined with field values, 94–95
  in Update To cells, 185
  used in filtering, 108–9
  used with SetValue action, 157

field data
  expressions in Update To cells not matching type, 185
  label controls next to text boxes explaining requirements of, 281
  in tables, unable to add or edit, 56–57
Field/Expression column (Sorting And Grouping dialog box), 208–9
field names
  appending spreadsheets or text files to tables, 148
  automated indexing based on, 283

Is as reserved word, 108, 109
Is Not Null, 262–63, 275
Is Null function
    adding to query selection criteria, 223
    in expressions for skipping over blank fields, 96, 97
    IIf function and, 21, 37, 96, 97
    in parameter queries to view all records in results, 193

Join Properties dialog box, 221, 226–27, 245
joins, 221, 226–27, 238–39. *See also* tables, relationships

Keep Together property, 257, 265
keyboard shortcuts. *See* shortcut keys
keys. *See* primary key fields
keystrokes, sending to dialog boxes, 151

L, creating input masks with, 51
label controls, next to text boxes explaining requirements
        of field data, 281
labels
    adding titles for reports when saving crosstab queries, 209
    attached to text box controls, 22
    of charts, 5
    defined, 9
    for fields, not repeating in each group in a report, 209
    for legends, 4, 6–7
    mailing labels, 96–97, 262–63
    placing above text boxes, 123
    text boxes lining up with, 120–23
    x-axis in graphs, 4
Label Wizard, 263
Label X and Label Y properties for text box controls, 123
Last function, 198
legend in charts, 9
legend labels, 4, 6–7
length. *See* size and sizing
Less Than Or Equal To operator (<=), conditional
        formatting using, 19
library files, 39, 40–41
Like operator, 218
limits and limiting
    field size, 56–57
    length of text in memo fields, 86, 87

limits and limiting, *continued*
    modules in Visual Basic, 42
    number of characters in message boxes, 153
    number of indexes, 42, 43
    number of records displayed when filtering, 105
    values in fields using validation rules, 46–47
Limit To List property, 130, 131
line breaks, indicating in multiline messages in message
        boxes, 152–53
lines. *See also* gridlines
    drawn across reports, 246–47
    drawn below records, 137
    in group footer sections of multiple-column reports, 265
Link Child Fields and Link Master Fields properties
    compared, 72, 73
    designating fields charts are linked to, 10, 11
    in subforms, 77
Link dialog box, 141
linked items
    defined, 181
    forms, 118–19, 136, 137
    OLE objects, 174, 175
    tables, 101, 139, 140, 143, 149
linking
    fields in query design, 202, 203
    filtering on fields from linked tables, 101
    filters returning wrong records from linked tables, 139
    importing compared to, 143
    index and memo files, 141
    messages about not finding linked files, 139
    record-bound charts to multiple fields, 11
    subforms to forms, 136, 137
    tables, 143
links. *See* hyperlinks
Links dialog box, 175
list boxes
    delay in display of items in, 23
    entering records in, 130–31
    #Error or *#Name?* displayed in, 16–17
    order of rows in, 14–15
    using list items in calculations, 15
lists, resetting command buttons in, 291
literal values, interpretation of, 94
locked fields, cutting from or pasting into, 61
Locked property, 180
locked records or tables, 56
lookup fields
    filtering records in queries based on, 235, 270
    in parameter queries, 192, 193
    references and, 68
    searching for, 67–68
    sorting on, 234–35, 270–71
    source of values in, 235
    values displayed in, 270
lookup list, 235
Lookup tab, 235
LTrim function, eliminating spaces using, 263

macros. *See also specific macros*
AutoKeys, 158, 159
"Can't find the macro" error message, 154–55
correcting names in property boxes, 155
Ctrl+C not copying, 158
documenting, 150
grouping, 155, 158, 159
printing information about, 150
putting multiline messages in message boxes, 152–53
SetValue macro running at wrong time, 156–57
turning off warning messages about, 151
mailing labels, 96–97, 262–63. *See also* labels
margins
affecting multiple-column reports, 265
fixing after converting to Access 2000, 35
printer settings causing blank mailing labels, 262, 263
of reports causing blank pages, 258–59
Match box, 69
mathematical calculations. *See* calculations
Max function, 198, 200
Medium Date format, 63
Memo data type, 284
Memo fields
associated files for linked tables, 140, 141
creating indexes on, 283
finding records with two values in, 216–17
formatting, 49
relating tables with, 243
sorting on, 270, 271
text truncated when designing queries based on, 243
text truncated when exporting tables to Excel, 86, 87
viewing all text in, 67
memory, error messages about being out of, 42–43, 174, 175. *See also* disk space, saving
Menu Bar property box, 168
menu bars, 161, 162–63, 166, 167
menu commands. *See also* command buttons; *specific command names*
defined, 162
displaying without expanding list of commands, 167
hidden, 166–67
missing, 161, 165
restoring, 171
menus. *See also specific menu names*
added to built-in menu bars, 167
adding and moving to different menu bars, 166, 167
built-in, 164–65, 166–67
custom, 168–69
defined, 162
down arrows on, 166
hidden, 164–65, 166, 168–69
resetting and restoring, 164–65, 170–71

menus, *continued*
shortcut, 166, 170–71
startup settings changed to not display, 166
merge feature, forms and reports not exported, 83
message boxes, xiii, 152–53, 281
messages for users in Validation Text property box, 47
metafiles, 179
Microsoft Access 2.0 databases, 36–37
Microsoft Access 97, xiv, 16
"Microsoft Access can't append all the records in the append query" error message, 186, 189
"Microsoft Access can't create this relationship and enforce referential integrity" error message, 244
"Microsoft Access can't find the macro" error message, 154–55
"Microsoft Access can't update all the records in the update query" error message, 187
"Microsoft Access encountered errors while converting data..." error message, 53
"Microsoft Access was unable to append all the data to the table" error message, 149
Microsoft DAO 2.5/3.5 Compatibility Library, 39, 41
Microsoft DAO 3.6, 39
Microsoft Excel, 86–89, 138, 147
Microsoft Graph, 2–3, 4–5, 9
Microsoft Office, 255. *See also* Office Links; *specific software titles*
Microsoft Troubleshooting Web site, xv
Microsoft Visual FoxPro, 140, 142
Microsoft Web sites for support, xv
Microsoft Word, exporting to, 82–83, 88–89
Microsoft Works, exporting tables to, 85
migration. *See* converting
Min function, 199, 200
minus sign (-)
allowing in fields, 51
as wildcard characters, 219
modifying. *See* editing
modules, 36, 42
More Buttons button (>>), 292–93
moving toolbars, 293, 295
MsgBox macro action, 152–53
MsgBox Wait argument of SendKeys action, 151
Multi Row property, setting to show all tabs at once, 29

#Name?
evaluated expressions causing, 93
in fields instead of field values, 16–17
Name AutoCorrect feature, 16, 144, 145
name maps, 144, 145
Name property of subdatasheets, 70, 71

names
  of controls
    in expressions in same control, 92, 93
    linking forms and subforms, 136
  of fields
    appending spreadsheets or text files to tables, 148
    entered incorrectly in expressions, 16
    in expressions, 95
    length allowed in dBASE and Paradox, 84, 85
    renaming, 16, 17
    sorting on memo or hyperlink fields in reports, 271
  of legend labels, renaming, 4, 6–7
  of macros, correcting in property boxes, 155
  of modules and procedures in Access 2.0, 36
  of queries, changed or deleted, 10, 11
  of tables
    changed or deleted, 10, 11
    in Expression Builder, 93
    length allowed in dBASE and Paradox, 84, 85
    renaming, 143, 145
navigating subdatasheets, 77
Navigation Buttons property, 137
New Row Or Col property, 265
@;"None" displaying None as field value, 49
Not Like operator, 218
Now() function in expressions, 91
Null values. *See also* blank fields
  avoiding by requiring field values, 249
  blank calculated fields in report previews, 248–49
  blank results from calculation queries, 196–97
  in Column Heading field of Crosstab cells, 204–5
  converting databases created in earlier versions of Access, 37
  counting number of non-Null values, 201
  field indexes excluding records with, 276–77
  in forms or reports, 20–21
  in primary key fields, 278, 279
  query selection criteria including records with, 223
  searching for, 69
  text in blank fields, 20
  in Validation Rule property value list, 47, 281
Number data type, 284
Number fields
  default size, 285
  Field Size property for, 35
  relating to text fields, 185, 194–95, 242–43
  summarizing functions used with, 200
numbers. *See also* calculations; dates
  currency values, symbols for, 49
  emphasizing negative with special formatting, 45
  exporting to Excel, 87, 88–89
  exporting to text files, 80–81
  long decimal numbers as result of date expressions, 98–99
  in text fields, sorting on, 272–73
Nz function, 20, 21, 97, 197, 248–49

object libraries, 39, 40–41
Office Links, 83, 89. *See also specific software titles*
OLE Object fields, 200, 271, 283
OLE objects, 174–75, 180–81. *See also* images
"Once you enter data in a table..." error message, 52
On Load event, 156
On Open event, 156
Open dialog box options, 56
opening. *See* opening *under specific topics*
operators. *See also specific operators*
  enclosing in square brackets or quotation marks during queries, 215, 219
  forward slashes preceding, 91
optimizing disk space, 179, 233
option groups, 26–27. *See also specific box and button types*
Order By and Order By On properties, 270, 274, 275, 285
order of columns and rows. *See* sorting
Or operator
  And operator compared to, 108
  conditions combined using, 109
  described, 217
  in Filter By Form, 102–3, 108
  multiple validation rules combined using, 47, 280
  selection criteria combined using, 216, 222
  separating lists of values, 47
Or row (query design grid), 216, 217
outer joins, 221, 238–39
Output All Fields check box, 231
overwriting
  chart changes because of settings precedence, 4–5
  data in existing Excel files when exporting, 87
  old databases when converting to Access 2000, 39
  Paste Errors table, 60

page captions, seeing all at once, 29
Page Header. *See* headers
pages
  blank when printing reports, 258–59
  grouped records split over, 256–57
  printing header information on, 251
Paradox
  exporting to, 84–85
  importing tables from, 144–45
  linking and restoring index and memo files, 141
  opening and updating linked tables in, 140, 142
parameter prompts
  action queries causing, 185

source fields, 188, 189
space, disk. *See* disk space, saving
spaces
  eliminating, 263
  in event property boxes, 154–55
  in field or control names, 16, 17
  placeholders for, 48, 49
spacing
  of columns correcting wrong margins, 35
  between controls, 120, 260–61
  between text boxes, 122
speeding up display
  of forms or reports, 27
  of information in list or combo boxes, 23
  of simple select query results, 232–33
  of value lists, 112, 113
speeding up queries, 282–83
spreadsheets, 138, 146–47, 148–49
SQL statements
  editing to change legend labels, 7
  in Row Source property box, 131
  speeding up display of information based on, 23
square brackets ([]). *See* [] (square brackets)
startup settings, changed to not display menus and
        toolbars, 166, 292
static images, 180, 181
stored values, 67, 68
storing. *See* saving
Stretch setting, 182
styles of command buttons, 291, 297
Subdatasheet Expanded property, 73, 76
Subdatasheet Height property, 77
subdatasheets. *See* datasheets, subdatasheets
Subform Field Linker dialog box, 136
subforms. *See* forms, subforms
Suggest button in Subform Field Linker dialog box, 136
Sum() function in expressions, 92
SumOf<*fieldname*>, 6, 7
Switch function, 212–13
symbols. *See also specific symbols*
  for concatenation, 94, 196, 197
  for currency values, 49
  for formatting fields, 48, 49
  for input masks, 51
synchronizing forms, 118–19

tab controls, 28, 29
Tab Fixed Height and Tab Fixed Width properties, 29
Tab Index property, 127
table design view, testing validation rules, 47
Table Properties dialog box, 187
tables
  adding field data in, 56–57

tables, *continued*
  adding to queries, 230
  appending, 148–49, 188–89
  backup copies, 190, 191
  choosing data types and properties in, 284–85
  closing, 273
  deleting primary keys, 277
  editing field data in, 56–57
  exporting, 84, 85, 86–89
  expressions containing identifiers, 93
  filters not saved with, 110–11
  forms bound to, 134–35
  identifiers in expressions, 93
  importing, 139, 143, 144, 145
  index files for, 140, 141
  linked, 101, 139, 140, 143, 149. *See also* linking
  locked, 56
  multiple-field indexes, 282–83
  names and naming
    changed or deleted, 10, 11
    in dBASE and Paradox, 84, 85
    in expressions, 93, 95
    imported tables, renaming, 145
    linked tables, renaming, 143
    linking forms and subforms using names, 137
  properties, choosing and setting in new tables, 284, 285
  relationships. *See also* joins
    ambiguous outer joins, error messages about, 238–39
    building in queries, 242–43
    changing Join properties, 220–21
    clarifying, 237
    deleting, 237
    deleting fields in, 277
    deleting records in, 240–41
    duplicate values in fields, 202, 203
    editing, 237
    editing records in, 240–41
    index limits and, 42, 43
    many-to-many, 202
    one-to-many, 202, 203, 226–27, 241
    one-to-one, 202
    primary keys and, 278, 279
    query results altered by, 220–21
    referential integrity and, 186, 187, 244–45
    sequence affecting queries, 238–39
    unclear, 237
  reports inheriting properties from, 274, 275
  sorting fields in, 8–9
  sorting on memo or hyperlink fields in, 271
  sorting records in, 269, 273, 274
  updating data in, 56–57
  validation rules for fields in, 280–81
  validation rules for records in, 46, 47
  viewing all text in memo fields, 67
tab order on forms, 126–27
tabs, 28, 29, 127
Tab Stop property, 127
Test Validation Rules command (Edit menu), 47, 281

text
    combined with field values in expressions, 94–95
    on command buttons, 291
    comparing text criteria with Count function results, 195
    in expressions, 94
    formatting, 48, 49, 51, 67, 153
    in legend labels, 6–7
    in memo fields, 67, 86, 87
    in message boxes, 153
    from wrong column displayed in combo boxes, 12–13
text box controls
    adding without attaching labels, 22
    aligning, 115
    bound, formatting field values in, 20
    changing settings for default position, 123
    emphasizing values with special formatting, 18–19
    #Error or *#Name?* displayed in, 16–17
    label controls next to, explaining requirements of field
        data, 281
    labels attached to, 22
    labels lining up with, 120–23
    labels placed above, 123
    moving with group of controls, 120–21
    not resizing based on text display, 13
    resizing to fit contents, 260, 261
Text data type, 284, 285
Text fields
    creating input masks for, 50–51
    default size, 285
    finding records with two values in, 216–17
    formatting, 48–49
    relating to number fields, 185, 194–95, 242–43
    size limits, 56, 57
    sorting in numeric order, 272–73
    summarizing functions used with, 200
text files, 80–81, 146–47, 148–49
Text Only (Always) style of command buttons, 291
Text Only (In Menus) style of command buttons, 291
"The expression you entered has an invalid... value" error
        message, 219
"The record cannot be deleted or changed because table
        '*tablename*' includes related records" error message,
        240
"There is no primary key defined" error message, 278
"The Save As command can't process any subforms..."
        error message, 82
"The value you entered isn't appropriate for the input
        mask..." error message, 62
time and time values, exporting to text files, 81. *See also* dates
Time fields (Date/Time fields), 50–51, 200, 284
titles
    of charts, 5, 9
    of controls, 25
Toolbar Properties dialog box, 162–63, 289, 295
toolbars. *See also* command buttons; *specific toolbars*
    customizing, 293, 294–95
    displaying and hiding, 287, 295
    docking, 286, 295

toolbars, *continued*
    More Buttons button (>>), 292–93
    moving, 293, 295
    resetting original structure, 288, 289, 290–91
    resizing, 293, 295
    startup settings changed to not display, 292
"Too many crosstab column headers" error message, 205,
    206
Top Values box (Query Design toolbar), 199
Top Values query property, 199
Track Name AutoCorrect Info, 145
Trim function, eliminating spaces using, 263
troubleshooting. *See also specific topics in this index*
    Help button in error message boxes, xiii
    tips, xiii–xv
    What's This? button in dialog boxes, xiv
truncation. *See also* wildcard characters
    of decimal points in text files, 80–81
    of text in memo fields exported to Excel, 86, 87
    of text in memo fields when designing queries based on,
        243
"Type mismatch in expression" error message, 185,
    194–95, 242–43

unbound
    forms, 134
    objects, defined, 181
    OLE objects, 174, 175
underlining, periods replaced with, 7
Unfreeze All Columns option, 57
Unhide Columns option, 61, 70, 74
Unicode, converting to Access 97 from Access 2000, 41
unique index fields. *See* index fields
Unique property, 283
Unique Records and Unique Values properties, 225
universal *don't do it* symbol (circle with diagonal slash), 56
Update To cells, 185
updating. *See also* converting
    action queries, 185
    data in crosstab queries, 209
    data in tables, 56–57
    linked tables, 140, 142
    records with values already in destination table, 186–87
User and Group Permissions, 41

Val() function, 272, 273
Validation Rule property
    enclosing text in quotation marks, 280

About the author

Virginia Andersen saw her first computer in 1951, and she's been infatuated with them ever since. Grace Hopper, the inventor of the compiler concept, told her that there was a future to be found for women in "high-speed digital computers."

Virginia began writing computer books after she retired from her job as a computer systems analyst and programmer in the defense industry. During her years in that profession, she used computers for interesting projects, such as mapping the surface of the moon in preparation for the Apollo landing, undersea surveillance to detect enemy submarines, weapon system simulation, and system reliability modeling. During those years, she also taught mathematics, systems analysis, and computer science at several universities in southern California.

Becoming an author was a great step forward: she didn't have to wear power suits and nylons to the office anymore. Virginia has authored and contributed to more than 30 books about PC-based applications, mostly database management systems such as Microsoft Access, dBASE, and Paradox. She is a certified Microsoft Office User Specialist (MOUS) Expert in Access 97 and Access 2000.

These days, Virginia and her husband, Jack, enjoy their home in southern California. Each summer, they load the computer and the cats into their trailer and head for the High Sierra. In between her book assignments, they find time to hike, bird-watch, and fish for the famous Eagle Lake trout.

The manuscript for this book was prepared and galleyed using Microsoft Word 2000. Pages were composed using Adobe PageMaker 6.52 for Windows, with text in ACaslon Regular and display type in Gill Sans. Composed pages were delivered to the printer as electronic prepress files.

Cover designer

Landor Associates

Interior graphic designer

James D. Kramer

Principal compositor

Carl Diltz

Principal graphic artist

Joel Panchot

Copy editor

Crystal Thomas

Indexer

Kari Kells

Target your
solution and fix it
yourself—fast!

When you're stuck with a computer problem, you need answers right now. *Troubleshooting* books can help. They'll guide you to the source of the problem and show you how to solve it right away. Use easy diagnostic flowcharts to identify problems. Get ready solutions with clear, step-by-step instructions. Go to quick-access charts with *Top 20 Problems* and *Prevention Tips*. Find even more solutions with handy *Tips* and *Quick Fixes.* Walk through the remedy with plenty of screen shots to keep you on track. Find what you need fast with the extensive, easy-reference index. And keep trouble at bay with the Troubleshooting Web site—updated every month with new FREE problem-solving information. Get the answers you need to get back to business fast with *Troubleshooting* books.

Troubleshooting Microsoft® Access Databases
(Covers Access 97 and Access 2000)
ISBN 0-7356-1160-2
U.S.A. $19.99
U.K.   £14.99
Canada $28.99

Troubleshooting Microsoft Excel Spreadsheets
(Covers Excel 97 and Excel 2000)
ISBN 0-7356-1161-0
U.S.A. $19.99
U.K.   £14.99
Canada $28.99

Troubleshooting Microsoft® Outlook®
(Covers Microsoft Outlook 2000 and Outlook Express)
ISBN 0-7356-1162-9
U.S.A. $19.99
U.K.   £14.99
Canada $28.99

Troubleshooting Microsoft Windows®
(Covers Windows Me, Windows 98, and Windows 95)
ISBN 0-7356-1166-1
U.S.A. $19.99
U.K.   £14.99
Canada $28.99

Troubleshooting Microsoft Windows 2000 Professional
ISBN 0-7356-1165-3
U.S.A. $19.99
U.K.   £14.99
Canada $28.99

Troubleshooting Your Web Page
(Covers Microsoft FrontPage® 2000)
ISBN 0-7356-1164-5
U.S.A. $19.99
U.K.   £14.99
Canada $28.99

Troubleshooting Your PC
ISBN 0-7356-1163-7
U.S.A. $19.99
U.K.   £14.99
Canada $28.99

Microsoft®

mspress.microsoft.com

Target your
solution
and fix it
yourself—
fast!

U.S.A. **$19.99**
U.K. £14.99
Canada $28.99
ISBN: 0-7356-1162-9

Trouble with your e-mail system? TROUBLESHOOTING MICROSOFT® OUTLOOK® can help you fix it. This plain-language book will guide you to the source of your problem—and show you how to solve it right away. Use easy diagnostic flowcharts to identify your e-mail problems. Get ready solutions full of clear, step-by-step instructions. Go to quick-access charts with *Top 20 Problems* and *Prevention Tips*. Discover even more solutions with handy *Tips* and *Quick Fixes*. Walk through the remedy with plenty of screen shots to keep you on track. Find what you need fast with the extensive, easy-reference index. And keep trouble at bay with the Troubleshooting Web site—updated every month with new FREE solutions.

mspress.microsoft.com